The Fourth Gospel:
Tales of a Jewish Mystic

Also by John Shelby Spong

Honest Prayer

Dialogue in Search of Jewish-Christian Understanding
(with Rabbi Jack Daniel Spiro)

Christpower (compiled and edited by Lucy Newton Boswell)

*Life Approaches Death: A Dialogue in Medical
Ethics* (with Dr. Daniel Gregory)

The Living Commandments

The Easter Moment

Into the Whirlwind: The Future of the Church

Beyond Moralism (with the Venerable Denise Haines)

*Survival and Consciousness: An Interdisciplinary Inquiry into
the Possibility of Life Beyond Biological Death* (editor)

Living in Sin? A Bishop Rethinks Human Sexuality

*Rescuing the Bible from Fundamentalism: A Bishop
Rethinks the Meaning of Scripture*

*Born of a Woman: A Bishop Rethinks the Virgin Birth
and the Role of Women in a Male-Dominated Church*

This Hebrew Lord: A Bishop's Search for the Authentic Jesus

Resurrection: Myth or Reality? A Bishop Rethinks the Meaning of Easter

Liberating the Gospels: Reading the Bible with Jewish Eyes

Why Christianity Must Change or Die: A Bishop Speaks to Believers in Exile

The Bishop's Voice: Selected Essays (1979–1999)
(compiled and edited by Christine Mary Spong)

Here I Stand: My Struggle for a Christianity of Integrity, Love and Equality

*A New Christianity for a New World: Why Traditional
Faith Is Dying and How a New Faith Is Being Born*

*The Sins of Scripture: Exposing the Bible's Texts
of Hate to Reveal the God of Love*

Jesus for the Non-Religious: Recovering the Divine at the Heart of the Human

*Eternal Life: A New Vision—Beyond Religion,
Beyond Theism, Beyond Heaven and Hell*

Re-Claiming the Bible for a Non-Religious World

The
Fourth Gospel:
Tales of a
Jewish Mystic

John Shelby Spong

HarperCollins*PublishersLtd*

While I have relied heavily on the Revised Standard Version, the New Revised Standard Version and the King James Version in quoting scripture, I have in every case used whatever wording seemed to my ear to be most faithful to the original text.

THE FOURTH GOSPEL: TALES OF A JEWISH MYSTIC.
Copyright © 2013 by John Shelby Spong.

Published by HarperCollins Publishers Ltd

First Canadian edition

HarperCollins books may be purchased for educational, business, or sales promotional use through our Special Markets Department.

HarperCollins Publishers Ltd.
2 Bloor Street East, 20th Floor
Toronto, Ontario, Canada
M4W 1A8

www.harpercollins.ca

Library and Archives Canada Cataloguing in Publication information is available upon request

ISBN 978-1-44342-399-1

Printed in the United States of America.
RRD 9 8 7 6 5 4 3 2 1

For Christine
with
my deepest love

AND FOR

St. Peter's Episcopal Church, Morristown, New Jersey

AND

St. Paul's Episcopal Church, Richmond, Virginia

These two churches have nurtured my life most significantly
and for the longest number of years and have thus
helped me to grow into the wonder and
mystery of God.

Contents

PART III

THE FAREWELL DISCOURSES AND
THE HIGH PRIESTLY PRAYER

PART IV

THE PASSION NARRATIVE: FROM DARKNESS
TO LIGHT, FROM DEATH TO LIFE

PART V

RESURRECTION: MYSTICAL
ONENESS REVEALED

Preface

I have placed most of what would normally constitute the preface of this book into the first chapter. I have done that because it sets the stage for this book and I do not want my readers to skip over this material because they regard any preface only as a throat-clearing operation on the part of the author. Chapter 1 is vital to the work of the whole of this book. So in this preface I will only mention those people who have assisted me in the task of preparing this book and those people and institutions to which this book is dedicated.

I must say that with this book, my twenty-fourth, I feel a sense of completion. I have arrived at a place both spiritually and theologically with which I am content. My life is still a journey along the Christ path into the mystery of God, and that continues to be an ever deepening reality, but the more I walk this path the less I find that words are my communication vehicle of choice and I slip into the wonder of wordlessness. I think those who have been my great teachers must have felt the same thing, for John A. T. Robinson entitled one of his last books *In the End, God* and Paul Tillich entitled one of his *On the Boundary*. I resonate significantly with the retired bishop who once said to me, "The older I get the more deeply I *believe,* but the less *beliefs* I have." That, I think, is the mystical oneness to which all religious systems point and is thus the final goal of the religious journey. I can now see that boundary.

I have wrestled with the Christian faith for all of my now eighty-two years and I find myself at this moment, to the surprise of my traditionalist critics, I'm sure, more deeply committed to my Christ and to my faith than ever before. My commitment is, however, to a new understanding of both the Christ and Christianity. I am increasingly drawn to a Christianity that has no separating barriers and that does not bind me into the creeds of antiquity. It is a Christianity that cannot be contained by or expressed through traditional liturgical forms. I have no desire to find certainty or to embrace religious security. I choose rather to live in the unbounded joy of embracing the radical insecurity that is the nature of human life and by doing so to discover that I am in fact walking the Christ path. I also have no desire to walk any other faith path. I have discovered, however, that if I walk the Christ path deeply enough and far enough, it will lead me beyond anything I now know about Christianity. I see that not as a negative statement, but as a positive one. Jesus walked beyond the boundaries of his religion into a new vision of God. I think that this is what I also have done and that is what I want to celebrate. God is ultimate. Christianity is not. The only way I know how to walk into the ultimacy of God, however, is to walk through Christianity. I claim not that the Christian path is the exclusive path, but that it is the only path I know and thus the only path on which I can walk. I claim for myself without equivocation the title "Christian." I define human life through the lens of the Christ experience and that satisfies me. I can honestly say with deep conviction that I am who I am because of my relationship with one called Jesus of Nazareth and that it is through him that the meaning of what I call God has been opened for me.

It is because of that conviction that I have dedicated this book not just to my very special wife, but also to the two churches in which I have lived for the longest number of years and which have nurtured me in the deepest and most significant ways. Churches, by which I mean congregations, are not always given the credit they deserve for introducing their people to the transformative power of the God they exist to serve. Maybe that is so because so many of them are struggling maintenance organizations, but beyond these struggles they do represent something wondrous and something real. That is what I, at least, have experienced in all of the churches that have shaped my life. Before I speak of the two churches that were the most formative and thus to which my debt is the deepest, let me in this preface say just a word about each of the other congregations in which my life has been lived.

My first experience of Christian community was in the Church of the Holy Comforter, then on South Boulevard in Charlotte, North Carolina, but now located on Park Road. Here I was baptized as an infant and my earliest memories of church rise out of my Sunday school experience in this place. One lay couple stands out for me above all others. Estelle Darrow was my kindergarten teacher for the three years between ages three and five. I remember little content from that time, but I remember loving to go to Sunday school and always being eager to see Mrs. Darrow. Her husband, Herbert, directed the church school, led the opening exercises and was my fifth grade Sunday school teacher. Our subject that year was the Ten Commandments. Mr. Darrow skipped the seventh commandment and went directly from "You shall do no murder" to "You shall not steal." Noting this omission, I raised my hand and asked, "Mr. Darrow, you skipped commandment number seven. What does it mean to commit adultery?" It was an innocent question. I had no idea what adultery meant. His response, however, was indelible. "You will learn about that when you get older!" he said.

I left this church shortly before my twelfth birthday, not for any negative reason, but in order to sing in the boys' choir at St. Peter's, the downtown Episcopal church in Charlotte. In a very short time I was so drawn by that choir and by the experience of singing in that church that I decided to be confirmed there, rather than at Holy Comforter. My father died about four months after I was confirmed and my choirmaster, a lovely, white-haired musical genius named William Wall Whiddit, was a pastor to me long before I knew what a pastor was. My life was significantly rooted in this church and it became a haven of security for me in my radically anxious and insecure young life. In early 1946 this church also brought into my life my first great mentor. His name was Robert Littlefield Crandall, a former navy chaplain during World War II, serving on the carrier *Wasp* in the South Pacific. The war being over, this man at the ripe old age of thirty-two returned to civilian life to be my rector. He was there during all of my years in high school and college, leaving for Louisiana in late 1952. More perhaps than he ever realized, he was my role model, the one who created in me the desire to be ordained and the one on whom, both consciously and unconsciously, I patterned my priestly life and career.

I was ordained to the diaconate in St. Peter's in 1955. Robert Crandall came back from Louisiana to be the preacher at that service, so he and that church literally launched me into my professional career. I have been able to return in my later life to St. Peter's in Charlotte on several occasions to tell them what they meant to me. These were wonderfully satisfying moments. I also spoke in this church at the burial of my mother.

In September of 1949 I left Charlotte and St. Peter's Church to enroll at the University of North Carolina in Chapel Hill. While at that great university I attended regularly the Chapel of the Cross, the Episcopal church located literally on its campus. The rector, David W. Yates, and the university Episcopal chaplain, L. Bartine Sherman, were both incredibly gifted men to whom I looked up with appreciation.

In my senior year at the university I served on the weekends as the "lay reader in charge" at St. Mark's Church in Roxboro, North Carolina, located about thirty miles from Chapel Hill, and there I had my first experience of what it means to lead a congregation. The people at St. Mark's were kind to put up with both my inexperience and my immaturity and I have many happy memories that bind me still to that lovely church in that wonderful small town.

While studying for the priesthood at Virginia Theological Seminary from 1952 through 1955, I had two "field work" assignments, as we called them. The first was at St. Paul's Episcopal Church in downtown Alexandria, Virginia. The rector of this church was William Henry Mead, who would later become the bishop of Delaware. He was a brilliant orator whose sermons introduced me to the power of the pulpit, a force I would never forget.

The second was a rural chapel in Culpepper County, Virginia. St. Paul's Church, Raccoon Ford, was its name, and there I spent the Sundays of my senior year in seminary. Leaving my home in Alexandria about 5:00 A.M., I would drive into the beautiful Virginia countryside to get to Raccoon Ford in time to teach Sunday school, to conduct the morning worship service, to preach, to have Sunday dinner with a church family, to visit parishioners on Sunday afternoon and finally to lead the youth group on Sunday evening. I would then drive back to my apartment near the seminary, arriving about 10:00 P.M. on Sunday night, exhausted, but also exhilarated. There were many dynamics in that rural congregation that helped me to understand how communities work. My supervisor was the Rev. David Lewis, then the rector in Culpepper, who later became the suffragan bishop of Virginia. He and his wife, Carol, were wonderful, gracious and gifted people whose friendship I treasured.

St. Joseph's Episcopal Church in West Durham, North Carolina, located quite literally between Duke University and the Erwin Cotton Mills, was the first church I served after ordination. It was also the place in which I was ordained as a priest on December 28, 1955, with the same David Lewis, my former supervisor, serving as the preacher on that occasion. St. Joseph's welcomed my newly-minted ministry and tolerated my excessive zeal and intense ambition to be the best priest I could be. The location of this church was both its challenge and its opportunity. My two church wardens symbolized this community. Milton (Piggy) Barefoot, a lifelong member of the mill community, was my senior warden, and Dr. Herman Salinger, the head of Duke University's German department and a published poet, was my junior warden. In this first assignment I had the challenge and the opportunity of bringing these two worlds together and I learned much from both.

Next came Calvary Parish in Tarboro, North Carolina, and its neighboring church, St. Luke's. Calvary was the place on my career path in which I grew up and I owe so very much to the members of that congregation and community, especially to those longtime members who were quite sure that I was "over the top." The late 1950s and early 60s were not an easy time in history in America. Early in my ministry in Tarboro I had the honor of being named "Public Enemy Number One" in Edgecombe County, North Carolina, by the local branch of the Ku Klux Klan. Before departing, however, I was named Tarboro's "Man of the Year" by the Junior Chamber of Commerce. My indebtedness to that church is enormous.

One diagonal block away from Calvary Church was St. Luke's Episcopal Church, an African-American congregation built to illustrate and to maintain segregation, but the identity, impact and witness of that congregation remains both alive and vital in me to this day. The world has moved on from that dark time in Southern history: Today the members of St. Luke's are now completely welcome in Calvary Church and many friendships bind the two congregations together. I served these two congregations, however, from 1957 through 1965, when segregation was breaking up and frightened, hostile feelings were running high. The people of St. Luke's quite literally loved the racism out of me and inspired me to see both the role and the power of the church in the relentless quest for human justice. The members of St. Luke's gave an integrity to the rest of my ministry that it could never have had without them. While in Tarboro I also served three rural missions in Edgecombe County: St. Mary's Church in Speed, Grace Church in Lawrence and St. Ignatius' Church in Old Sparta.

St. John's in Lynchburg, Virginia, was the next step in my career, and a wonderfully significant step it was. St. John's was filled with bright, well-educated, somewhat affluent social leaders who had, so far as I could tell, never been required to think much about their faith. During those years I shared this town with the late Jerry Falwell and I watched him grow from a local preacher into becoming a nationally known religious and political figure. I also made the decision in this congregation to organize my developing ministry around teaching and so I inaugurated a Sunday morning adult Bible class dedicated to sharing with the people in the pews the same biblical scholarship available in the academies of higher learning. This class grew to an attendance that constantly overran the space in our large auditorium. It also shaped my future ministry, convincing me that if I tried to protect either God or educated laypeople from truth, because it was inconvenient, I would never be an effective leader of the church of the future. I was at St. John's less than five full years, but it was a major building block in my life. That now brings me to the two churches to which this book is dedicated.

I moved to St. Paul's in Richmond in the fall of 1969. No church

I have ever served or known has meant what this one meant and still means to me. St. Paul's stood literally across the street from the capitol building of the state of Virginia. It has been the spiritual home to people like General Robert E. Lee and Confederate President Jefferson Davis, as well as to many of that state's governors, since it is not only in the heart of downtown Richmond, but is also quite literally less than a block from the mansion where Virginia's governors live while in office. Yet despite its deep history and rather traditional understanding of the Christian faith, this church had a reputation for calling young, liberal-minded, challenging clergy and then engaging them deeply until the tension between the liberal rector and the conservative, but thoughtful, congregation produced an incredible quality of both life and growth for both. Five of the six rectors who were privileged to serve that church between 1920 and 1976 were chosen to be bishops in such diverse places across our nation as Pennsylvania, Ohio, Arkansas, Arizona and New Jersey. It was the greatest church I have ever watched operate and I was incredibly fortunate to have been its rector for seven years. My indebtedness to St. Paul's, more than any other congregation that I served, is immeasurable. The early books that inaugurated my writing career were the direct by-product of the adult class I taught from September through May of each year that I was there. Leaving that church to become the bishop of Newark in 1976 was one of the most difficult things I have ever had to do. St. Paul's present rector, Wallace Adams-Riley, and its associates, Kate Jenkins, Melanie Mullen and Claudia Merritt, are in the mold of this church's clergy over the years. Wallace is young, bright, energetic, outspoken and progressive. He is clearly a future leader of the Episcopal Church. His kindness to me and his constant invitations to return to be part of his Lenten program or to teach the still extant adult Bible class on a Sunday morning are deeply appreciated. Two of our daughters continue to live in Richmond with their families and that draws us back to that city with regularity. To continue to be part of a church I love so deeply, almost forty years after my departure as its rector, is a rare experience for which I am grateful. So I thank this congregation and its present rector for making this continuing relationship possible.

When I was elected bishop of Newark in 1976 we bought a home in Morristown, New Jersey, just four blocks from St. Peter's Church, a nineteenth-century neo-gothic structure located on South Street near the town center. The rector at that time was Hughes Garvin, a tall, dignified and loving man, who welcomed me and my wife, Joan, into this church and into his affections. As my wife's sickness developed and began to move toward the inevitable moment of her death, Hughes' kindness and understanding were deeply appreciated. When she died in August of 1988 we had her funeral in St. Peter's and its congregation nurtured me in both my grief and my loneliness. The associate minister during the early years of my association with this church was the Rev. Dr. Philip Cato, a brilliant man whose PhD from Duke was in the Intellectual History of Western Civilization, a very ostentatious subject for a doctorate! Philip, however, may have actually been the brightest priest with whom I was ever associated. He was three years younger than I, but as fate would have it, I had actually known him since he was nine years old! At that tender age he had joined the boys' choir at St. Peter's Church in Charlotte, North Carolina, when I was a "senior chorister." It is a small world! In his Morristown career, Philip gave to St. Peter's Church an intellectual toughness so often missing in Christian congregations, and week after week his sermons were powerful, provocative and memorable. He also taught the adult class on Sunday morning and he insisted that the Sunday school for children was to be an educational venture of the first order. To assist him in this task he recruited, trained and raised to signifi-cant leadership in that church a laywoman named Christine Mary Barney, who soon directed the entire educational program for ages one to ninety-nine, as she has said. She was twice elected to serve on that church's vestry. In 1990 I married Christine Barney in St. Peter's Church, so it is fair to say that this church also gave to me my wife, whose abilities and affection expanded my life and my career in ways I could never have predicted. In time, she even became my editor. My books and the weekly columns that I have written over the past fourteen years bear the imprint of her genius and her uncompromising love has made me a whole person, intro-ducing me to aspects of life that I had never known before.

Next St. Peter's Church gave me the friendship of a rector named David Hegg and his wife, Judith. David was probably the best and most effective overall parish priest that I have ever known.

Today this church is served by my current rector, Janet Brod-erick, and her associate, Melissa Hall, and in my retirement both of these gifted priests have welcomed me into a leadership role in this congregation, which now includes many of our clos-est personal friends. Both Christine and I feel a deep sense of belonging in this faith community, and so through the words of this preface and the dedication of this book to St. Peter's in Mor-ristown and to St. Paul's in Richmond I now express my gratitude publicly to all those who make up these two wonderful and vital congregations.

There is one other church to which I feel a sense of indebted-ness. St. Martin's Episcopal Church, located in the small Vermont town of Fairlee, is the church we attend when visiting our Ver-mont children and grandchildren. I have never seen more than thirty people at a worship service in this church, not even on Christmas Eve, but what a gracious and loving congregation it is. That quality stems directly from its part-time rector, a priest who is also a retired public school teacher, named John Morris. Together with his elegant wife, Susan, they have built in this part of rural Vermont a community of theological openness, liturgical integrity and the kind of caring that creates life. One of the treats of visiting our grandchildren is to experience worship with them in this place. I dedicate this book to St. Peter's and to St. Paul's, but I salute with thanksgiving each of these other churches that have touched my life so deeply.

There are some additional individuals to whom gratitude for this book is also due.

First to Andrew Scrimgeour, the Dean of the Libraries at Drew University, who has been my personal research assistant, making available to me the treasures not only in the university library, but also in the theological library. The Theological School at Drew University, while affiliated with the United Methodist Church, is universal in its resources and in its appeal. Andy, who is also Chair of the Board of the Westar Institute, and thus of the Jesus Seminar, has encouraged me in any number of ways. He has provided me with study space, given me my own library carrel, done research for me, allowed the long-term use of certain volumes and been a good friend in the midst of it all. I am delighted to thank him in this way quite publicly.

Second I thank those clergy and places at which lectures on the material now in this book first found public expression: the Gladstone Library in Hawarden, Wales, where Peter Francis serves as Warden; the Lutheran Church in New Market, Ontario, served by Pastor Dawn Hutchins; the Plymouth Church in Victoria, British Columbia, served by Pastor Michael Coveney; St. Paul's Church in Chattanooga, Tennessee, served by Rector Susan Butler; First Congregational United Church of Christ in Hendersonville, North Carolina, served by Pastor Richard Weidler; the

Clemson United Methodist Church in Clemson, South Carolina, served by Pastor Keith Ray; the Church of the Incarnation in Highlands, North Carolina, served by Rector Bruce Walker; my own St. Peter's in Morristown, served by Rector Janet Broderick; and last St. Paul's Church in Richmond, served by Rector Wallace Adams-Riley.

Third to Lydia Yorke, a doctoral student at Drew Theological School, whom I hired to turn my handwritten legal pads into the legible type of Microsoft Word.

Fourth to the members of my family I extend my profound appreciation for their love, support and caring. I have already referred to my wife, Christine. Now let me add that her love is the most sustaining gift I have ever had and I return it to her with a fervor that sometimes seems unusual for people of our ages, and I am grateful beyond measure for all that she is and all that she does.

Next, I express my gratitude to my three very unusual and wonderful daughters, Ellen, Katharine and Jaquelin, whose careers in banking, law and science still amaze me. One of the greatest gifts of life is to become good friends with your adult children. We have shared in that privilege with all three and with their husbands and partners, Gus Epps, Jack Catlett and Virgil Speriosu. They have also given us grandchildren, granddogs and grandcats. So to Shelby and Jay Catlett, to John and Lydia Hylton and to Jersey Rose, Elsie Lou, Brown Dog and Nolan the Cat, I express my appreciation.

Finally, my marriage to Christine gave me the pleasure of being a stepfather to two incredible people, Brian Yancy Barney, probably the most patient and gentle six-foot-four son anyone has ever had, and Rachel Elizabeth Barney, who has packed more into her now forty-one years of life than almost anyone I've ever known. To them I also say a genuine thank-you. Brian, who works for the telephone company in rural Vermont, is married to Julieann Hoyt, a brilliant and still growing young woman, and they are the parents of twins, Katherine and Colin, who are now ten years old and who have given us a second chance at the wonderful task of grandparenting.

Rachel is now practicing medicine in Delaware after careers as a paramedic in the South Bronx and a helicopter pilot in the United States Marine Corps (which included three tours of active combat in the Second Iraq War), followed by going to medical school in Beer Sheva, Israel.

There is no greater blessing in life than the gift of a family. Christine and I feel every day the enormity of this blessing.

John Shelby Spong
Morris Plains, NJ
2013

PART I

Introducing the
Fourth Gospel

Chapter 1

Setting the Stage

Throughout most of my professional career I was not drawn to the Fourth Gospel; indeed I found it almost repellent. This gospel presented, I believed, a Jesus whose humanity was no longer intact. John's Jesus claimed pre-existence—that is, he said he came to this earth from another life in another place. He was portrayed as possessing clairvoyance—that is, he knew about people's lives and their pasts before he met them. He was even said to know what they were thinking while he was talking to them. The Jesus of John's gospel also seemed to endure crucifixion without suffering. He displayed no anxiety about having to meet his destiny, no unwillingness "to drink this cup," as he described it; indeed John has him state that this was the purpose for which he had been born.

The place where I experienced the most negative impact of the Fourth Gospel was in the role it played in the development of both the creeds and the imposed dogmas of the church. Because this book was thought to have spelled out "orthodox Christianity," John's gospel also helped to fuel such dreadful events in Christian history as heresy hunts and the Inquisition. As the centuries rolled by, John's gospel seemed to make meaningful discourse on the nature of the Christ figure almost impossible. Every creed developed in church history appears to have been created primarily to falsify the Jesus experience by forcing that experience into time-bound and time-warped human words. The original creed of the Christian church was just three words: "Jesus is messiah." I believe that this is still the best creed the Christian church has ever developed. When Christianity moved from a Jewish world, where the meaning of the word "messiah" was understood, into a Gentile world where that word was strange and unknown, "Jesus is messiah" became "Jesus is Lord." That shift in turn opened Christianity to a very new and different understanding of Christology, that is of the person of Jesus. The next stage in creedal development grew out of baptismal formulas in the second and third centuries, which later evolved into what we call today the Apostles' Creed, though I think it is fair to say that none of the actual apostles would have recognized it as expressing their understanding of Jesus.

Then came the more convoluted Nicene Creed adopted by the Council of Nicaea in 325 CE and still later its potential successor, the three-page attack on any deviation from "the catholic faith" known as the Athanasian Creed of the late fourth century, which, thank God, never found its way into corporate worship. These later creeds—the Apostles', the Nicene and the Athanasian—all reflected both a three-tiered universe and Greek dualism, as they attempted to define Jesus of Nazareth as the incarnation into human form of the theistic God who lived above the sky and later as the second person of "the divine and eternal Trinity." It was the Fourth Gospel more than any other biblical source that Athanasius, the fourth-century "champion of orthodoxy," quoted almost exclusively in these formative debates. Creeds, by definition, are always barrier-building vehicles. By this I mean that creeds are ecclesiastical attempts to draw the theological lines so firmly in the sand that it becomes easy to determine who is in and who is out, who are the "orthodox" believers and who are the "heretics." The Nicene Creed defined Jesus over and over again in "loophole-closing rhetoric." Listen to its repetitious words: Jesus is "eternally begotten of the Father, God from God, light from light, true God from true God, begotten not made, of one being with the Father, through whom all things were made." It was "for us and for our salvation" that Jesus "came down from heaven." In these definitions the finger of the debate points to and the vocabulary of the debate reveals the influence of the Fourth Gospel in every line. Those creedal connections served to dim my enthusiasm for this gospel, if for no other reason than that imposed orthodoxy is never real and never vital.

That creedal system seemed to me to have locked Jesus into a pre-modern world, to have defined God as an invasive, miracle-working deity from outer space, and to have made the work of engaging the world in dialogue not only very difficult, but almost impossible. The discipline of theological study known as "apologetics" was meant to be the study of how we can recast the meaning found in the Jesus experience into the thought forms of contemporary society, but instead it has become the activity of defending ancient and dated formulations. This meant that throughout most of my career, both as a priest and as a bishop, I saw John's gospel more as a problem in ministry than as an asset. So my tactic was to avoid it, if possible, to ignore it whenever I could not avoid it, and simply to resign myself to the reality that it was in the canon of scripture. Sometimes I walked around this gospel. At other times I attacked it or at least attacked those I thought misunderstood and/or misused its message. I certainly never wanted to spend much time on it. I was given a copy of Rudolf Bultmann's commentary entitled *The Gospel of John* by a dear friend in early 1974. I placed it on a shelf and did not crack its cover until 2010, a period of thirty-six years! For one who thinks of himself as intellectually curious, that is quite a record.

A number of things challenged this understanding near the end of my active career. One was disillusionment with the perspective known as salvation or atonement theology. Atonement theology concentrates on human depravity and weakness and portrays God as a "divine rescuer" on whom we are totally dependent. Most people, while not using those words, would recognize atonement theology as the primary way they have learned to think about Christianity. It is present in most liturgical forms used in the majority of churches. Later in this book, when it is appropriate to do so, I will spell out the origins, the development and the power of this pattern of thinking and relate it to its own scriptural sources. I will also show why it has collapsed under the onslaught of the expanding knowledge of the Western world, which has caused the concept of God employed in its theological understanding to become both "homeless"—that is, without a place to live above the sky—and "unemployed"—that is, without any work to do in a post-age-of-miracles world.

As I became aware of the bankruptcy of this dominant way of understanding the Christian story in the latter years of my professional career and as my writing turned to trying to formulate what I called "A New Christianity for a New World," several things happened which nudged my mind open and invited me to look at the Fourth Gospel in a new way.

First, I began to see John's gospel increasingly as a Jewish book. It was not, as scholars in the early twentieth century had begun to assert, primarily a Gnostic work, a text influenced by Hellenism, nor even a book shaped by Philo, a first-century Jewish philosopher who tried to merge Jerusalem with Athens. Rather, it was, as I began to discover, an authentically Palestinian-Jewish book. Having in an earlier book developed an understanding of Mark, Matthew and Luke as liturgical works shaped by the worship life of the synagogue and organized around the liturgical year of

Jewish festivals and fast days,* I now wondered if I could find a similar background clue that might unravel John for me. I then came across a 1960 book written by Aileen Guilding entitled *The Fourth Gospel and Jewish Worship: A Study of the Relation of St. John's Gospel to the Ancient Jewish Lectionary System.*† As I devoured that book, it created a new window into John's gospel for me. Still, however, I did not know what to do with the pre-existent divine claims made for Jesus, or with John's ideas of Jesus being the word of God *enfleshed* and thus one who shared in the oneness of God.

Next I began to work on my book that was published in 2009 under the title *Eternal Life: A New Vision—Beyond Religion, Beyond Theism, Beyond Heaven and Hell,* which plunged me into a study of the origins of life. I read astrophysics and biology. I traveled to remote places in the world, including the Amazon Rain Forest, the Galapagos Islands, Kruger Park (the world's largest game preserve, located in South Africa), and the Great Barrier Reef in northern Queensland, Australia, to examine life in a variety of forms. In each of these settings, my agenda was to study every manifestation of life—plant life, insect life, animal life, even single-cell life. I studied the development of consciousness, then of self-consciousness and finally opened myself to the possibility of there being something called a universal consciousness. I began to rethink and ultimately to dismiss the theistic definition of God and started moving away from an understanding of God as "a being" to an understanding of God as "Being itself," or as Paul Tillich, the formative theologian of my early training, would say, as "the Ground of Being."

From here I began to look anew at mysticism, at claims of new

---

* My reference here is to my book *Liberating the Gospels: Reading the Bible with Jewish Eyes.* See bibliography for details.

† See bibliography for details.

dimensions of consciousness achieved in the mystical experience and more specifically at forms of Jewish mysticism present in the first century. With that background, quite suddenly John's gospel began to unfold before me as a work of Jewish mysticism and the Jesus of John's gospel suddenly became not a visitor from another realm, but a person in whom a new God consciousness had emerged. Now, seen from that new perspective, the claim of oneness with the Father was not incarnational language, but mystical language. Such Johannine statements as, "If you have seen me, you have seen the Father," as well as the "I AM" sayings by which John's gospel has Jesus claim the name of God for himself, and even the purpose of John's Jesus to bring to life a new wholeness, all became provocative new doorways into what this gospel might actually mean.

So, armed with those insights from multiple sources, I entered upon a study of John's gospel that consumed over five years. It was one of the richer learning experiences of my entire life. Other than the daily newspaper and books that I had agreed to endorse or review, I read nothing in those years but Fourth Gospel materials. I have now read almost every recognized major commentary on John's gospel that is available in English from the nineteenth, twentieth and twenty-first centuries. I have roamed through learned biblical and theological journals for articles on John published over the last century. Even at that I have only scratched the surface of what is available.

I have no pretensions about this book. It is not a new commentary. Learned commentaries abound, but those for whom I write are not going to read them. Bultmann's commentary never translates the Greek text, for example, making it a real struggle even for one like me who has a background in Greek. Without that background it would be impossible. Raymond Brown's commentary, *The Gospel According to John,* is in two volumes totaling over eleven hundred pages, all in very small print and with copious notes. Urban von Wahlde's commentary is in three volumes, containing over two thousand pages, and deeply repetitious. Several commentaries from the late nineteenth and early twentieth centuries were written in two columns; set up like encyclopedias or dictionaries, they do not encourage readers to look at more than brief passages. My readers want meaning, not technical facts nor excessive knowledge of the various elemental stages in the development of John's book. So I have read the commentaries for them and have tried to distill the meaning. John's gospel is about life—expanded life, abundant life, and ultimately eternal life—but not in the typical manner that these words have been understood religiously. I see a new paradigm arising in Christianity and I try to speak to that paradigm and to ground it in the tradition by breaking open the Fourth Gospel to a new interpretive process. I found the Fourth Gospel a book to be lived as much as it was a volume to be mastered.

To get to this place, however, given the way in which the Bible is understood in the religious culture of our world, will not be a simple task. So much superstition has been laid on the texts of the Bible and so many of the fears of men and women have been invested in this book as people seek a certainty in the Bible, which neither life nor religion can ever provide, that genuine biblical knowledge is hard to attain. Both of these must be set aside before biblical understanding can be gained. This setting aside, however, is not easily accomplished. It will cause traditionally religious people to feel threatened, attacked and even angry and they will resist these pages with a vengeance, that will even express itself in the character assassination of those whom they perceive have done this to them. Meanwhile, those people, who have long ago dismissed most traditional religious categories as irrelevant to their lives, are not motivated to enter a study that is this complex, because they do not think the conclusions they might reach will be worth the effort. Both of these groups I want to urge to persevere and journey with me as I seek to lay the groundwork for a new way to look at Christianity and a new way to read the gospel of John. I can assure you that for me the reward has been worth the labor. I can only hope that this will also be so for my readers.

Those who define themselves in traditional religious language may well be scandalized by this book, even as those who think of themselves as members of the "Church Alumni Association" may well be intrigued, as both groups learn in these pages that the gospel of John was written in different layers by different authors over a period of about thirty years. It, therefore, cannot contain in any sense the literal "words of God." They will also learn that none of the sayings attributed to Jesus in this gospel was in all probability ever spoken by the Jesus of history. They will learn that none of the miracles, called "signs" in this book, and attributed to Jesus, ever actually happened. They will learn that most of the characters who populate the pages of this gospel are literary or fictionalized creations of the author and were never real people who ever lived. They will learn that the language of an external deity entering into the flesh of our physical existence, which shapes the way most people both understand Christianity and the way they read this gospel, is not even close to what the writer of this gospel intended.

With these words of both introduction to my methods and warning about my conclusions, I now invite you to turn the pages, read on and walk deeply into the background of what we call the gospel of John.

CHAPTER 2

John: One Gospel, More Than One Author

The Fourth Gospel has been traditionally read and understood by most people as if it were the work of a single author. That assumption, however, is not shared by the vast majority of Johannine scholars. They tend to see this gospel as a book that went through a series of editorial revisions by different authors over a period of years until it reached the stage of development in which we have it today. To support their theories, these scholars point to contradictions in the body of the gospel itself, places in the text that give us the impression of forced unity and places where editorial additions appear not to have been woven into the text seamlessly. For example, in some parts of this gospel we find what scholars call a "low Christology." By this they mean that in portions of the Johannine text the life of Jesus is seen and described primarily in terms of well-known Jewish messianic images: the new Moses, the new Elijah, the prophet of whom Moses spoke. While all of these images point to an extraordinary life, none of them necessarily claims for Jesus a divine status. There are, however, other passages in this gospel that reveal what scholars call a "high Christology." By this they mean that the life of Jesus is seen and portrayed primarily in divine, supernatural terms. Jesus is frequently pictured as claiming a special and unique relationship with God that borders on complete identification. Clairvoyance is also attributed to Jesus in several episodes. In still other places the claim is made for Jesus having known pre-existent or pre-earthly life, prior to his birth into this world.

In this gospel alone, countless numbers of times Jesus is made to employ the divine name "I AM" as if it were his own. The opening prologue makes claims for both his pre-existence and his divine nature: "The word was with God and the word was God" (John 1:1), and "the word became flesh and dwelt among us" (John 1:14).

One might argue that each of these claims, the low Christology and the high Christology, is true, and in some sense that is what creedal Christianity sought to express with its assertion that Jesus was both "fully human" and "fully divine." That, however, is a dualistic theological idea that came to dominance about three hundred or so years after the crucifixion of Jesus and could hardly have reflected the thought of a person living in the latter half of the first century, when John's gospel was written.

Scholars have become quite convinced that they see behind the present form of John's gospel earlier sources that were incorporated into the final text. One of the postulated pre-Johannine sources is called the Book of Signs, and much of the material in chapters 2 through 11 of John's gospel is believed by these scholars to reflect this source. If that premise is true, and no less a scholar than Rudolf Bultmann makes a strong case for it, we need to recognize that this would account for the material beginning with the story of Jesus turning water into wine at a wedding feast in Cana of Galilee and concluding with the story of Jesus raising from the dead a man named Lazarus. That represents just under half of this gospel.

Clues that lead these scholars to the conclusion that the Book of Signs was originally a separate source are found in that part of the gospel narrative itself. The text of John's gospel refers to the water into wine story as "the first of the signs" that Jesus did in order to "manifest his glory" (John 2:11). In response to this sign we are told in the text that the disciples "believed in him." Later references speak of Jesus' "second sign," but admittedly the numbering gets a bit vague by the time we arrive at the last sign, the Lazarus story in chapter 11.

In this proposed "independent" signs book, a sign is depicted as a mighty act, done quite publicly, that points to something even bigger and more important. At the same time, as we shall note later in this book, the signs accounts are filled with strange references, enigmatic words, unusual actions and dramatically drawn characters, all of which appear to mitigate against these signs ever having been understood as literal events that occurred inside the normal flow of history. Stories that the synoptic gospels portray as miracles with no great hesitancy are much more obscure in John. The word "sign" stands for this obscurity.

Another aspect of this Johannine strangeness is found in the dramatically heightened imagery of the signs related in the Fourth Gospel. It is as if these signs were exaggerated for a purpose that is not readily understandable. There is no question that there are some things about these signs that are quite different and distinct from the miracle stories in the earlier gospels. One argument is that this difference reflects an older written tradition (such as the aforementioned Book of Signs) on which John drew, which was quite different from the synoptic tradition of the first three gospels. The fact is that while there are some similarities between some of John's signs and some of the miracle stories in the other gospels, most of them are very different and some of them are unique to this gospel alone. So the conclusion is drawn, at least by some Johannine scholars, that the original author of John's gospel was using a written source no longer available to us that has been preserved only in the Fourth Gospel. I think it is fair, however, in working out gospel theories, to be suspicious of the assertion of a now-lost source, whether it be a lost book of signs or a lost book of sayings. Suspicion does not mean that I reject this conclusion either as possible or as probable, but it does mean that I hold loosely to theories that require the existence of a now-lost document as the cornerstone for their verification.

There is also material in John's gospel that appears to have been cobbled together—material that does not really fit or has been clumsily inserted into John's text—which again gives credence to the speculation that there was more than one source for this work. The geographical references in chapters 4, 5 and 6, for instance, would make more sense if the order were 4, 6 and 5. As another example, modern scholars do not consider the story of the woman taken in the act of adultery, a narrative that is mentioned only in the Fourth Gospel, to have been an original part of John. It appears in the text of the King James Version as John 7:53–8:11, but it has been removed to a footnote in more modern translations like the Revised Standard Version and the New Revised Standard Version. A study of ancient manuscripts reveals that the earliest copies of the gospel of John did not include the story. It makes its first appearance in the text of John's gospel only well into the Middle Ages. In at least one other ancient manuscript it actually shows up in Luke's gospel, not in John's. The story is a beautiful one, with its climax having Jesus say to the execution-oriented mob: "Let the one who is without sin cast the first stone," but it also feels authentic. That response sounds very much like an authentic word that might well have been spoken by Jesus. Its original setting as a part of John's corpus, however, is today universally dismissed in scholarly circles.

Still another illustration that suggests the merging in this gospel of some originally not connected parts is found in the midst of what are called the "Farewell Discourses," which include chapters 13–16, and perhaps even chapter 17 (generally referred to as the "high priestly prayer"). These discourses represent a time when Jesus turned away from the crowd and concentrated solely on his disciples. John develops this farewell material both elaborately and intensively, portraying Jesus as not only preparing his disciples to deal with their grief over his death and departure, but also equipping them to live without him.

Yet in many ways these Farewell Discourses seem to reflect far more the difficult times that the Johannine community itself would endure near the end of the first century than they do the things that Jesus might have said to his disciples before his death. The point is, however, that there is internal evidence in these discourses that points to the conclusion that they are not the work of a single author. At the end of chapter 14 Jesus says: "Rise, let us go hence" (John 14:31). This suggests that these discourses are over, but alas they will continue for at least two more chapters. I will return to this issue with more amplification when we come to that point in the text.

Further internal evidence that John's gospel was written in stages is found in the resurrection narratives. Once again I will go into these narratives in more detail later, but for now simply file in your memory bank that all of the resurrection stories in the Fourth Gospel look like unrelated episodes.

A final problem in trying to determine the integrity of the Fourth Gospel as a whole comes when one tries to understand the relationship between its last two chapters, 20 and 21. There is almost no possibility that the same person wrote both of these mutually contradicting chapters.

While scholars are today largely unified in the conclusion that more than one author or major editor lies behind the Fourth Gospel, the debate rages as to how many primary authors and different editions there were (Raymond Brown says five, Urban von Wahlde says three) and which parts of John are to be assigned to which editor. That debate is probably more than the average reader cares to engage. My point in this chapter is simply to signal that in all probability the Fourth Gospel is a composite of more than one source and that it reflects in its various editions quite distinct episodes in early Christian history. I will in this book assume a minimum of three stages, plus the addition of the Epilogue. I spell out here very briefly the conclusions to which my study has led me as a way of introducing readers to the background against which this book was written.

There was first, I believe, a deeply Jewish, synagogue-related stage that lies at the origin of this gospel—a stage that can still be discerned. In this first phase, which I would date in the early to mid-70s, Jesus is seen as the fulfillment of Jewish messianic images; he is defined as the promised one on whom Jewish hopes were pinned and to which they believed Jewish scriptures pointed. I see this phase particularly when the story of Jesus is related to specific festivals in the life of the synagogue.

On top of this earliest tradition was then superimposed the material that grew out of the rising hostility between the followers of Jesus and the leaders of the synagogue. That tension was exacerbated by the fall of Jerusalem and the destruction of the Temple by the Romans in the year 70 CE, and it increased until the followers of Jesus were literally expelled from the synagogue, which seems to have occurred no later than 88 CE. Echoes of this expulsion are certainly present in a number of places in John's gospel that will be obvious when we get to them. As a consequence of this excommunication, this gospel reflects a rising hostility between the disciples of Jesus and those that this gospel calls simply "the Jews." This conflict, like all religious disputes or family arguments, was filled with pain, recriminations and bitterness. Those of us who have observed religious disputes closely know that the levels of hostility that mark these disputes cannot be minimized. In this conflict both sides probably said terrible things about the other.

What we have in John's gospel is the product of only one side of the conflict. We need, therefore, to understand when we are reading this material that these are the raw feelings of the followers of Jesus toward the excommunicating synagogue leaders. These passages were later read as a conflict between Christians and Jews and as such produced and fed a deep and virulent anti-Semitism that expressed itself in torture, murder, inquisitions, expulsions, ghettoizations and ultimately the Holocaust. It is a history that should fill all Christians with a deep sense of shame and guilt. I do not minimize this shame and guilt one bit. I do believe, however, that to read John's gospel as the place where this anti-Semitism is rooted in the New Testament is to misread the text. Keep in mind that the followers of Jesus in the Johannine community were themselves overwhelmingly Jews. This talk of "the Jews" in the text of the Fourth Gospel did not mean the ethnic Jews, for that would have included the community itself. It meant rather those Jews who were the synagogue leaders and thus the people who had excommunicated the followers of Jesus. This split shaped the Johannine community dramatically and not surprisingly it also shaped the gospel narrative that this community produced as that text journeyed toward its final form. If we were to translate the words "the Jews" as "the orthodox party that ruled the synagogue," we would be far more accurate historically. In the editorial revision that occurred in this stage of excommunication, huge amounts of negativity entered the text.

The third major editing of this gospel developed later still. It came when these excommunicated Jewish followers of Jesus began the task of defining themselves apart from the traditional background of Judaism of which they had heretofore always been a part. They now understood that they needed to ground their Jesus experience in something more universal than what their Jewish background and expectations could provide. It was in this third editorial phase, I believe, that they began to move into a form of Jewish mysticism that enabled them to pass beyond all tribal boundaries and to reach a new and transcendent sense of the reality of God. That was what gave to the final form of this gospel its high Christology. That high Christology in turn was used in later Christian history to define Christian orthodoxy and thus to turn Christianity into the imperialistic Christian church of creeds and dogmas that it was destined to become. Christianity itself was thus victimized by the same forces of history that created anti-Semitism. Part of my task in this book is to pull the anti-Semitism out of Christian history and to pull creedal orthodoxy out of Christianity. I think it can be done by going deeply into the origins of this Fourth Gospel. The followers of Jesus had to learn how to live apart from Judaism. That was more than some Jewish members of the Johannine community could tolerate and so they split off and returned to the synagogue. I am increasingly convinced that the followers of Jesus today must learn how to live apart from Christianity, at least the kind of creedal orthodoxy that through the centuries Christianity has unfortunately become. That is more than some Christians today can tolerate and so many split off into more fundamentalist sects.

In this third stage of gospel revision we locate the tension that the gospel reflects between those who claimed to see Jesus as a God-infused human life and those who maintained that Jesus was a divine life—pre-existent with God in glory. I now believe that this was when the prologue was added and the divine name "I AM" was appropriated and applied to Jesus directly. It was a bold and a daring claim, but I do not think it was a false or foreign claim to those who understood what these concepts meant in the mystical tradition in Judaism from which the followers of Jesus had drawn them. Only when these concepts were later literalized in a dualistic, Greek-thinking world did Christian orthodoxy become identified with creedal and doctrinal exclusiveness.

Finally, and to complete this understanding of the sources behind the Fourth Gospel, I am increasingly convinced that the last addition to this book was the epilogue, the twenty-first chapter, which was not the product of any of the three previously described sources.

I will in this book acknowledge the layers of this gospel's formation as the key to its proper understanding. I will seek to rescue this book from the myths of fundamentalism that have been historically imposed on it. I will, however, also relate to the book as a whole, because that is the way the church received and began to use it. In that wholeness I will seek to discover something radically different from that into which Christianity finally developed. I find this gospel to be a book not about religion, sin and salvation, but about life, expanded life and expanded consciousness. I believe that this book leads us in an entirely different direction from the one traditional Christianity has followed from Nicaea to this day.

I want my readers to know these essential elements in the background of John's gospel, but more importantly I want them to know the meaning of John's gospel as a whole and to experience it as a doorway into a new dimension of life. It is also a journey into the heart of life, a journey beyond the boundaries of life and ultimately a journey into both a new consciousness and a whole new understanding of what Christianity is. The traditional understanding of Christianity is dying. Out of that death a new Christianity, rooted uniquely, I believe, in John's gospel, can be born. To bring that meaning to our awareness is why I have undertaken to write this book.

CHAPTER 3

Separating John from the Other Gospels

In the minds of most Christian people throughout the world, the gospel tradition of the Christian church has undergone a great blending process. Few people can listen to a gospel passage being read and readily register whether it comes from Mark, Matthew, Luke, or even John. I say "even" because John's gospel is quite different from the other three, which are collectively known as "the synoptics." Both Matthew and Luke had Mark in front of them when they wrote, and they incorporated great chunks of Mark into their narratives, Matthew utilizing about ninety percent of Mark and Luke about fifty percent. Both of them also added material to their own distinctive versions. One finds some echoes of this primitive tradition in John, but this gospel reveals no primary dependence on any of the previous gospels. While no one can be sure whether John was familiar with the synoptic tradition, I find it inconceivable that at least the final editor of John's gospel was unaware of the other three, and I will document my reasons for this opinion as this book unfolds.

The experience of most people, clergy and laity alike, is that when the gospel for the day is read in a church setting, the congregation hears only a brief passage without context; there is no sense of what came before or what will follow after that passage. Even though the liturgical announcement proclaims: "The Holy Gospel of our Lord and Savior Jesus Christ, according to . . . ," and then the gospel source for that day is stated as being Mark, Matthew, Luke or John, this source identification makes little impression on most Sunday worshippers.

It is also true that in traditional liturgical usage involving such high holy days as Christmas, Holy Week and Easter, the blending of scriptural sources is so total that our minds are programmed not even to try to separate them. When one looks at the annual Christmas pageant dramatically reenacted each December in most churches, the blending is remarkable. The typical pageant is a nightmare of homogenization of material which might have had integrity in its isolated, original form, but in its blended presentation has lost that integrity.

The normal pattern of Christmas pageants is to take the storyline from Luke, even though Matthew's account of Jesus' birth entered the tradition much earlier, and then to tack Matthew's wise men onto the pageant as the final scene. That way the audience does not have to deal with Matthew's more gory elements, like the slaughter of the innocent children in Bethlehem by Herod in his attempt to eliminate God's promised deliverer! In this blending process, however, Matthew's narrative is totally compromised. In Matthew, for example, there is no journey to Bethlehem by Mary and Joseph and no inn or manger to adorn his story. This author assumes, rather, that Mary and Joseph live in Bethlehem in a house distinct enough for a star to stop over it and to shine its light directly on that dwelling. This, of course, gives Matthew a problem that Luke did not have, for Matthew knew that Jesus was referred to both as a Galilean and as one who came from the town of Nazareth. So he has to develop a story that has Jesus travel first to Egypt, then back to the family home in Bethlehem, then on to Galilee and ultimately to the town of Nazareth, all in an effort to escape the threat of Herod, who is portrayed, strangely enough, as one who is fearful that this infant, born in relative poverty, represents a threat to his throne. That is, of course, the stuff of fairy tales, but not of history.

Luke, on the other hand, assumes that Mary and Joseph live in Nazareth. He, therefore, has to deal with the expectation that the messiah must be heir to David's throne and so must be born in David's city of Bethlehem. To accomplish this Luke develops a storyline that allows this Nazareth-based couple to be in Bethlehem when the promised child is born. He adopts the ruse of a government-ordered enrollment that requires everyone to return to his or her ancestral home, including Joseph, who is said to be a direct heir of King David. This narrative, which is clearly mythological, reveals how far reality must be stretched in the attempt to make mythology credible. First, please note that there would be about fifty generations between David and Joseph. Assuming David's many wives and the large number of his own sons and daughters, the direct heirs to David after fifty generations would, if they had all survived, which of course they didn't, be in the billions. If they all returned to Bethlehem, as this story implies, there would obviously be no room in the inn! Second, Luke tells us that this enrollment occurred when Quirinius was governor of Syria, but historical records inform us that Quirinius did not become governor until 6–7 CE, by which time Jesus would have been ten to eleven years old. Third, this story, if taken literally, assumes that Joseph would have taken his near-term wife, who was "great with child," on a ninety-four-mile donkey ride to get from Nazareth to Bethlehem. None of these details in Luke's story can pass the test of history, and many parts of his story are immediately recognizable as quite incompatible with Matthew's story. These stories, the only two biblical accounts that purport to chronicle

Jesus' birth, are separated in time by about a decade and represent quite different growing traditions. That, however, does not stop pageant directors from bringing the wise men to the stable as the last scene of the Christmas pageant. One certainly would not want a good pageant to be compromised by biblical scholarship!

A similar blending has occurred in our understanding of the crucifixion and the final moments of Jesus' life. For centuries, Christian churches observed Good Friday with sermons or meditations based on what were called the "seven last words" spoken, presumably by Jesus, from the cross. As with the Christmas pageant, a homogenization of the separate gospel accounts of the cross gradually occurred. Factually, there never were "seven last words." We get that total from combining the gospels' four separate passion stories—accounts that were never intended to be combined. The overwhelming probability is that nowhere is there recorded a single word that Jesus actually spoke from the cross. All of these "words from the cross" are the products of human mythmaking. The earliest gospel, Mark, suggests that no one could have recorded the final words of Jesus because Jesus actually died alone. Mark tells his readers that when Jesus was arrested, "*all* of the disciples forsook him and fled" (Mark 14:50), meaning there was no one left to watch or to listen by the cross. The early Christians argued that this undoubted desertion occurred in order to fulfill the prophets and a text of Zechariah was quoted as proof. In that text, the prophet wrote: "Strike the shepherd that the sheep may be scattered" (Zech. 13:7). Usually one does not work out a rationale for behavior if that behavior is not so deep in the tradition that it cannot be ignored.

There is also the fact that the first actual account of the story of the crucifixion, written by Mark (14:17–15:49), reveals that it is not itself an eyewitness account at all, but is rather an attempt to tell the story of the crucifixion as the fulfillment of the Jewish scriptures, especially of Psalm 22 and Isaiah 53. This first passion story to be written is thus a liturgical interpretation, not remembered history.

It is in this Marcan interpretive narrative that the first "word" that Jesus was supposed to have spoken from the cross is mentioned. It is what we call the cry of dereliction: "My God, my God, why have you forsaken me?" This verse turns out to be nothing but the first verse of Psalm 22—and the first instance, but not the last, in which Psalm 22 is used by Mark to frame the crucifixion story.

When Matthew writes his story of the passion, with Mark's gospel as his guide, he too asserts that only this plaintive question about being forsaken by God is said to have been spoken from the cross by Jesus.

By the time the third gospel, Luke, was written in the late 80s or early 90s, the idea of Jesus' suffering a sense of separation from God or even of his having felt forsaken by God was more than the Christians of that later generation could bear. It was also far too human a cry to fit into the growing understanding of Jesus as a divine being, so the original saying, "My God, my God, why have you forsaken me?" disappears. Luke simply dismisses it from his narrative, even though his source, Mark, included it. He then substitutes for this cry of anguish three different sayings never before heard or recorded in the Christian tradition. First Luke has Jesus speak a word of forgiveness to the soldiers: "Father, forgive them, for they know not what they do" (Luke 23:34). Then he records a word of hope spoken to one of the two thieves, a man Luke, and Luke alone, describes as having become penitent: "Today you will be with me in paradise" (Luke 23:43). Finally he has Jesus speak a word of trust at the moment of his death: "Father, into your hands I commend my spirit" (Luke 23:46). That is a far cry from "My God, my God, why have you forsaken me?"

When the Fourth Gospel is written, its author finds none of

these sayings appropriate for the portrait of Jesus that he is painting, so he drops them all and adds three of his own. The first
is Jesus' words as he commends his mother to the care of the
"beloved disciple": "Woman, behold your son. Son, behold your
mother" (John 19:27). Next there is the anguish of "I thirst"
(John 19:28), uttered, says John, to fulfill the scriptures—specifically, Psalm 69:21, which John then quotes. Finally John records
the climactic words "It is finished" (John 19:30), which brings
this story not to a tragic but to a triumphal end. One will never
understand any gospel and most especially the Fourth Gospel
until the bondage of our own blending process, which actually
makes straightforward Bible study all but impossible, is shattered
and we can begin to know each gospel in its uniqueness.

So in this chapter, in a stark way, with bullet points and only
brief details, I want to isolate the Fourth Gospel from all the
others until we can see this gospel and feel it in its pristine individuality and thus be able to embrace its particular message.

- There is in John no account of a miraculous or virgin birth. It
  is inconceivable to me that at least the last author or editor of
  John had not heard of this story, since it had been introduced
  into the Jesus tradition some ten to fifteen years earlier. So
  we have to wonder why there is no allusion to it. Not only is
  there no supernatural birth story in John's gospel, but on two
  occasions (John 1:45 and John 6:42) Jesus is referred to in a
  rather matter-of-fact way as "the son of Joseph."

- In the Fourth Gospel John the Baptist never baptizes Jesus as
  he does in the first three gospels. All he does in John is bear
  witness to Jesus.

- In the Fourth Gospel there is no account of the temptation of Jesus in the wilderness and no account of the transfiguration of Jesus when he spoke to Moses and Elijah.

- In the Fourth Gospel there are no short provocative sayings of Jesus, no parables and no version of the Sermon on the Mount. Instead, Jesus is portrayed as uttering long, sometimes convoluted theological dialogues or monologues.

- In the Fourth Gospel the story of the cleansing of the Temple is not associated with the final week of Jesus' life as it is in all the other gospels. It occurs rather in chapter 2, near the beginning of his public ministry.

- In the Fourth Gospel the setting is mostly Jerusalem, with Jesus retreating to Galilee only to escape the hostile presence of the Judean authorities. In the three earlier gospels Jesus goes to Jerusalem only once, and that is for the Passover, at which time he is crucified. He is in Jerusalem for three Passovers in John.

- In the Fourth Gospel there is no description of the Last Supper. Nowhere in this gospel does Jesus share the Passover meal with his disciples in an upper room. In place of the institution of the Last Supper, this gospel tells us of the foot-washing ceremony and attaches all of Jesus' teaching about the Eucharist to the story of the feeding of the five thousand in chapter 6.

- In the Fourth Gospel miracles are transformed into "signs," which describe a dramatic truth that is breaking into human consciousness in Jesus. Most of the signs correlate very poorly with earlier miracle stories.

- In the Fourth Gospel there is no anguish in the Garden of Gethsemane and no prayer in which Jesus asks to be spared his fate. Instead Jesus is recorded as rejecting that synoptic tradition and saying that he was born for the purpose of being crucified (John 12:27).

- In the Fourth Gospel Jesus' glorification is portrayed to be the moment of his crucifixion. It is when Jesus is lifted up on the cross that he draws all people to himself. It is not a suffering Christ who is seen on the cross, but a glorified Christ whose work is somehow completed in his death.

- In the Fourth Gospel a host of memorable characters are introduced who are mentioned nowhere else in the New Testament. This parade of characters begins in chapter 1 with a man named Nathaniel and concludes with a character known as the "beloved disciple," who is introduced in the Farewell Discourses and who then plays a major role in the story of the passion and resurrection of Jesus. To understand this gospel we must deal with these unique Johannine creations.

- In the Fourth Gospel this author also gives content and even personality to several other people who have appeared previously in the tradition, but without any of the defining characteristics which John attaches to them. Among them are Andrew, the mother of Jesus, the brothers of Jesus, Philip and Thomas. We will examine the role that this gospel alone assigns to them as the story develops.

These are some of the marks of the Fourth Gospel that set it apart from all the others. What are these unique features about? From where do these distinguishing marks arise? How are they used by this author to tell his story? For now we file these questions along with the differences we have outlined and the remarkable examples of character development to which we have pointed. In many ways they hold the key to the understanding of this gospel.

CHAPTER 4

The Work of a Palestinian Jew

Once we can see the context of the Fourth Gospel in clear relief, separated from the blending processes of the Christian culture, there are still three significant interpretive tools that must be deployed in the study of this book. The first is to recognize that this book is the peculiar and specific creation of a mind that is profoundly influenced by the Jewish experience.* The second is that a popular first-century form of Jewish mysticism has shaped in a dramatic and significant way the message of the book. The third is that literalism can never be applied to this book and the author(s) tell us, on almost every page, that a literal approach to the reading of this book is worthy only of ridicule. In the remaining chapters of this stage-setting section, we will look at these three subjects in detail, with the treatment of Jewish mysticism being the most thorough, since for most people it will be the least familiar and the thing

---

* *Even though this book will reveal my conviction that John's gospel has more than one primary author, I am going to write as if the author is a single person and the finished work has a layered but unified integrity. The final author/editor accepted the text as a whole and that is the way most people throughout history have related to this gospel.*

most easily to be misunderstood. We begin by making the case for
the Jewishness of this book.

I think it is fair to say that John's gospel reveals on almost
every page of its text a persistent and deep familiarity with things
in Jewish Palestine in general and in Jerusalem in particular. It
draws on images out of the Jewish scriptures with which only a
Jewish person would normally be familiar. Wherever this gospel
writer suspects that a Jewish concept might be misunderstood or
misinterpreted by his audience he explains it.

This gospel is also Jewish in the liturgical style it describes,
revealing a special knowledge of the life of the synagogue including a genuine familiarity with Jewish holy days. Its author understands and appeals to this liturgical flow of synagogue worship
and he tells his Jesus story against the background of that flow.
One not familiar with the ordered life of Jewish worship will miss
many of John's nuances.

The internal evidence of Jewishness in this gospel is so powerful and so overwhelming that it amazes me that any other possibility for its origin was ever seriously advanced in Christian
history. If one reads Johannine commentaries from the nineteenth
and early twentieth centuries, however, one will find learned
scholars unable to make sense out of its message without reading into this gospel Hellenistic or Gnostic elements or applying a
syncretism intended to bring together the Hebrew scriptures with
Greek philosophical thinking.

Overwhelmingly the passage in John's gospel that generated
these alternative possibilities was the prologue (John 1:1–18)—in
particular the word *logos,* on which the author builds the emphasis of the prologue. *Logos* can be interpreted or translated not
only as "word," but also as "reason," "the rational principle,"
"the first emanation of God" and "the self-disclosure of God."
It was thus said to have been similar to and to have come out

of Greek philosophy. There is certainly no doubt that when the Christian movement finally began to turn away from its Jewish origins to embrace the Greek world, the Fourth Gospel, as it was typically interpreted, formed the primary bridge that connected the two worlds.

Let me be clear—some Greek influence was always and obviously present from the beginning of Christianity, since Greek was the formal language of the entire Roman Empire. Recall that the letters of Paul, all of the gospels, the non-Pauline letters, the book of Acts, the general epistles and the apocalyptic book of Revelation were all originally written in Greek. There is no substance, we can now say with certainty, to the periodic claims made for the existence of an Aramaic original that might lie behind any one of the gospels. To work in the Greek language, as those early writers did, inevitably meant that they absorbed Greek concepts and were unconsciously shaped by a Greek worldview. To be forced to use Greek vocabulary also meant that people were forced to make Greek assumptions. It is, therefore, impossible to rule out some Greek influence even at the beginning of the Christian movement. It was not, however, until after the period of gospel writing was complete that people in the Christian church who were Gentile converts (and, consequently, almost completely ignorant of Hebrew traditions and Hebrew customs) began to read the Jewish scriptures through a Gentile, Greek lens. The transition to Greek interpretations reached a new and dominant height by the fourth century, when creeds were being written and the theological images that would dominate classical Christianity were being formed. Only during the last half of the twentieth century and the early years of the twenty-first century has it been possible to challenge that classical perspective and thus begin to recover the original Jewishness of the New Testament in general and of the Fourth Gospel in particular. Actually it was a study of the Dead Sea Scrolls, found in the 1940s in a cave at Nag Hammadi near the Dead Sea by an Arab shepherd named Muhammad Ali (not to be confused with the great heavyweight boxing champion of the 1960s and 70s), that caused the weight of scholarship to begin to swing back dramatically to the affirmation that the Fourth Gospel must be seen as clearly reflecting Jewish origins. In this chapter I want first to document the overwhelming Jewish content found in this gospel; then to relate this gospel to the liturgical flow of the synagogue, and finally to explore even the prologue for its Jewish roots and meaning. One must develop Jewish eyes, I believe, if one is going to understand the Fourth Gospel.

Please notice that even the prologue is interrupted by words that only a Jewish person would use and that only a Jewish person would understand. This interruption focuses on John the baptizing one, but be aware that this gospel never calls him John the Baptist. He was clearly a known figure in first-century Jewish life, and perhaps his movement was an early rival to the Christian movement or at least to the Johannine community that produced this gospel. Early in the prologue the baptizing one begins to be downgraded. No movement treats an important figure that way unless its members feel some threat from the one they seek to diminish. Listen to this gospel's words: "He was not the light, but came to bear witness to the light" (John 1:8). The role assigned to John in this gospel is simply "to bear witness" to the Christ, nothing more. He is not even allowed in this gospel to baptize Jesus of Nazareth. That would be to affirm a more powerful role for this John than the author of the Fourth Gospel was willing to provide. He could and did only point beyond himself to the one "who comes after me," though that one "was before me" (John 1:15, 16). When the Fourth Gospel relates the account of this John being interrogated by the priests and Levites from Jerusalem, the questions asked are all in terms of concepts that a non-Jew could neither conceive of nor understand: "Are you the messiah?" "Are you Elijah?" "Are you the prophet?" Only Jews used the term "messiah." Only the Jews developed a mythology around their messianic hopes that involved the return of the prophet Elijah to prepare the way for the messiah. Only the Jews would understand "the prophet" to be the one whom Moses was said to have promised that God would raise up in the last days (Deut. 18:15). When John, the baptizing one, finally identifies himself, he does so in the words of the prophet Isaiah that, again, only Jews with their knowledge of the Jewish prophets would understand. He was, the baptizing one said, "the voice of one crying in the wilderness, to make straight the way of the Lord" (John 1:23, see Isa. 40:3).

When this John actually meets Jesus in the Fourth Gospel, he refers to him as "the lamb of God who takes away the sin of the world," a reference that Jews, and only Jews, would immediately recognize, since it comes out of both their liturgical synagogue life and a messianic interpretation of their scriptures. I shall develop these deeply Jewish concepts later in this book. For now, however, let me simply establish the fact that a non-Jewish, Gentile author could not possibly have turned the Jesus story into one that was thought to fulfill the sacrificial aspects of Jewish liturgical worship patterns. So our study of John must begin with the simple embrace of the overwhelming reality of the Jewishness of this gospel.

Later in this same first chapter of John's gospel, with no explanation, other Jewish titles are introduced for Jesus, the assumption of the author being that his audience would understand them quite well. The author of the Fourth Gospel does explain that the title "rabbi" means teacher (John 1:38), but he then goes on to have Andrew tell his brother Peter: "We have found the messiah," while Philip says to Nathaniel: "We have found him of whom Moses in the law . . . wrote" (John 1:45). This gospel then demonstrates that both Nathaniel and those to whom he spoke were apparently familiar with the tensions between Galilee and Jerusalem, because Nathaniel can articulate the Judean prejudice by asking: "Can anything good come out of Nazareth?" (John 1:46). Among the titles Nathaniel attributes to Jesus is "king of Israel" (John 1:49). Can anyone imagine a non-Jewish writer using this language? Jesus later says that Nathaniel will see greater things than those which he has seen thus far, and he describes these "greater things" by alluding to the Genesis story in which Jacob has a dream of a ladder to heaven on which angels ascend and descend (John 1:51, see Gen. 28:12). To portray this level of familiarity with the Jewish scriptures is the mark of a writer who can only be Jewish. All of these details are found just in chapter 1 of the Fourth Gospel!

With that point established I will skip more quickly over other Jewish references that confirm again and again the Jewish authorship of this book. We find in chapter 2 a reference to the water pots that are used for the Jewish rites of purification (John 2:6). In John 2:13 there is the first of three references to the Passover and Jesus' need to go up to Jerusalem to celebrate it. In Mark, Matthew and Luke, there is only one Passover observance. When we examine Mark closely we find that the one Passover is the climax of a series of Jewish holy days and feast days. Mark opens his gospel with a Jesus story that has echoes of the Jewish observance of Rosh Hashanah and then in proper order tells Jesus stories for the other festivals and penitential observances of the liturgical year of the synagogue. So there is next in Mark material appropriate to be read at Yom Kippur, the Day of Atonement, with a series of healing and cleansing stories, including the call of Levi from the receipt of customs in the employ of unclean Gentiles to leave his uncleanness in order to become one of the twelve disciples (Mark 2:14). Mark's narrative then moves to Sukkoth, the eight-day harvest festival, which he covers with the long parable of the sower and his harvest (Mark 4). Then he takes note of the winter festival of light, called the Feast of Dedication then, but Hanukkah now, with the account known as the transfiguration, where he portrays the light of God descending not on the Temple, but on Jesus (Mark 9:2, 3). Finally, Mark relates the story of Jesus' crucifixion to the season of Passover (Mark 14–15). This means that Mark provides Jesus stories for liturgical use in the proper order from the Jewish New Year, Rosh Hashanah, all the way to Passover, which covers only about six and a half months of the year. Matthew and Luke both expand Mark to cover the entire liturgical year, which is why both of these gospels are forty percent longer than Mark.

John, however, seems to be under the influence of a different Jewish liturgical pattern. For while part of the Jewish world did use a one-year Torah reading cycle (as reflected in Mark, Matthew and Luke), other parts of the Jewish world used a three-year Torah reading cycle. John appears to be relating his version of the Jesus story to this three-year cycle. It is this liturgical practice that determines the form through which this gospel tells its Jesus story.

John's gospel makes a reference to the Feast of Tabernacles (John 7:2), which is another name for Sukkoth, the harvest festival, and in that chapter relates Jesus quite specifically to that festival. Later, the Fourth Gospel makes a reference to the Feast of Dedication (John 10:22), which comes in the dead of winter. No one outside the world of Jewish worship traditions would be as conversant with these practices as our gospel writer clearly was.

Once one learns the pattern, the Jewish references leap out at the reader from almost every page. In a conversation with Nicodemus (John 3:1ff) Jesus is made to refer to the Holy Spirit as the "wind." The Jewish words *ruach* and *nephesh,* which mean respectively "wind" and "breath," or external wind and internal wind, are frequently used in the Hebrew scriptures as synonyms for spirit or the breath of God. Only a Jewish author and Jewish readers would know this.*

In the story of the Samaritan woman by the well, the author uses place-names with which only a Palestinian Jew would be familiar. He refers to a city named Sychar and to Jacob's well, which was nearby. In Jesus' conversation with the Samaritan woman the author reveals intimate knowledge of the relationship between Jews and Samaritans and of the places in which their debate was focused and around which hostility was most intense (John 4:7–42).

In chapter 5, after another feast of the Jewish liturgical calendar is mentioned, but not named (perhaps deliberately), the author reveals intimate knowledge of things in Jerusalem such as a pool by the Sheep's Gate called Bethzatha, which has five porticoes (John 5:1–3). He knows of the myth of the healing power of the troubled waters (John 5:7–9) and of the fierceness of the Sabbath day restrictions. He refers to the Jewish custom of searching the scriptures for the promise of eternal life (John 5:39). He is familiar with the intimate geographical details of the Palestinian landscape in the hills of Galilee (John 6:1ff), and with the details of the story of Moses providing manna in the wilderness (John 6:31–34). None of these details would flow naturally or easily from the pen of a non-Jew or even a fringe Jew. This is the database on which I form the conclusion that the author of the Fourth Gospel is deeply and profoundly Jewish.

When we reach chapter 9 we find a story that appears to reveal not the time of Jesus, but the contemporary experience of this gospel writer living at the end of the first century. The author, in presenting the case of a man born blind (was it due to sin—and if so, whose?), is clearly aware of the conflict that resulted in the

---

* See Gen. 2:7, Ezek. 37:1–10.

expulsion from the synagogue of the followers of Jesus mentioned in this story (John 9:22). Jesus is portrayed as engaging the Jewish authorities on the issues of the *author's* day, which resulted in expulsion, and he is portrayed as having done so in the quintessential form of the rabbinic debates of *his* day. The split between revisionist Jews and orthodox Jews which led to the followers of Jesus being expelled from the synagogue when this gospel was being written was both real and clear. This gospel reflects the pain and trauma of that expulsion, as well as the necessity for reformulating the Christ message so that it will endure in its new reality as a movement that is outside the synagogue.

The data is thus overwhelming that this gospel is a Jewish work. Its message becomes understandable only when it is placed inside the Jewish context that produced it. Yet this gospel also appears to reflect some early movement beyond the traditional boundaries of Judaism, but it was more experiment than contradictory, that is, a movement that would be recognized as being in a predominantly Jewish direction. Some, though not all, of this evidence is located in the prologue. Even here, however, the prologue reflects deliberately the creation story of Genesis 1 with which only Jews would have been familiar. Other evidence of a post-Jewish debate is seen in the unique use of the story from Exodus in which the words "I AM" became the assigned name of God—a name that this gospel then applies to Jesus. We have no record that it had occurred to anyone to do this prior to the writing of the Fourth Gospel.

The claims of pre-existence are related in the text of this gospel again and again, but frequently through the mouths of those who are the major heroes of the Jewish scriptures, people about whom non-Jews would not be conversant. One thinks of Jesus being made to say in John such things as, "Before Abraham was, I AM" and "Moses rejoiced to see my day."

The gospel of John is a foreign book to anyone except a Jew. Its author was clearly deeply knowledgeable of Jewish places, practices, and liturgical forms. So how was it possible that anyone ever saw this gospel as a book that reflected Greek Hellenized thinking, was compromised by Gnostic thinking or was influenced either by Philo or by those who produced Philo? It was the prologue that they misunderstood, so to discover the profoundly Jewish nature of the prologue we now turn.

CHAPTER 5

Tracing the Jewish Roots of the Prologue

The prologue to John's gospel is strikingly different from the words with which any previous gospel has begun. John, the one who baptizes in the wilderness, is introduced; yet this John is not the John the Baptist we have met in the earlier gospels. The idea of Jesus being pre-existent is also introduced in the prologue, and later developing Christian doctrine regarding the divinity of Jesus is significantly rooted in this idea. If, as I have sought to demonstrate, the Fourth Gospel is a profoundly Jewish piece of writing, then why, we must ask, would its Jewish author write such a non-Jewish-sounding prologue?

There are two possible answers to that question. The first suggests that the prologue was originally not a part of this gospel, but was the work of a later editor who had a quite different agenda. Urban von Wahlde, a Johannine scholar at Loyola University in Chicago, maintains in his brilliant analysis that not only the prologue, but all of the "I AM" passages, in which Jesus is made to claim the divine name, are indeed the work of a third major editor. Nowhere, however, does von Wahlde suggest that this editor was writing material that was alien to the rest of the book. Von

Wahlde asserts only that this editor was drawing out the implications that he was convinced were in the book itself. Such scholars as E. F. Scott, C. H. Dodd and Rudolf Bultmann also agree that the themes in the prologue are developed fully in the body of the book and that the prologue is to this gospel what an overture is to an opera, serving to introduce what will be encountered later.

The second answer counters the underlying assumption that the prologue sounds non-Jewish and asserts, to the contrary, that it is fully in keeping with Jewish tradition. The possibility is thus raised that over the centuries its words have been misread and misinterpreted by a Gentile, deeply anti-Semitic Christian church in a way that not only was ill-informed about Jewish thought, but was also deeply distorted by that very anti-Semitism. That is the conclusion to which my study has led me and the insight that ultimately helped me to engage this book as I have done.

My first step was and is to recognize that the concept of the "word" (*logos*) of God shaping and entering human life runs all through the various strands of the Jewish tradition. The Torah (the so-called books of Moses), with which the Old Testament opens, starts with the words "In the beginning, God . . ." John's prologue thus counters the first words of Genesis by saying, "In the beginning"—not just God, but the "word." No one should miss this obvious and very Jewish contrast. John then goes on to give a radical and expanding definition of the "word," describing it as being "with God" at the beginning. Through the "word," he says, "all things were made," and without the "word" nothing was made (John 1:3). The prologue then personalizes the "word" "In *him* was life" and this life "was the light" of human beings. It was this light that illumined darkness and the darkness could not extinguish it or overcome it (John 1:5).

Now read the creation story of Genesis 1 in its fullness. In a more modern idiom, this is what it says:

In the beginning God created the heavens and the earth. At the beginning the heavens and the earth were without form and void, and darkness covered the face of the deep. The spirit then hovered over the water like a hen perched on a nest of eggs out of which life was to emerge. And God said, "Let there be light."

In the beginning there was the oneness of God. Then out of God came God's word, "Let there be light." Now the singularity of God shared creation with a new power. The "word" of God came out of God and stood over against God. That "word" began to shape the world, separating light from darkness, creating a firmament to divide the waters above from the waters below, which had the effect of separating heaven from earth. Then God spoke again and ordered the earthly waters to be gathered together so that dry land could appear. Next God spoke to create the sun and the moon—one to give light to the day, and the other, to the night. God then began to bring life out of the sea and to form birds to populate the air and finally creatures to populate the earth, "beasts of the field" and "everything that creeps upon the earth," the creation story calls them. Finally late on the sixth day God spoke, and this time in response to the "word" of God human life was born—male and female together and instantaneously. To this first couple was then given stewardship over all the earth.

I do not mean to suggest that this creation story is a narrative about how the world literally came into being. The astrophysicists and the biologists know far more about that today than did the ancient biblical writers. I do mean to suggest that the anonymous Jewish writers who wrote this creation story attributed to the "word" of God enormous creative power, seeing it as separate from God, but of God's very essence.

The prologue to John's gospel makes this same Jewish claim as a prelude to this gospel's attempt to describe that which the followers of Jesus believed they had experienced in the life of Jesus of Nazareth. The Hebrew word for "word" was *dabar.* The Greek word for "word" was (as we have seen) *logos.* The Hebrew concept of *dabar* indicated that this "word" had power to shape the world, to reveal the presence of God, to call people to a heightened sense of selfhood, a heightened consciousness. So much of that which we find in the Greek word *logos* was not as foreign to the meaning of *dabar* in Jewish thought as once was supposed.

Later in their history Jewish writers, telling the sacred story of this nation, looked for and created symbols that expressed their conviction that God was not simply an external being, but an ever-present reality. During the wilderness-wandering years of their national life, when the Jews were between their captivity in Egypt and their settlement in what they called "the promised land," these writers symbolized God's presence in their midst with a mobile tabernacle into which they placed holy objects. God was not fixed in a place because these people at that time were wanderers, themselves not fixed in a place. I suspect that every people in the hunter-gatherer phase of their anthropological history had some replication of this conviction that the holy God was on their journey with them.

For the Jews this tabernacle was connected, so their mythology proclaimed, with the deity that they, like all other ancient people, located beyond the sky. It was said in the Bible that this connection was accomplished with a pillar of cloud by day and a pillar of fire by night (Exod. 13:21). God was, if you will, both transcendent (that is, external) and immanent (that is, within). Following the Sinai experience, described in the book of Exodus beginning in chapter 18, Moses, who was thought of as the Jewish people's primary human link to God, had just begun the process of delegating his authority to "able men out of all of Israel" whom he had made "heads over the people, rulers of thousands, of hun-

dreds, of fifties and of tens," and, we are told, "they judged the
people at all times" (Exod. 18:25–26). Moses still remained the
judge of final appeal.

When the authority to judge is removed from a single leader
and distributed among the people, the problem of subjectivity
always arises, and with subjectivity comes the need to objectify
the law—that is, the will of God. This need is met in the story
of God dictating the law to the chosen people from Mount Sinai.
Since God was thought to live above the sky, to climb to the top
of the mountain would be to come as close to God as a human
being could come. Moses first gathered the people at the foot of
the mountain and then God was said to have come down from
above the sky to the top of the mountain. This divine presence
was symbolized in Exodus 19 by all kinds of mysterious natural
phenomena: thunder, lightning and thick clouds that covered the
mountain. Sinai was said to have been wrapped in smoke and to
have quaked visibly. Only then was Moses invited to come to the
mountaintop, while the people of Israel were warned to keep their
distance. The priests were bidden to go through various acts of
consecration and finally Aaron, the high priest, was asked to accompany Moses in order to receive the "word" of the Lord.

That was the prologue to the Jewish story of how the Torah
was given. It began with this introduction: "And God spoke all
these words" (Exod. 20:1). First came the Ten Commandments,
which spelled out the human duty toward God and the human
duty toward one's neighbor. Over the years, even the centuries,
these commandments would be endlessly expanded to cover every
conceivable set of circumstances and every possible ethical decision with which life would confront the Jews. Finally, spiritual
and liturgical directives were given to cover every aspect of their
worship life. That was how the "word" of God evolved into being
the Torah. Now the "word" of God, which had created the world,

was said to have been captured in human words designed to govern every concrete human situation. Those who were to judge the people of Israel had an objective standard by which to make their judgments.

These words of God, as spoken to Moses and amplified in the Torah, were codified in the law, which was called the "word" of God. Gradually the Jewish people, as time passed, began to see the law as being as sacred as God. These words, the tradition suggested not altogether accurately, were said to have been placed by Moses into the mobile tabernacle to be carried by the people wherever they went. God's "word" was thus always present with God's people. When the Temple of Solomon was completed in the latter years of the tenth century BCE, the tabernacle, now called the "ark of the covenant," was brought to the Temple with great ceremony, its contents removed and placed in the Temple, including the symbols of the law: "the two tablets of stone." That meant that now the "word" of God had a permanent dwelling place in this settled nation. So did God, for in the Temple of Solomon there was an outer court into which all people could come, the holy place into which only Jews could enter, and finally the inner sanctum, known as the "holy of holies," where God was believed to dwell quite literally and into which only the high priest could enter (and he only once a year on the Day of Atonement and then only after elaborate ritual cleansing activities).

It was out of this history that the Jews began to use the word "tabernacle" as a verb, speaking of God as "tabernacling" with God's people. God was not only the external, transcendent God, but had now also become the immanent and ever-present God. While the highest heaven might not be able in the minds of the Jews to contain God's majesty, they were convinced that the Temple contained God's earthly throne and that the law, now placed within it, contained God's "word."

The Jews were destined to learn, as all people must, that God cannot be possessed, nor can the "word" of God ever be reduced to propositional statements. So God continued, according to the biblical story, to operate outside official religious channels in the lives of the prophets. These prophets would constantly rise up outside the boundaries set by the religious hierarchy and they would speak the "word" of God in and to the citadels of power. In previous books I have traced the rise of the prophetic movement in the Jewish world and sought to demonstrate how the "word" of God, which was thought to have "possessed" the prophets, was spoken in such a way as to redefine the holy God in ever new and substantial ways.* While God may not be subject to change, the human perception of God is; and history, even the history of the Bible, is the story of the ever-changing human perceptions of God. That biblical story journeys from the fierce tribal God who sends plagues on the Egyptians, including "murdering" the firstborn male in every Egyptian household on the night of the Passover (Exod. 12:12), to stopping the sun in the sky to allow Joshua more daylight in which to slaughter more of his Ammonite enemies (Josh. 10:12–14), to the prophet Samuel ordering King Saul to carry out genocide against the Amalekites (I Sam. 15:1–3), to a sense of God's universality found in Malachi, and finally to the commandment to "love your enemies" and "to pray for those who persecute you" (Matt. 5:44). That is quite a journey. So was the journey from the idea that the "word" of God had been captured in the Torah to the "word" of God that was spoken through the prophets. This prophetic "word" appeared to be a time-limited experience. The "word" came, but only for a season, until the power of the "word" had been delivered.

As these Jewish ideas evolved, the next stage and the next

---

* *Re-Claiming the Bible for a Non-Religious World.* See bibliography for details.

change-agent in their understanding of God came when the messianic idea was born within Judaism. In the concept of the messiah, the externality of God began to be tempered.

The word "messiah" at its inception meant nothing more than "the anointed one." It was a reference to the process of anointing a king with oil at his coronation as a sign that he possessed the ability to rule in God's name. Recall that Samuel the prophet had anointed Saul, a Benjaminite and the son of Kish, to be Israel's first king (I Sam. 10:1ff). When that rule failed, Samuel anointed David, the youngest son of Jesse, a member of the tribe of Judah, to be the second king (I Sam. 16:13). So the anointed one, "the messiah" (*maschiach*), was, as the term was first used, nothing more than a royal title for the king of the Jews.

The royal family had become established about 1000 BCE when the reign of King David began, and it came to an end around the year 586 BCE with the destruction of Jerusalem by the Babylonians. As part of the Babylonian attempt to destroy the Jewish state completely, these conquerors of the Jews rounded up all the sons and other presumed heirs to the throne of the final Davidic king, a man named Zedekiah, and murdered them before Zedekiah's eyes. They then put Zedekiah's eyes out and took him blind and in chains to a Babylonian prison where he died, bringing to an end the house of David (II Kings 25:7). Since the concept of "the anointed one" was no longer bound to the history of a specific king, it now began to flow freely in Jewish mythology. The people envisioned an ideal ruler who would someday come and who would represent God in a far more specific and complete way. That was how the Jewish idea of a messiah actually began.

The images of the messiah, however, varied widely in the fantasy life of the Jewish people, ranging from a conquering military leader who would reestablish the Jews' earthly power, all the way to the figure of the suffering servant, who would absorb the world's anger and pain and transform it into love and life. This messianic tradition also took the phrase "son of man," introduced in Ezekiel (where it meant nothing but a human being), and developed it into an eschatological figure who would bring the world to an end and inaugurate the kingdom of God on earth. By the time we arrive at the book of Daniel (165 BCE), this figure even seemed to possess supernatural power and to share in God's divinity. Behind all of these messianic symbols, however, lay a yearning for wholeness and a sense of oneness with God, who was still primarily conceived of as an external being. As one of the images of wholeness, the prophet Isaiah described the dawning of the kingdom of God in these terms: "The wilderness and the dry land shall be glad, the desert shall rejoice and blossom like a crocus. . . . Then the eyes of the blind shall be opened, and the ears of the deaf unstopped; then shall the lame man leap like a hart, and the tongue of the dumb [that is, the mute] shall sing for joy. For waters shall break forth in the wilderness and streams in the desert" (Isa. 35:1–2, 5–6). This messiah, who would inaugurate the kingdom of God, was a future promise, however—one who would come at the end of time. Jewish thought had to go through one more transformation before John's gospel could say something like: "In the beginning was the word, and the word was with God, and the word was God . . . and the word became flesh and dwelt among us." That final transformation would arrive when this new understanding of the immanence of God, the permeating presence of God, infiltrated and finally challenged the primary definition of God as an external being. This came with the rise of both the wisdom literature and the development in the Jewish people of something that came to be called Jewish mysticism. To that discussion we turn next.

CHAPTER 6

Permeating Wisdom: The Doorway into Jewish Mysticism

M ysticism appears to be part of every religious system, existing usually on the fringe of acceptability. In some sense it is always a commentary on the adequacy of traditional definitions. I am certainly not the first to suggest that the gospel we call John was a reflection of this mystical emphasis. In the second century Clement of Alexandria, seeking to distinguish John from the synoptics, referred to the Fourth Gospel as a "spiritual gospel." Origen, a third-century theologian, called the Fourth Gospel a "mystical gospel."* Twentieth-century American scholars John Sanford and L. William Countryman picked up that same ancient theme and developed it in their books. Sanford, a Jungian analyst, entitled his work *Mystical Christianity* and clarified his perspective in his subtitle, *A Psychological Commentary on the Gospel of John,* while Countryman's title was *The Mystical Way in the Fourth Gospel,* with his explanatory subtitle being *Crossing Over into*

---

* Both Clement and Origen are quoted in Jey J. Kanagaraj's book, *Mysticism in the Gospel of John,* p. 22. See bibliography for details.

God.* On the opposite side of this debate there have also been a number of eminent Johannine scholars, including B. F. Westcott, Edwyn Hoskyns, R. H. Lightfoot and Raymond Brown, who saw no place for mysticism in their understanding of John's gospel. C. H. Dodd and C. K. Barrett were neutral on the subject, while an English scholar of Indian background, Jey J. Kanagaraj, perhaps assisted by his roots in Eastern religion, made a powerful case for reading this gospel through the lens not just of mysticism, but of a very specific school of Jewish mysticism. Kanagaraj identifies this school as "merkabah mysticism," or "throne mysticism," a school that New Testament scholars once considered historically irrelevant to the study of John's gospel. They assumed a much later date for the development of this form of Jewish mysticism, one well past the time of the writing of the New Testament. With the discovery of the Dead Sea Scrolls, however, this impression was corrected and it was quite conclusively demonstrated that merkabah mysticism had been known in the first century.

I will not end this debate, but I will bear witness and cast my vote on the mystical side. My study has convinced me, first, that the gospel of John is a deeply Jewish book and, second, that by reading it through the lens of Jewish mysticism, our generation is given new doors for the understanding of this gospel. Mysticism and mystical writing by definition can never be literalized, which offers us another interpretive clue which I will develop in the next chapter. When that chapter is joined to this one, my readers will know and understand why I have entitled this book *The Fourth Gospel: Tales of a Jewish Mystic.*

For now I want to show how mysticism developed in Judaism, why it developed, what need it met and what determined the form that it would ultimately take. If my thesis is correct that the third

---

* See bibliography for details.

major editing of the Johannine text took place when the excommunicated followers of Jesus turned to the far more unbounded and universal themes of Jewish mysticism to translate the Jesus experience, then we need to understand Jewish mysticism. How did mysticism enter into Judaism? How did it evolve through Judaism in order to be present and available, not only as an option for understanding Jesus, but as the option of choice? How did this mysticism transform Christianity in ways that those early Christians could not then have fully understood? John's gospel did all of these things and thus occupies a unique place in the development of Christianity.

The gospel of John was then tragically distorted, I now believe, by the Nicene and post-Nicene fathers, who used it to formulate their creeds. As Greek thinkers, these early Christian leaders had little appreciation for things Jewish and as far as we can tell no understanding whatsoever of Jewish mysticism. As dualists, they saw God and human life, spiritual things and material things, souls and bodies as two separate and divided, even antagonistic, realms. Not knowing the language of Jewish mysticism, these religious leaders could not possibly hear the Johannine mystical tradition, which saw Jesus not as an invader from another realm, but as the "defining" human life, bringing together into oneness the human with the divine, nor could they understand the divine as a permeating presence that opened its recipients to a new dimension of consciousness. These concepts would have been completely foreign to them.

Jewish mysticism was never a majority movement inside Judaism. As mysticism tends to be everywhere, it was resisted and resented by the hierarchy of the Jewish priesthood and marginalized in the traditional Jewish community. It was, however, an option to which a Jewish community might turn when they were forced out of their normal boundaries by excommunication. That excommunication, I now believe, actually compelled the Jewish disciples of Jesus to redefine Jesus and their Jesus experience in a new, transcendent, mystical and universal language.

The doorway through which mysticism entered Judaism was what is called the "wisdom tradition," and it featured the "wisdom literature" that was composed by Jewish people in the post-exilic phase of their history. To understand how "wisdom" is used in this context, we need to go back a bit in history.

The Jewish scriptures always reflected the history of the Jewish people. The Jews had to adapt their understanding of God to the current realities in their common life. So God was their "comfort" in the days of slavery in Egypt, their "vindicator" and "guide" in the exodus and wilderness years and their "conquering, heroic warrior" in the defeat of the Canaanites. God was also, however, the one who was transformed by the insights of the prophets and the one who sustained the people in their exile in Babylon, finally being perceived as the power that worked through Cyrus the Persian to free them to return to what they believed was their promised land.

The idea of a changing God is not exclusive to the story of the Jews; it is inherent in the story of human life. God is never static in human history, but is always changing, ever evolving, and the reality that forces this change in our understanding of God is always found in the changing circumstances of human life. The events of history coupled with the expansion of human knowledge serve as the twin change-agents.

A brief survey of the religious history of human beings will make that thesis abundantly clear. Hunter-gatherer people always had to have an unfixed deity, one who could wander with them. Animism served that circumstance well. Settled agricultural communities, as they evolved, needed a deity who was attached to the land they were farming. The fertility cults and the earth mother goddess religions met that need in a very specific way.

Tribal deities emerged when the need to defend a group's tribal land and their life-providing food supply became a bigger issue than producing the crops or expanding the flocks. The tribal chief, who always emerged in battle as a successful military leader, formed the next image of God. Such chiefs were thought of (and began to think of themselves) as the incarnation of the tribal god who lived above the sky. That is what produced ideas such as the divine right of kings and even the suggestion, most powerfully expressed in Japan, that the emperor himself was divine, the son of God. Human beings always create God in their own image and in an attempt to meet their own needs.

As the world became smaller, these local tribal gods evolved into a sense of God's universal oneness. That has happened in world history. It has also happened in Jewish history.

A journey through the Hebrew Bible will reveal most of these stages, side by side in the same book, in all of their contradictory eloquence. It is a journey we have previously chronicled. This basic understanding of the Bible as an evolving story counters the literalism of those who want to make inerrant the text that they see as "the word of God." The changing understanding of God throughout human history renders nonsensical any religious claims to the "infallibility" of a particular religious leader.

So look now at how it was that within Jewish history wisdom literature developed and out of wisdom literature Jewish mysticism grew.

Following the Babylonian exile, the voices of the prophets fell silent. The law—the Torah—was codified to speak to every conceivable circumstance of both life and ritual. The law was thought of as the dictated "word of God," and God increasingly was seen as a distant and even uninvolved deity. God is always easier to see in times of victory than of defeat, in power more than in powerlessness. There was an ache of emptiness in the Jewish soul. The development of the "wisdom tradition" was the response, the next phase in Judaism.

Wisdom was perceived as an aspect of the God who was immanent, within them, a God who could touch their lives deeply. To walk in wisdom for the Jews came to mean to walk in or with God. To learn wisdom was to learn God. To listen to wisdom was to listen to God. The God that the universe itself could not contain, much less a temple made by their own hands, began to be perceived not only as a "being" present with them, but as a permeating presence in all of life. So in the literature of this period of Jewish history, wisdom came to be made very human and very personal. Wisdom was perceived as a manifestation of God that informed even the tiniest events of daily life. God had come out of the heavens and had become a reality closer than their breath. People walked with God's wisdom. People lived inside God's wisdom. People partook of God as they partook of God's wisdom. Wisdom was thus another aspect of God, like the law given at Mount Sinai. The law, however, was an external body of data that could be studied; wisdom was a permeating presence of the divine that was experienced only when it was internalized. In the law God's will was proclaimed; in wisdom God's life was lived. It was a new dimension of Jewish thought. In the book of Proverbs, the unknown author penned a hymn to wisdom as a manifestation of God. In it wisdom was personified and became, if you will, an "incarnation of God." It was not, however, the way we would later understand incarnation, a God invading the world from some distant abode, because between wisdom and God there was thought to be no separation.

The book of Proverbs portrays wisdom as calling to us "in the heights, in the paths . . . beside the gates . . . and at the entrance of the portals" (Prov. 8:1–3). There was no escaping the divine presence. Out of the mouth of wisdom, it was said, truth moved and insight was gained—insight into ourselves. The journey into the self, however, was also perceived to be the same as a journey into God. This was the place where mysticism first entered the tradition. Of wisdom, the writer of Proverbs claims that "the Lord created me in the beginning of God's work"—before the earth was made. When God "established the heavens," wisdom was there. "In the beginning was wisdom and wisdom was with God and wisdom was God." This personified wisdom was daily God's delight and this is spelled out as the eighth chapter of Proverbs unfolds. In wisdom was life, while death was found in the absence of wisdom. All of the major themes found in the prologue of John's gospel are found in the book of Proverbs as the attributes of a God experienced as immanent in the heart of life itself. God's self-revelation, the "word," was part of the external God from the beginning of the universe. God, experienced as immanent in the creation, however, was "wisdom." Both the "word" and "wisdom" were manifestations of God. Both the "word" and "wisdom" were pre-existent. Both the "word" and "wisdom" were calls to life, to love and to being. The prologue to John's gospel was a hymn to the "word" based on a hymn to "wisdom" in the book of Proverbs (8:21–32), and thus it was a deeply Jewish concept. Both hymns began to hint at the growing awareness that God was not to be perceived as a being, no matter how majestic, distant or otherworldly. God must be understood as a verb, calling, informing and shaping us and all creation into being all that we were created to be. In wisdom was life and that life was the light of all people. The "word" takes flesh. "Wisdom" expands life.

This was not to speak of a divine invasion in human form, as if the divine and the human were two distinct realities; that is, this was not an experience of Hellenistic dualism. Jesus was not being portrayed in John's prologue as related to God in the same way that Clark Kent is related to Superman—in other words, God in disguise as a human being. The author of John's gospel, in his prologue, is either using or creating an early Christian hymn based on a hymn to wisdom in the book of Proverbs to express the mystical unity that human life can have with God and asserting that this was in fact the unique thing about Jesus of Nazareth. It is that life-expanding oneness with God to which the author of the Fourth Gospel believed that Jesus was calling us. The Christ life, so envisioned, cannot be found in ritual activities, as we will see as John's story develops. It was his understanding of Jesus that in him dwelt both the presence of this "word of God" and the presence of the "wisdom of God." Both had been lived out by Jesus of Nazareth. That is the secret of John's gospel and the invitation in this gospel to us is to come into this presence.

Onto this picture of God as "word" calling us to life and as "wisdom" empowering us to live, Jewish people added the dimension of Jewish mysticism. Early Jewish mysticism focused on the visions found in the Old Testament where oneness with God was thought to have been experienced. There was Jacob's dream, described in Genesis 28, in which Jacob saw a ladder connecting heaven and earth, and angels ascending and descending on this ladder as God and human life came together. The author of the Fourth Gospel, still in chapter 1, has Jesus say to Nathaniel: "You will see heaven open and the angels of God ascending and descending on the son of man" (John 1:51). Another important feature in Jewish mysticism was the story told in the book of Exodus in which Moses requests to see God face-to-face (Exod. 33:17–24), something the Jewish people believed to be beyond the limits of human life. In this narrative that request is denied, but Moses is allowed to gaze on God's back as God goes around the bend in the mountain. Mystics could see only where God had been.

Still another focus of Jewish mysticism was the vision attributed to Isaiah in which the prophet was said to have seen God "high and lifted up," surrounded by angelic beings who covered God's face lest the vision be more than Isaiah could absorb (Isa. 6:5). Ezekiel spoke of seeing a wheel in the sky (Ezek. 1:15ff) and of seeing his nation revived from the status of a valley filled with dead, dry bones into a spirit-filled, living people called to a new dimension of life by the wind of the spirit that blew over the valley (Ezek. 37). Daniel's vision in the Temple (Dan. 7) took the title "son of man," which had originally meant only a human being, and used it to envision one who had entered into divinity. Daniel, who referred to God as the "Ancient of Days," now saw God revealed in this human form.

A Jewish mystical tradition had certainly developed by the first century, and it centered on the idea of God's enthronement. The Fourth Gospel would take the enthronement image and transform the death of Jesus by describing it as a mystical enthronement on a cross. The cross became the moment of Jesus' glorification and in the process of his interpretation of the crucifixion John transformed the Jesus story. This gospel writer's images were, however, still Jewish, borrowed, as they were, from the enthronement images of Jewish mysticism. This meant that a form of Jewish mysticism became the lens through which the final writing of this gospel was to be read. To say that "the word was made flesh and dwelt among us" is to say that in the life of Jesus people saw the will of God being lived out and they heard the word of God being spoken. To exhort people to be born again or to be born of the spirit (as we will later hear John do) was not to call them to a conversion experience that would make them spiritually superior to others; rather, it was to invite them to escape life's limits and enter a new level of consciousness where they would begin to see themselves as a part of who God is and to experience God as a part of who they were. Jesus, in this Jewish sense, was the place where God once again came to "tabernacle" with God's people. Jesus was the place where the human and the divine flowed together as one, so that Jesus could be heard as speaking with the voice of God. Jesus could be heard as saying that the oneness with God that he offered would satisfy the deepest human hunger and quench the deepest human thirst. In John's mind it was by relating a person to this understanding of God that a person was introduced to life that is eternal. Finally, it was this mystical oneness that enabled the Johannine followers of Jesus to perceive Jesus as being part of who God is.

The "word of God" had thus come to dwell among the people in the person of Jesus. That was John's affirmation. Yet those who had seen this reality and who had entered it could not force this mystical experience into the religious words of their day. They tried, but they succeeded only in expanding their words beyond the breaking point, beyond traditional religious recognition; and when this effort resulted in their expulsion from the synagogue, they decided not to turn their backs on this vision, but to continue their journey into Jesus, which was destined to be also a journey into mysticism. Now this community could redefine itself and redefine its experience of Jesus in such a way that not only the boundaries of the rejecting synagogue could be transcended, but so also could all religious boundaries, as well as all of the limits that have been placed on human life. The members of this community were then ready to write this new vision of who God is and of how Jesus was a part of that God in a dramatically new way. That is the meaning of the Fourth Gospel. They wrote their story self-consciously, without denying their Jewish roots, but at the same time without being bound by their Jewish frame of reference. The writer who placed the *final* stamp on the Fourth Gospel wanted to point to new consciousness, to what it means to be born from above. In the prologue, which this final editor,

I believe, added to the text, he announced his intentions. Jesus was the word of God spoken to the world. The bearer of the word and the word itself must be seen as one. It is interesting to note that the word *logos* is never used again in this gospel after the prologue. It was, however, *lived,* and it is to the living of that word in the life of Jesus to which the prologue points. John's work is a fascinating gospel, Jewish to its core, mystical in its meaning.

CHAPTER 7

John the Non-Literalist

One cannot be mystical in one's approach to God and still be literal about the symbols one uses for God. Indeed the very idea of the mystical means that words cannot capture it. Mysticism expands words beyond their normal limits and calls the mystic into the ultimate experience of wordlessness. The best that words can do is to point beyond themselves to a new reality that words can never contain or even describe. Literalism suggests that words, which are only pointers, can in fact be made concrete, thus establishing assumptions that can never be demonstrated. Literalism commits us to the presumption that any religious form can not only capture truth, but also explain it fully. It is out of the distortions that literalism inevitably creates that most religious violence originates. Religious literalism requires infallible leaders and inerrant scriptures. Literalism is thus always the enemy of faith, which is ultimately the opposite of certainty. John's gospel, perhaps more than any other part of the biblical text, makes a mockery of literalism, constantly holding it up to ridicule. If one seeks to impose any kind of literalism on this book, one closes one's eyes to its profound and yet affirming meaning. Mystical eyes can never be literal eyes, and this gospel is the product of mystical eyes—more specifically, Jewish mystical eyes.

So deeply rooted in a literal or quasi-literal view of the biblical story are most Western people that literal assumptions are always creeping back into the narrative. The recognition of the non-literal aspects of the gospel tradition in general, and of John's gospel in particular, is usually accompanied in Christians by a sense of the guilt and sometimes even despair that mark traditional believers. Some deeply religious people even respond to the insights that challenge a literal understanding of Christianity with anger, a dead giveaway that it is their religious security that has been disturbed, not religious truth. So let me begin this chapter on the non-literal reading of John with some statements designed to be provocative. I am certain they will be.

A preponderance of biblical scholarship now indicates that John the Baptist had no sense that he was ever the forerunner of Jesus; that no water was ever turned into wine in Cana of Galilee; that Jesus never rebuked his mother because his "hour had not come"; that Jesus never literally drove the money-changers out of the Temple, either at the beginning of his ministry as John asserts (John 2:13–22), or following his entry into Jerusalem as the other gospels portray (Mark 11:1–19, Matt. 21:1–13, Luke 19:28–46); that Jesus never identified his body with the Temple; that Jesus never had a conversation with a man named Nicodemus or with a Samaritan woman by the well; that Jesus never fed the multitude by multiplying loaves and fish, nor did he liken his flesh to bread and his blood to wine; that he never engaged the people of Jerusalem in debate about his origins; that he never said any of the "I AM" sayings; that he never restored sight to a man who was born blind; that he never raised from the dead a man named Lazarus; that there never was a triumphal entry into Jerusalem; that we have no idea what, if anything, Jesus said from the cross, and that no tomb was ever supplied by a rich man from Arimathea.

What we have been doing, when we assume that the things recorded above are actual events, is to confuse storytelling and parable with history. We have failed to recognize the impact of both liturgy and preaching on the recorded memory of Jesus. We have failed to embrace the need of first-century people to create memorable images both of Jesus and of those who were said to have been around him. We have failed to understand that these images were shaped by the sacred scriptures of the Jews and were then transformed by the members of the Johannine community into messianic expectations that found their fulfillment in Jesus.

When people hear the contents of the above list, which could be considerably expanded, they often respond with a startled look and the obvious questions: What is left? What is true? What is real? Can we have confidence in anything? Those questions reveal, however, only that most of us begin reading the Bible with a set of literal assumptions. When biblical scholarship opens us to new possibilities, literalists experience this as chipping away at the foundations until there is little or nothing remaining and the believer stands suspended over a bottomless pit in religious free fall. That sensation, if unaddressed, will make fundamentalists out of all who want to remain believers.

Most Christians, in my experience, are fundamentalists, but they draw the literal line at different places. For some, every word of the text must be taken literally; no deviation from that standard is allowed. For others, the line is not quite so rigid; some biblical phrases are recognized as "figures of speech." When Paul said: "Pray without ceasing," he did not mean being on one's knees in prayer twenty-four/seven! For still others who recognize the forty- to seventy-year journey through which the memory of Jesus traveled before achieving written form or the fact that our earliest texts of the gospels are in Greek, a language neither Jesus nor his disciples spoke, there is a kind of relaxed fundamentalism;

so they have no trouble seeing the miracles, for example, as illustrations more than as supernatural happenings. Others draw a line in the sand to defend the historicity of the virgin birth or the physical resurrection.

John's gospel, I now believe, challenges literalism at *every* point and invites the reader into a radical, strictly non-literal encounter with Jesus of Nazareth. This gospel sees in Jesus both an invitation into and a doorway through which we can walk into a new dimension of what it means to be human. Escaping the prison of literalism is the first step in that process. This invitation to walk beyond the need for literalizing is a constant Johannine theme. Let me lift some of the passages that make this point clear into your conscious awareness.

In the conversation between Jesus and Nicodemus (John 3), Nicodemus is portrayed as one who is not yet ready to become a follower. He, therefore, comes to Jesus "by night," to pay his respects and to ask his question. To him Jesus is said to have responded: Nicodemus, you do not have the eyes that can see or the consciousness needed to hear the answer. "You must be born again!" You must develop a new angle of vision. Nicodemus is a literalist, and so John has him respond: Born again! Don't be absurd! I am a grown man. "Can I climb back into my mother's womb and be born a second time?" Literalism can never endure such a transition. Nicodemus chooses to remain in the darkness.

The same concept is developed with different content in the story of the Samaritan woman at the well (John 4). She too is said to have engaged Jesus in conversation. She too was a literalist. Jesus asks for water to quench his thirst. She reminds him of the boundary between Jew and Gentile. Jesus is made to respond to her by saying: "If you knew the gift of God and who it is that is saying to you, 'Give me a drink,' you would have asked him and he would have given you living water." The literal-thinking

Samaritan woman looks at him. She hears his words but not his meaning, since her mind is bound inside its literal prison, and so she responds (loosely translated): "Man! You don't even have a bucket!" That is literalism once more being held up to ridicule by this gospel writer.

The non-literal perspective finds expression again in the same narrative when the disciples of Jesus return to find him talking with this Samaritan woman. They are shocked to find their cultural protocols being violated. In this case it is the fact that she is a woman more than the fact that she is a Samaritan that provides the offense. The disciples are concerned that Jesus has had no food and so they exhort him to eat. He seeks to lift them beyond the crude level of literalism and responds to their concern by saying: "I have food to eat of which you do not know!" The disciples respond: "I wonder where he got that food. Who brought it to him?" That is literalism being exposed.

Again and again John pounds on this theme. Jesus says to the Jerusalem Jews attending an unnamed Jewish feast: "You search the scriptures because you think that in them you have eternal life" (John 5:39). That is the behavior of biblical literalism—quote the scripture, show how well you are acquainted with "God's word." Justify your prejudices with the perfume of the Bible; that is what literalists do. Ultimate truth, however, cannot be captured in finite human words. The scriptures point to truth, but they cannot capture it. Truth will always break open the literalism of the Bible. The Fourth Gospel asserts that these scriptures point to what Jesus has come to reveal, but his hearers will never see it until their eyes are opened to a reality that literalism can never, ever see.

Jesus later identifies the meaning of his message with his flesh and his blood and tells the disciples that they must eat his flesh and drink his blood. That, he says, is "the doorway into eternal life" (John 6:54). The disciples hear this as a form of cannibalism and call it "a hard saying." That is literalism. Jesus in the Fourth Gospel exposes literalism, while religion, then and now, hides in it. John is not about literalism. His understanding of Jesus is not about what Jesus literally said or what Jesus literally did. John is a Jewish writer, writing a Jewish book that transcends literalism at every point, and he draws his major images from Jewish mysticism, as he seeks to tell the story of Jesus' life as one who transcends limits, breaks barriers and invites us all into a new place that he represents. This gospel is not about God becoming human, about God putting on flesh and masquerading as a human being; it is about the divine appearing in the human and calling the human to a new understanding of what divinity means. It is about bringing God out of the sky and redefining God as the ultimate dimension of the human. It is about the spirit transcending the limits of the flesh, not in some pious or religious sense, but in opening the flesh to all that it means to be human. It is about seeing Jesus as the doorway into a new consciousness, which is also a doorway into God, who might be perceived as a universal consciousness.

So in order to read this gospel, we must in a radical act of faithfulness lay literalism aside. There is probably not a single word in the Fourth Gospel that Jesus ever spoke. The fellows at the Jesus Seminar made that clear when they published their monumental work *The Five Gospels*.[*] In that color-coded text,[†] they rendered only one saying of Jesus from John's entire gospel in pink (the color designated for a text that may be close to an authentic saying by the Jesus of history), and that saying was self-referential; it was not at the core of John's message at all (John

---

[*] Edited by Robert Funk and Roy Hoover. See bibliography for details.

[†] Red means they heard in this text the legitimate voice of the Jesus of history. Pink means this is close to Jesus' words, but has been tempered by history. Gray means that the evidence points away from this being an authentic word of Jesus. Black meant that there is no way the Jesus of history could have said this.

4:44). Every other saying of Jesus in this gospel was colored either gray or black, indicating that these sayings may well reflect the meaning of Jesus, but he never spoke any of them. To embrace this gospel as completely non-literal will produce a very different angle of vision, but it will also lead us to the heart of this Jewish mystical work. Jesus' journey into the reality of God will be portrayed not only as a journey beyond literalism, but also as a journey beyond scripture, beyond creed, beyond doctrine and beyond religion itself. It will be a journey into life, into a higher consciousness, into a permeating reality for which we have traditionally used the word "God" as a symbol.

Before completing this chapter on literalism, we need to look at another dimension of the Fourth Gospel and address a second question. If all of the recorded words and sayings of Jesus in John's gospel are to be viewed as having never been spoken in literal history, which I am confident is the case, then what are we to make of these characters who dot the Johannine landscape and through whom he tells his story? Some of these characters appear in no other written Christian source of which we are aware; others, who do appear in previous Christian writings, have been newly defined in John's gospel with images that have never before been attached to them. In the case of the first category, how many of these characters, we must ask, are simply symbols or literary creations drawn by the magnificent skill of this author, but with no more historical reality than Hamlet, Lady Macbeth, Jane Eyre, Nicholas Nickleby, Sherlock Holmes or Harry Potter? In the latter category, how many of the characters already introduced in the tradition, but who are mentioned in John contain a redefinition that comes from history? A book that seems to take great pains to warn against reading its pages literally might surely also invite us not to literalize the various characters who make cameo appearances in the Johannine text.

In the course of this book I will go into these characters more thoroughly. They are the keys, I believe, to that portion of John called the Book of Signs, which includes chapters 2–11. John opens the possibility that none of these characters should be treated as historical figures by developing his first mysterious character in chapter 1 and then introducing his last mysterious character in the Farewell Discourses.

Neither of these "Johannine bookends" has been mentioned in any prior identifiable biblical source, yet in the Fourth Gospel they frame John's narrative. The one introduced in chapter 1 is called Nathaniel, a name which means "the gift of God." The one introduced in the Farewell Discourses is never named, but is referred to only as "the beloved disciple" or "the disciple whom Jesus loved." Because "the beloved disciple" is so crucial in the climax of this gospel, I will save a discussion of him until he emerges at the end of John's story.

Nathaniel, however, is introduced in the first chapter, I believe, to give us a key to understanding all of the characters that challenge our literal reading of John's characters that appear in the Book of Signs. He is not a person of history, I am now convinced, but a symbol that bound primitive Christianity to the Johannine community.

First, notice what this author says about Nathaniel. Just as Andrew was said to have brought Peter to Jesus, so this gospel says that Philip brought Nathaniel to Jesus. Philip's invitation to Nathaniel is accompanied by these words: "We have found him of whom Moses in the law and also the prophets wrote" (John 1:46). Nathaniel demurs. He will not be a quick convert. Hearing from Philip that Jesus is from Nazareth, Nathaniel asserts his anti-Galilean prejudice and responds: "Can anything good come out of Nazareth?" (John 1:46). Nonetheless, he accompanies Philip to see Jesus.

When the two of them arrive, Jesus says of Nathaniel, with absolutely no introduction: "Behold an Israelite in whom there is no guile" (John 1:47). Surprised by this designation from someone he has never before met, Nathaniel asks: "How do you know me?" (John 1:48). To which Jesus responds by saying: "Before Philip called you, when you were under the fig tree, I saw you." We need to be aware that the phrase "under the fig tree" is a synonym for the place where the rabbis studied the Torah. Surely this was not intended to be read as literal dialogue.

Nathaniel immediately breaks forth in an extravagant confession of faith: "Rabbi, you are the son of God, you are the king of Israel" (John 1:49). To these words, Jesus responds: "Because I said I saw you under the fig tree do you believe? You shall see greater things than these" (John 1:50). Then, as if not to keep his readers in suspense, John has Jesus say what these greater things will be: "You will see the heavens opened and the angels of God ascending and descending on the son of man" (John 1:51). It is a reference to that familiar vision of Jacob in the book of Genesis, a reference popular in Jewish mysticism and one that will appear again and again in John's gospel.

With such a dramatic introduction of Nathaniel, we surely must ask who he was in the mind of the author of the Fourth Gospel. Is he a real person? He is surely ranked by John with the twelve. He is among the very first called to be a disciple. Yet his name has never been on any other gospel's list of the twelve, nor has he received any mention anywhere prior to this Johannine narrative. In John Nathaniel is called by Jesus himself, quite personally, into discipleship. At the beginning of this episode, he is portrayed as one who is opposed to and contemptuous of any man from Nazareth, but he is won over, we are told, not by the disciples, but by Jesus himself. He is portrayed as predestined for Christianity even while he was deeply engaged in the study of the

Torah under the fig tree—in other words, hiding in the shadows of the law. He is described as an "Israelite in whom there is no guile." It is predicted of him that he will see the heavens opened. Could Nathaniel be a symbol of someone else, someone who has played a very significant role in Christian history and someone John wanted to acknowledge as one of his scriptural ancestors? I believe that this is at least a possibility, one first introduced to me by E. F Scott, a Canadian scholar who wrote near the beginning of the twentieth century.

Only one other person in biblical history is described in such extravagant Jewish terms (even if that latter description is self-imposed), and his name is Paul. "A Hebrew of the Hebrews," Paul says of himself, one who was possessed of zeal for the law. He calls himself one who had "advanced in Judaism beyond many of my own age" (Gal. 1:14). Paul also claims an excessive piety for himself: "as to righteousness under the law," he pronounces himself "blameless" (Phil. 3:6). Who else might be "an Israelite in whom there is no guile"? It was to Paul, according to the book of Acts, that the vision was given, in which "the heavens opened" and Jesus appeared. Perhaps John wanted to tip his hat to Paul in the first chapter, but because he would ultimately disagree with Paul on the meaning of salvation, he did not want to use his name; furthermore, there is no historical data suggesting that Paul ever met Jesus. John, however, could have chosen in this manner to signify his appreciation of Paul and at the same time reveal to his readers that this Johannine character and John's entire gospel needed to be read non-literally. This is my speculation, and it is only that; but I think that as this book unfolds and other Johannine characters are introduced and examined, it will be seen to be a worthy speculation.

To carry this speculation just one stage farther, the later Paul—the author of the epistle to the Philippians—does begin to turn in a mystical direction that connects him more deeply to the Johannine community. He speaks of Jesus as the self-emptying of God (Phil. 2:5–11). He refers to Jesus as sharing somehow in the divine nature of God. Paul does not appear to be the author of the epistle to the Ephesians,* but that text seems to stand midway between Paul and John. It speaks of the God who chose us before the foundation of the world, which John's prologue seems to echo. The theme of Ephesians is that, in Christ, God has "made known to us, in all wisdom and insight, the mystery of his will according to the purpose which he set forth in Christ, as a plan for the fullness of time, to unite all things in him" (Eph. 1:10). Ephesians is a major step toward the kind of mystical Christology that John will develop in the Fourth Gospel.

There is a strong tradition that locates the Johannine community, and thus the writing of the Fourth Gospel, in Ephesus. I do not want to jump to conclusions, but simply to allude to the possibility that the later Paul moved in a mystical direction and that the author of the Fourth Gospel wanted to acknowledge his dependence on this aspect of Paul's teaching. For that reason he introduced a heretofore unknown and unheard-of character that he called Nathaniel, "a gift of God," and then he told the story of Nathaniel's call to follow Jesus that (for those in the know) would seem to be a tip of the hat to Paul.

At the very least we are placed on guard to embrace the realization that John will fill his work with literary, not historical, characters and he will weave around them his interpretations of Jesus.

John's gospel, his methods and techniques have now been introduced. We enter next the Book of Signs, in which John's meanings begin to take form.

---

* We are not sure that this particular epistle was originally addressed to the church in Ephesus, and many believe it to have been written by one of Paul's disciples. The document nevertheless wound up in Ephesus.

PART II

The Book of Signs: Mythological Characters Wrapped Inside History

CHAPTER 8

The Mother of Jesus: Introduction to the Book of Signs

The prologue is complete. The disciples have been chosen. The witness of John the baptizer has been made. Nathaniel has been introduced. The groundwork for understanding has been laid. Now the author of the Fourth Gospel moves into material called the Book of Signs. If this material once circulated separately, as I have discussed previously, then we need to note that it has been deeply incorporated into this gospel's finished whole. There is, for example, a similarity and a consistency of both themes and vocabulary between the completed gospel and the Book of Signs. Indeed the Book of Signs actually provides the Fourth Gospel with its primary storyline. If John's content has gone through major revisions, as most scholars today assert, then we need to note that each of the major editors carefully preserved the integrity of the whole, which they were, perhaps unknowingly, collectively creating, even as they expanded and deepened its meaning. Perhaps the secret to this coherence was that each of the editors was also a member of the Johannine community and therefore each shared in a common growth and understanding.

The first of the "signs" chronicled in John is the well-known narrative of water being changed into wine at a wedding feast in Cana of Galilee. While this story is familiar in the cultural memory, primarily because of the jokes that have been made about it, for our purposes we need to see it as the place where many Johannine themes are introduced.

In this opening sign, for example, we meet the first of the characters that carry the gospel's storyline. We are forewarned that we will make a serious mistake if we literalize these characters, or indeed the signs of which they are so deeply a part. A clue to understanding the Fourth Gospel is to recognize that this author uses literary license to create memorable personalities who become the pillars around which he relates the themes of his Jesus story. Our interpretive task will be to "read" these characters as John, their creator, intended them to be read. So let me turn our spotlight first on the person who in this gospel is described only as "the mother of the Lord." What is the role assigned to her by John?

The "mother of the Lord" makes two appearances in John's gospel, one in this opening Cana story and the other at the foot of the cross near the end of the gospel. In neither episode is she ever called Mary. That is not as unusual as it might seem to some, for she is not nearly as significant a figure in the New Testament as Christian history has portrayed her. Let me briefly trace her story biblically in an effort to set the stage for understanding her role in the sign to which we are introduced at the wedding feast in Cana of Galilee.

Paul, who wrote all of his authentic epistles* ten to twenty years before the first gospel was written, never mentions the par-

---

* Only seven of the fourteen epistles attributed to Paul are actually the work of Paul. They are I Thessalonians, Galatians, I and II Corinthians, Romans, Philemon and Philippians.

ents of Jesus. The only reference we will find to Jesus' family of origin in the Pauline corpus is his mention of James, the brother of the Lord (Gal. 1:19, 2:12). Later in that same epistle, Paul refers to Jesus as one who was "born of a woman" and "born under the law" (Gal. 4:4). The word he uses for "woman" is the word from which we get the English word "gynecology," and it has absolutely no connotation of virginity attached to it. Paul clearly means here that Jesus, like every other human being, is the child of a woman and, like every other Jew, is born under the power of the law.

When we move to the gospel written first, Mark, we find that the mother of Jesus is described in chapter 3 as thinking that her son has become an embarrassment and is, perhaps, even "demon-possessed." This text in Mark refers to Jesus as "beside himself," a first-century synonym for "mental illness." So, accompanied by his brothers, the mother of Jesus comes to take him away. Jesus, according to Mark, is told that his mother and his brothers are asking for him. He refuses to go out to them, claiming that his real mother and his real siblings are those "who do the will of God" (Mark 3:31–35). A few chapters later (Mark 6:1–4) Jesus is said to have created a stir by preaching in his hometown synagogue in Nazareth. People wonder where "this local boy" could have received both his knowledge and his oratorical power. A voice in the crowd is said to have cried out: "Is not this the carpenter, the son of Mary and the brother of James, Joses, Judas and Simon, and are not his sisters here with us?" This is the first and only time the mother of Jesus is called Mary in any New Testament source until the ninth decade of the Common Era.

Embrace this fact and face the reality that this is the sum total of what we know about the mother of Jesus until the ninth decade, when the gospel of Matthew begins to develop her image mythologically via miraculous nativity stories.

In Matthew, the birth narrative makes its first entrance into the Christian tradition, but even in Matthew, while the name Mary is established—Matthew uses it four times in the birth story—the mother of Jesus still plays quite a secondary role. In this gospel the annunciation is made to Joseph (Matt. 1:18–25), who is called "the husband of Mary" (Matt. 1:16). It is Joseph who makes the decision to flee from the wrath of Herod by traveling to Egypt (Matt. 2:13–15). It is Joseph to whom the angel reveals the death of Herod and thus the possibility for this family to return to their Bethlehem home in safety (Matt. 2:19). It is Joseph who is then told that the child's safety requires another move, and so he relocates the family to Nazareth of Galilee (Matt. 2:23). Matthew, having now introduced (and given familial prominence to) the figure of Joseph in the first birth narrative in Christian written history, must refocus the statement that he found in Mark, which provided the first biblical reference to the fact that the name of Jesus' mother was Mary. As we have just noted, Mark had a nameless voice in the crowd say: "Is not this the carpenter, the son of Mary?" (Mark 6:3). When Matthew writes his line, he has that same voice say of Jesus: "Is not this *the carpenter's son,* whose mother, Mary, is here with us?" (Matt. 13:55). This sparse data is the sum total of the biographical details relating to what we can discover biblically of the mother of Jesus prior to the late ninth or early tenth decades, when Luke wrote his gospel. My readers also need to be aware that there is no reputable biblical scholar today who believes that these Matthean birth references are factual accounts of historical happenings. Stars do not announce human births, nor do they wander across the sky so slowly that wise men can follow. So in the absence of facts, myths were already revolving around Jesus' family of origin in the latter years of the first century.

The figure of Joseph as the earthly father of Jesus, who is first introduced into the tradition by Matthew, is also upon analysis revealed to be little more than a recreation of the character of Joseph the patriarch from the book of Genesis (37–50). Of the patriarch Joseph and the literary, earthly "father of Jesus," three distinguishing marks are said to be primary. First, they both have a father named Jacob (Gen. 30:24–25, Matt. 1:16). Second, both are deeply associated with dreams (Gen. 37:5ff, 40, 41; Matt. 1:20, 2:13, 2:19, 2:22). Third, both are assigned the role of saving the promise of Israel, either as the people of the covenant or as the messianic figure, by fleeing for safety to Egypt (Gen. 45, Matt. 2:13–15). The other obvious fact is that the story of the wicked King Herod, who tried to extinguish at his birth the promised "deliverer of his people" by killing all the boy babies in Bethlehem (Matt. 2:16–18), is regarded as little more than the retelling of a portion of the Moses story, for Moses at his birth also had to escape the killing of all the boy babies by a wicked king, this time a pharaoh, in his attempt to extinguish the life of the one God had chosen to be the rescuer of Israel (Exod. 1:15ff). By the early ninth decade when the presumed parents of Jesus are first introduced, it is not history that is being written, but a great and growing mythology that is already surrounding both of the parents of Jesus.

When Luke writes, sometime between 88 and 93, the mother of Jesus begins, for the first time, to play a central role in the story of the life of Jesus. It is to his mother, now clearly known as Mary, and not to Joseph as Matthew had suggested, that the angel Gabriel makes the annunciation. Joseph has not disappeared, but he has faded significantly into the background. Here Luke identifies Mary as a virgin, as she was in Matthew, but uses none of Matthew's attempts to defend that status with biblical quotations. There is no proof text drawn from Isaiah (7:14) that she is supposedly fulfilling. She is portrayed as being accepting of and obedient to her destiny, despite her plea that a virgin who is with child seems quite impossible. "How can this be," she is made to ask, "since I know not a man?" (Luke 1:34). She then is said to have received a salute from the not-yet-born John the Baptist from the womb of his mother, Elizabeth (Luke 1:41). Mary sings a song in perfect meter that we call the "Magnificat," in which she refers to herself as one who possesses "a low estate," but one whom God has raised to great significance (Luke 1:48). According to Luke, she bears this child in Bethlehem, wraps him in "swaddling cloths" (Luke 2:7) and lays him in a feeding trough, called a manger, for the world at his birth, like the world at his death, had no room in it for this Jesus of Nazareth. She then receives the witness of the shepherds and is said to have pondered all these things "in her heart" (Luke 2:19). Finally she is said, with her husband, Joseph, to have accompanied the twelve-year-old Jesus to Jerusalem for the Passover. In this narrative she rebukes her son for getting lost on this journey (Luke 2:48), only to learn of his peculiar relationship with his heavenly Father (Luke 2:49).

Luke's story, just like Matthew's, has a deep affinity for scripture and for messianic expectations. The Magnificat, Mary's song, is modeled after the song sung by Hannah, the mother of Samuel, at his birth (I Sam. 2:1–10). The manger seems to come out of Isaiah (Isa. 1:3). The "swaddling cloths" seem to come out of the Wisdom of Solomon (7:4–5). The story of Jesus' boyhood trip to Jerusalem appears to be little more than a retelling of a Samuel story (I Sam. 1:24ff). Luke even gives the grandfather of Jesus in his genealogy (Luke 3) the name Heli, or Eli, which is the name of the old priest that the young Samuel served. Once again, we recognize that there is little history connected with this gospel writer's portrayal of the mother of Jesus. She is a mythological figure in the gospel tradition long before she makes her first appearance in John's gospel. John continues to develop the myth by building into his characterization of her the things he needs her to be and do in order to develop his story.

There is no suggestion in John's gospel that the mother of the Lord was a virgin. Indeed her first appearance in this gospel is not in a narrative of Jesus' birth, but in the aforementioned wedding feast in Cana of Galilee. Not only is the mother of the Lord present at this wedding, but also Jesus' disciples are said to be in attendance. The mother of the Lord is, however, cast in a central role. The symbols are obvious. This transformation of water into wine will occur "on the third day" (John 2:1). There are six stone jars present that are meant to be used for the Jewish rites of purification. The mother of Jesus stands at the nexus between the shortcomings of the ritual activity of the Jews and the celebration of the new life that Jesus came to bring—new life that is symbolized by the marriage ceremony. The "old wine" has been spent. There is no more for the celebration. The mother of Jesus pushes her son to act in this crisis. He rebukes her, calling her "woman" and saying to her, in what seems like a harsh manner, that his "hour" has not yet come and no one can force it. The word "hour" is used many times in the Fourth Gospel to refer to Jesus' crucifixion and thus to the time of the ultimate revelation of who he is. When the Book of Signs is complete, Jesus finally announces that "the hour has come for the son of man to be glorified" (John 12:23), and the drama of the cross begins to unfold. Jesus in this earlier narrative must decline to have his mother determine the hour of his death, which for the Fourth Gospel will also be the hour of his glorification.

In this Cana of Galilee story his mother now retreats, but before doing so she is made to instruct the servants to "do whatever he says" (John 2:5). That is the moment when the water pots of Jewish purification are filled with water which is then transformed into wine. The wine steward tastes the new wine in the Jewish water pots, pronouncing it better than that first served at the wedding feast, and the glasses of the guests are refilled. The people wonder at the source of this wine, for if we literalize the measurements given, there would be more than 150 gallons of new wine, meaning that this symbol of new life was present in overwhelming abundance. This dramatic act, says John, creates in the disciples faith, and "they believed in him" (John 2:11). The first of John's signs is now complete, so Jesus, his mother and his disciples go down to Capernaum and remain for a few days. This is the final mention of the mother of the Lord until the scene of the crucifixion.

What is going on here? It is first of all not a miracle story. It is a "sign" pointing to something quite different from a supernatural event. Clearly in this story Jesus is the bridegroom, an image that we will see appear again shortly. He is calling Israel into a new status. The wine of the spirit has replaced the waters of purification. Who then is "the mother of the Lord"? I submit that, as she is developed in the Fourth Gospel, she is a mythological figure who stands for Israel, the faith tradition that gave birth to Christianity and thus is its mother. This transition from Israel to Christianity is one of John's interpretive keys. It must come, however, only when all else is ready. It is shrouded in secrecy in this narrative, for we are told that no one knows the source of this transformation. At the proper time all will know, but the ultimate revelation will come only when he—that is, Jesus—is lifted up on the cross. The seed of the idea, so central to John, that it will be in the death of Jesus that his glory will be revealed, is thus planted. That is a different note from any we have heard in the earlier gospels. John's unique message, his transforming understanding, begins to come into view. We will watch it emerge slowly and steadily as his story unfolds. For now recognize that the mother of Jesus in this gospel is not a person; she is a symbol. When she appears again at the foot of the cross, the meaning of that symbol will become abundantly clear.

CHAPTER 9

Nicodemus: What It Means to Be Born of the Spirit

T
he character known as Nicodemus is now brought front and center by John, following an account of Jesus cleansing the Temple of those selling oxen, sheep and pigeons. It is a strange introduction because in the Fourth Gospel that cleansing story has been shifted dramatically from the place it occupied in the earlier gospels, where it was a prelude to the crucifixion. It reminds us once again that we are not to read this gospel literally, or as if it were history. In John's cleansing of the Temple episode, Jesus is made to identify his body with the Temple. "Destroy this Temple and in three days I will raise it up" (John 2:19), he says. Various texts from the Hebrew scriptures are once more in evidence in the background. The disciples, we are told, recall Psalm 69:9, which portrays one who is consumed by zeal for his father's house. Luke has previously had a twelve-year-old Jesus claim the Temple as "my Father's house" when he was lost "for three days" (Luke 2:41–51). John now portrays this Jesus as an adult, but also at a Passover, still claiming the Temple as "my Father's house" (John 2:16).

In this manner the stage is set for John to introduce another of his mythological characters who will serve to contrast the old, which Jesus challenges, with the new, to which Jesus points. This character also contrasts those whose thinking is bounded by the limits of this world (with its literal mind-set) with those who are open to a new consciousness. This is the context in which Nicodemus, one of the more memorable figures in the entire New Testament, emerges. I don't think there is any possibility that Nicodemus was a person who actually lived in history. Around this figure, however, in characteristic style, the author of the Fourth Gospel continues to develop the themes of his narrative.

Nicodemus is described by John as a Pharisee, a ruler of the Jews, but also as one who was more than just a little inquisitive about Jesus of Nazareth. He was clearly a symbol of those in the synagogue, even in the hierarchy of the synagogue, who while impressed with Jesus could never take that final step into what the author of this gospel believed was the transformative Christ experience. Nicodemus was thus one who preferred the darkness to the light. So John has him come to Jesus "by night." Darkness and night are powerful images for this gospel writer, and they are always contrasted with light and day.

Nicodemus is drawn to Jesus, says John's storyline, perhaps against his better judgment. He is made to address Jesus as "rabbi," a position of great status in the Jewish world. He acknowledges that Jesus must somehow be related to God, for only if God were working through him could he do the "signs" that he did. Thus far in this narrative, those signs had been only one, the changing of the waters of purification into the spirited wine of new life.

Nicodemus obviously still conceived of God as a supernatural, external being through whom mighty works could be accomplished. These works, however, were viewed as somehow frightening by the religious authorities, for they did not fit the conventional religious patterns of control and happened outside the regular channels through which God was thought to work. Nicodemus' God needed to be harnessed, nuanced and feared. Divine acts had to be validated by ecclesiastical authority. Nicodemus would never understand the birth of a new consciousness. Jesus is portrayed as recognizing these attitudes immediately, and in the tension between Nicodemus' controlled world and Jesus' understanding of the power of new life, their conversation unfolds.

Jesus opens the conversation by going to the core of the issue. His opening words are introduced with the modern English translation "Truly, truly." I find these words to be a very weak rendition of what the King James Bible had rendered "Verily, verily." If someone began a conversation with me using the words "Truly, truly," I would immediately suspect that I was hearing anything *but* the truth. "Verily, verily" is actually better because it is an expression no one uses today, so it is surrounded with a sense of mystery. The Greek words that this gospel writer actually uses— the ones translated "Verily, verily"—are meant to signal that the conversation that is to follow is of the highest importance, that it cries out to be heard because it has a sense of ultimacy about it. When the words introduced by "Verily" are finally spoken, the message is in fact quite provocative. "Unless one is born anew," Jesus is portrayed as saying, he (or she) cannot see "the realm of God" (John 3:3).

I note first that the words translated "born anew" or "born again" can also mean "born from above." As for "the realm," the King James Version of the Bible and the Revised Standard Version render the Greek word *basileus* as "kingdom," but the New Revised Standard Version, seeking to escape the masculine connotations of a king (in the name of gender inclusiveness), renders the word "realm." No matter what route the NRSV translators took to get there, the word "realm" is a far more accurate rendition of what the Fourth Gospel was trying to communicate than is "kingdom." A kingdom is a place. A realm is more of an experience. The kingdom of God was normally represented in spatial terms as existing above the sky in a three-tiered universe. A realm could be an experience of new levels of consciousness, the ability to see beyond the limits of physical vision.

To be "born again" or to be "born anew" or even to be "born from above" is to claim a status that has had an interesting history in Christian circles. It has, I am quite convinced, nothing to do with what we today might call a "conversion experience." It adds no new pious dimension to a life as religious claims through the centuries have sought to establish. It does not draw a line between the "true believers" and the "pretenders." Being born again has been used in religious circles to encourage both immaturity and dependency. When one is "born again" one remains in childish mode. If one gets born again often enough, one never has to grow up. I loved reading a sign on a church wall once that proclaimed: "This church welcomes you, no matter how many times you have been born."

John was writing as a Jewish mystic and must be read in this way. He was speaking about a new dimension of life, not a new religious status. His words, however, have been read and interpreted against the background of a dualistic Greek worldview that contrasted the higher life of religion and God, and the lower life of desire and humanity. These ideas are not what the Fourth Gospel is suggesting. Jesus is from another realm, which he called the realm of God, but this realm must be understood experientially, not spatially. That is mystical, not dogmatic, theological language. It was destined, however, to be interpreted inside a Greek dualism that suggested there was an external realm of God to which Jesus belonged and that he had left that realm to enter the realm of flesh and blood. That is, I believe, to misunderstand this gospel completely. This view makes Jesus something of a divine visitor, masquerading as a real human being. Nothing could be farther from the mind of the author of the Fourth Gospel. The Christian church historically, however, walked this path, and what came to be viewed as Christianity's core beliefs, such as the doctrine of the incarnation and the idea that Jesus was and is the second person in a divine Trinity, are direct manifestations of this mentality. Indeed in the first five hundred years of Christian history, the "fathers" were so deeply dualistic in their thinking that they tried to figure out how divinity and humanity could come together in one person without compromising the integrity of either the divine or the human. The great classical heresies, such as Docetism, Nestorianism, Patripassianism and Adoptionism, were thought to err on the side of making Jesus so human that his divinity was falsified, or so divine that his humanity was lost.

The author of the Fourth Gospel would have understood none of this. John was a Jew, not a Greek. He was a mystic, not a rational theologian. What he did understand, however, is that Jesus represented a new dimension of humanity, a new insight, a new consciousness, a new way of relating to the holy; and all of this he placed into Jesus' conversation with his mythical character named Nicodemus. For you, Nicodemus, to understand who I am and what I am about, Jesus was saying, you must enter a transformative experience. You must see with insight or second sight. You must open yourself to a totally new perspective.

Nicodemus, who is portrayed as enjoying the darkness of his own religious night, is incapable of making sense out of these words. His response, the response of eyes bound by the limits of his own mind, is almost predictable. It was a frequent response present in the audience for which John was writing. So, as I noted earlier, John has Nicodemus say: "How can a man be born when he is old? Can he enter a second time into his mother's womb and be born?" It is an amusing image, expressing the absurdity of earthbound thinking, which is the inescapable boundary that literalism always provides.

John's Jesus tries again, once more employing the "Truly, truly" formula, hoping to gain new understanding. "Unless one is born of water and the spirit, he [or she] cannot enter the realm of God," he says. "Water" in this phrase is not a secret reference to baptism, which according to traditional church teaching is to be undergone at or near one's birth in order to commit the child to the Christ path; nor is "spirit" a secret reference to that conversion process when a decision is made to accept Jesus "as my personal savior," to use standard evangelical language, which is supposed to guarantee to the convert the gifts of the spirit, like "speaking in tongues." That is to misread this text in terms of non-Jewish piety.

To be "born of water" is simply to be born into the life of this world, a process achieved in the breaking of the maternal waters. To be "born of the spirit" is to step into a new dimension of what it means to be human. John makes that abundantly clear in the next sentence, when he has Jesus say: "That which is born of the flesh is flesh; and that which is born of the spirit is spirit." Then Jesus identifies the spirit with the mystery of the wind "that blows where it will and you hear the sound of it, but you do not know whence it comes or where it goes" (John 3:8). To be born of the spirit is this same kind of mysterious, mystical experience.

In a previous book* I have argued that to be human is to enter into self-consciousness. It is to live knowingly in the medium of time. It is to remember the past and to be able to relive it in one's mind. It is to anticipate the future and to revel in it before it arrives. To be human is also to embrace finitude and mortality. It is

---

* *Eternal Life: A New Vision.* See bibliography for details.

to know that while your mind can roam beyond the limits of your body, your body is bound in time and space. To be self-conscious is to view all of life from within the center of the self, to look out to the world from the perspective of one who is somehow separated and distinct from that world. To be self-conscious is to feel loneliness, to know anxiety and to be engaged in a chronic struggle for survival. It is to see oneself as related to the whole, but without losing one's identity inside the whole. It is *not* to be a raindrop in the sea of God. Self-consciousness, however, does open up the possibility of escaping all boundaries and touching, seeing and experiencing a universal consciousness, a radical new awareness of connectedness, a mystical sense of identity with that which is ultimate. That is an experience that only self-conscious human beings can have. That is also what John's Jesus is talking about in this conversation with the character Nicodemus, who has used religion to bind his ability to see inside his predictable boundaries of security. That is not what John believes he himself has experienced in Jesus, and so he has Jesus seek to open the eyes of the earthbound and flesh-limited Nicodemus.

Nicodemus is blinded by this potential vision. "How can these things be?" he asks. Jesus points to the limitations of religion in his response: "You are a teacher of Israel," a member of the religious elite, "and you do not understand this?" (John 3:10). I represent another realm of reality, he is saying. I have seen a new vision. Unless you, Nicodemus, are willing to undergo a transformative experience and thereby to escape your self-imposed boundaries, you will not believe. The lines in this conversation are clearly drawn.

Then Jesus is made to hint at the revelatory moment. Using one of the many references from the Hebrew scriptures that the followers of Jesus had mined to validate their Jesus experience, John has Jesus liken himself to the healing serpent that Moses had lifted up in the wilderness during a time of sickness and death (John 3:14). In that story the wandering Jewish people began to complain about their fate, preferring the security of bondage in Egypt to the anxieties that accompanied new life in the wilderness. As punishment for their faithlessness, asserts this story, found in the book of Numbers (21:4–9), God sent fiery serpents among the people, and those who were bitten died. In terror the people repented and came to Moses, begging him to ask God to remove the serpents. So Moses prayed and God instructed him to make a bronze serpent and put it on a pole so that those bitten might look upon it and live. Moses did just that and in time the bronze serpent on a pole became the symbol of the healing arts (and is used today to mark the medical profession). John sees Jesus symbolically as the serpent lifted up on his cross, drawing the venom out of human life, restoring wholeness. It is a powerful image.

John is here referring once more, I believe, to the "throne mysticism" of early Judaism. At the climax of his gospel Jesus will be enthroned, not on a throne of gold reflecting earthly power or even on a throne of bronze as was the serpent, but on a throne of wood fashioned into a cross, an instrument of execution through which he will reflect a new humanity. That will be the doorway into a new consciousness, a new oneness with all that God is, a doorway into that which is eternal. The God Jesus reveals is the source of love that comes not to judge human inadequacy, but to open the eyes of people to see that they are part of who and what God is so that they can enter the eternity that God represents. Judgment, says the Johannine Christ, is not a divine act but a human choice: It means to prefer the darkness to light, to choose security over freedom, to relate to what is and never to see what can be. The call of the Johannine Christ is to something quite different. Nicodemus, a Pharisee and a ruler of the Jews, is the perfect foil against which this insight can be processed.

Nicodemus will make two further appearances in the Fourth Gospel. The second occurs in the seventh chapter, in which Jesus has gone up to Jerusalem for the Feast of Tabernacles and has stirred up the authorities to the point that they are seeking to kill him. Nicodemus cautions them that the law does not charge a person without "giving him a hearing and learning what he does" (John 7:51). Nicodemus is always considering new possibilities, but he is never ready to act on his feelings.

The third time that Nicodemus appears in this gospel will come suddenly and in a quite different context, namely as part of the story of Jesus' burial. I will go into that narrative in more detail at the conclusion of the passion story. For now, let me simply note that there is in the burial account no hint of the birth of new life. After this Nicodemus is never mentioned again. He was always close to the presence of light, but he could not enter it. He, and those whom he symbolized, simply could not get beyond the flesh that they knew, which always ends at the grave.

John's story depicting those who prefer the security of the known darkness to the startling vision of life lived in the light of a new understanding of God is concluded. He now moves on beyond Nicodemus to the next mythological character who will walk across the stage in his drama and who will help to reveal Jesus' purpose.

CHAPTER 10

The Samaritan Woman by the Well: A New Dimension of the Jesus Experience

J esus and his disciples now move on from their encounter with Nicodemus. The author of the gospel seems to be doing a review before launching into the next dramatic episode, so in the last half of chapter 3 he revisits the figure of John the baptizer, who is made to bear witness to Jesus anew. The baptizer likens Jesus to a bridegroom and calls himself a "friend of the bridegroom," perhaps the person we would designate the "best man." The friend of the bridegroom, he says, rejoices in the experiences in the bridegroom's life. Then the baptizer announces that his own destiny is to decrease as the bridegroom's increases. He says, in language reminiscent of some of Jesus' conversation with Nicodemus, that he belongs to the earth, but Jesus belongs to another realm. Jesus, he says, utters God's words because he was sent from God. Jesus is the dispenser of the spirit, which means that because the spirit links us to that which is the source of life, Jesus is the doorway into that life which is eternal.

The baptizer's use of the analogy of the bridegroom segues nicely into the next story, which is filled with the intimate images of courtship and marriage. To tell this story, in his fourth chapter John has created another symbolic figure and thus another mythological character, one whom we call the "Samaritan woman at the well."*

Traditional voices, which are overwhelmingly male voices, tend to see this woman in sexual terms, as one who flaunts her sexual immorality. My reading of John's gospel leads me to the conclusion that this understanding violates the message of the Fourth Gospel and completely distorts John's meaning.

The first thing that needs to be grasped is that in the Hebrew scriptures, a well is the place where one goes in search of a wife, and the reference to this being Jacob's well (John 4:12) makes that abundantly clear. It also signals that this narrative is not the recollection of an actual event, but a story designed to provide a new insight into the Jesus experience.

To document the well as the place to seek a wife we need to be familiar with the folk tales of the Jewish people. In the book of Genesis (24:1–61) Abraham, the family patriarch, sends his senior servant to find a wife for his son Isaac. He does not want Isaac to marry a Canaanite—that is, one from among the people with whom Abraham is living. So this servant is dispatched to Abraham's place of origin to find a wife from among Abraham's own people. The only criterion is that the woman of choice must be willing to return with Abraham's servant.

The servant is equipped with provisions for the journey, gifts of gold, an entourage of support people and a train of ten camels. They journey to Mesopotamia, to the town of Nahor, and arrive at a well to which the women of the village come each day to draw water for their households. The servant is instructed to

---

* I am indebted above all others in this chapter to Sandra Schneiders, whose essay "A Case Study: A Feminist's Interpretation of John 4:1–42" was published in a book of essays on the Fourth Gospel edited by John Ashton. See bibliography for details.

follow a carefully set script in looking for a suitable woman. He is to ask each woman he singles out to give him a drink. If one does so and, in addition, offers to water his camels, she is the one. The suggestion is that God will control the choice through these code requirements. A young woman arrives. She is described as "fair to look upon and a virgin whom no man has known."* Her name is Rebekah and she follows the script implanted in the servant's mind perfectly. The servant asks her for a drink and she gives it to him. She then proceeds to water his camels. He inquires as to her identity and asks the names of her parents. He thus discovers that she is the granddaughter of Nahor (after whom the town is named), who was the brother of Abraham. Believing that God has blessed his journey, the servant completes the courtship by giving Rebekah a gold ring and two gold bracelets, and asks her if he can find lodging in her father's home for the evening.

The arrangement is made and Rebekah's brother, a man named Laban, comes out to greet and welcome Abraham's servant. He invites him first to a feast and then to a place of rest for the night. Before eating, the servant relates his story, tells his hosts of Abraham's great wealth and asks for Rebekah to be Isaac's wife, but only if she is willing to follow him back home. Rebekah's family comes to the conclusion, as the text says, that "this thing comes from the Lord," and they express their willingness for Rebekah to enter the marriage contract. Then gifts are presented: first jewelry made of both silver and gold, and then lovely raiment. Gifts are then given to Rebekah's brother Laban and to her mother. These gifts are identified as "costly ornaments." Finally, they all participate in a feast accompanied by much wine.

The next morning the servant, his mission accomplished, is ready to leave. Rebekah's family asks for a ten-day delay. The

---

* The text does not say how this fact was determined, but it was a pre-condition of the mating process.

servant demurs. Rebekah is then consulted and expresses her willingness to go at once. So they send her on the way with her maids, bidding her to be the mother of tens of thousands. In this episode the well is established in scripture as the place to find a wife.

The place of the well as the setting for a marriage contract is reiterated just five chapters later in the book of Genesis when Jacob, the son of Isaac and Rebekah, goes in search of a wife for himself (Gen. 29:1ff). The themes are similar. Esau, Jacob's twin brother, has taken a wife from among the local people. Jacob, through whom the promise of the covenant is to flow, is instructed by his father, Isaac, to seek a wife from among his own family's kin. So he journeys, just as Abraham's servant did, to the east, and he stops at a well which was covered by a large and heavy stone near the town of Haran. The well, once again, will serve as a place for mating.

Soon some shepherds come, remove the stone from the well and water their flocks. Jacob inquires as to the location of their home and is told that they live in Haran. Jacob knows that Rebekah's brother Laban, who is his uncle, lives there. He inquires about Laban and is told by the shepherds that they know him and that he is well. They then look up and see a young woman named Rachel coming with her flocks, and they inform Jacob that the approaching young woman is actually Laban's daughter. The matrimonial well is about to work its magic spell again. Jacob assists Rachel by helping to remove the heavy stone at the mouth of the well, and then he proceeds to water her sheep for her. Recognizing her as his kin, he kisses her and weeps, identifying himself as the son of Rebekah, the sister of her father, Laban. Rachel then runs to inform her family and they come out to invite Jacob to their house. There the marriage contract is negotiated. Rachel is found by Jacob to be "beautiful and lovely," and so he accepts a high bride's price. Jacob will work for his uncle Laban for seven years to gain Rachel as his wife.

A third story identifying a well as the place to find a wife is recounted in the life of Moses (Exod. 2:15ff). Forced to flee the wrath of the pharaoh, Moses heads into the wilderness, where he finds a well and sits down by it. To that well, predictably, come the seven daughters of a priest of the land of Midian to draw water. As they are about to be driven off by Midianite shepherds, Moses comes to their defense and scatters the shepherds. He then proceeds to draw water for the sheep belonging to these seven daughters. Returning home, these ladies tell their father of Moses' kindness to them. The father then goes out to find Moses and invites him into his home, and one of his seven daughters, a woman named Zipporah, becomes his wife.

As these examples show, in the scriptures when a man and woman meet by a well, the encounter is viewed as a "mating game." Keep that in mind and listen to these familiar biblical themes as John's story about the Samaritan woman at the well develops.

Jesus, apparently traveling alone from Judea to Galilee, comes to the town of Sychar in the region of Samaria and stops to rest by a well known as "Jacob's well." It is high noon. The Samaritan woman will not come to Jesus by night, as Nicodemus did; she will come in the clear light of the midday sun. She is about the routine task that women in that culture normally performed. She comes to draw the water that will sustain the life of her family. Jesus, using words identical with those used by the servant of Abraham in search of a wife for his master's son Isaac, asks her for a drink. Jesus is thus cast by the Fourth Gospel in the role of the bridegroom, inviting the Samaritans to become a faithful constituent part of the "new Israel," another name for the developing Christian covenant.

The Samaritan woman, recognizing that what is really happening is a courtship, cuts immediately to the chase and places into the conversation the history of the fracture between Jews and Samaritans. "How is it," she says, "that you, a Jew, ask a drink of me, a woman of Samaria?" The author explains that history briefly, noting that "Jews have no dealings with Samaritans" (John 4:9).

This fracture had its origins first in the secession from Judah of the ten tribes that constituted the Northern Kingdom of Israel, which occurred at the time of the death of Solomon around the year 920 BCE. That fracture meant that the northern part of the Israelite nation separated itself from the house of David, the city of Jerusalem and the Temple with its high priest who controlled the ecclesiastical structures. In time the citizens of the Northern Kingdom sought to build for themselves a capital city, which they named Samaria and which they hoped would come to rival Jerusalem. In time the name of that city became the name of the entire region. Next, they moved to transform the sacred shrines in this Northern Kingdom into their own indigenous holy places, in order to compete with the Jerusalem Temple. Finally, they sought to develop a royal family in which their national unity could be vested and which would rival the house of David. As they built these institutions, however, they were also aware of the danger of concentrating power too heavily in them, for it was against these very things that they had so recently rebelled. So they crowned a king, but they insisted that he be subject to the will of the people. This was a king who would rule not by "divine right," but by the consent of the governed.

As they tried to define themselves against Jerusalem, more and more these people of the north saw themselves as related primarily not to the royal house of David, but to the original patriarchs, Abraham, Isaac and most especially Jacob, who had changed his name to Israel. The rivalry between these two parts of what was once a single nation was intense. Secession of one part of a nation from the whole is almost always followed by warfare. In the war that followed this secession, the ten tribes of the Northern Kingdom were victorious and so their separation was secured. The hostility between the two nations, however, did not abate. Their history was one of constant warfare and frequently they found themselves allied with opposing powers (such as Assyria and Babylonia) that set northern descendants of Abraham (Israel) and southern descendants of Abraham (Judah) in deep opposition. Assyria, for example, was the Northern Kingdom's ultimate enemy and the Southern Kingdom's ally. Splits like this one also meant that both segments of the "chosen people" began to define themselves primarily against the other. Hatred, based on this rivalry, was deep. Prejudices developed that fed the survival needs of each.

That is the way human life works. We have seen it throughout history as the world has been regularly divided into competing groups with competing loyalties: Christian against Pagan, Catholic against Protestant, true believer against heretic, white against people of color, males against females and heterosexuals against homosexuals. In the insecurity of human life, our desire is to build ourselves up by tearing our rivals down. The citizens of Israel defined themselves against the citizens of Judah and vice versa. Each region's "self-definition" thus set the two "states" in constant tension with one another.

This already tense relationship then took a dramatic turn around the year 721 BCE, when Israel, the Northern Kingdom, was destroyed in warfare by the Assyrian armies, while Judah, Assyria's ally, looked on from a distance. Judah then accepted its status as a vassal state to Assyria in order to retain some semblance of independence.

In the style of that day, primarily to prevent future rebellions, the Assyrians transported many of the people of Israel into exile in Assyria and repopulated that part of these people's former homeland with peoples from other conquered provinces. In time intermarriage between the exiled people with their conquerors occurred and their DNA simply blended into that of the Middle East. Those exiled to Assyria in time became known in Jewish history and in folklore as the "ten lost tribes of Israel." Those Israelites who were allowed to remain in the land that once was the Northern Kingdom intermarried with the imported foreigners. From the point of view of the people of Judah, who now began to be called Jews, the people of the north became a "mongrel race" and their religious practices began to be syncretized with foreign ideas in which the purity of Israel's ancient faith was believed to have been badly compromised. Now both race and religion became barriers to unity and were developed as sources of enormous prejudice. There was, however, enough of the residual faith left in the people of the north that they retained their claim to be part of the original covenant rooted in the pre-Jerusalem patriarchs of Abraham, Isaac and Jacob. They centered their faith in a holy mountain in the north, not eager to claim kinship with that part of the covenant people who gathered around the house of David in the south and whose life was centered in the Temple of Jerusalem.

The tension between the two groups grew more intense in the early years of the sixth century BCE when the kingdom of Judah was destroyed by the Babylonians and its people exiled to the land of Babylon. This exile was, however, different in one essential way from the above-described mixing of races that typically followed war. These exiled Jews were determined to return to their home someday and that desire forced them to separate themselves radically from non-Jews in overtly distinguishing ways. This is what caused them to adopt such practices as strict Sabbath day observances, kosher dietary laws and mandated circumcision. In time, when these exiles were allowed to return to their homeland, they saw themselves as quite distinct from and superior to those who had remained in their conquered land, whose bloodlines were now suspect and whose religious practices were assumed to be corrupt. The term "Samaritan" was then applied to this group of people also, and the hostility between the returning Jews and the "half-breeds" who populated their former homeland was palpable.

All of these feelings are captured in this Johannine episode when the Samaritan woman responds to Jesus' request for a drink of water at the well of Jacob by shifting the conversation to the gaping divide between Jews and Samaritans. From this moment on, the conversation between Jesus and the Samaritan woman is a deep theological conversation about human boundaries and what role Jesus would play in the world of human tensions.

To the woman's hostile question as to why he, a Jew, would ask her, a Samaritan, for water, Jesus responds with a new invitation. He offers her "living water," a synonym for the spirit that binds human life together. The woman, not yet understanding the dialogue, notes that he has nothing in which to draw water from the well. His offer thus seems to her to be an empty one. Then she asks him the key question: "Are you greater than *our* ancestor Jacob, who gave us this well?" Note the use of the pronoun "our." She is identifying herself with the ancient covenant made with the patriarchs. The Samaritans were part of that covenant since they were the descendants, however corrupted, of Jacob.

Jesus responds once more by lifting the conversation beyond this ancient division. Jacob's well provides water that sustains life, but only momentarily. Those who quench their thirst with the waters from Jacob's well will thirst again, he says. Jesus is offering a kind of water that causes people to become so whole they will never again know thirst.

The woman, intrigued by this image, but still bound by her limiting literalism, says, in effect: That is a wonderful vision. Give me this water and I will never have to come here to draw from this well again. I will transcend the gift of Jacob!

Jesus, hearing this, asks her to call her husband. "I have no husband," she responds. Jesus, acting as if he has foreknowledge of her entire life, responds that she not only has no husband now, but she has had five husbands and the man with whom she now lives is not her husband. At this point, people forget that this woman is a mythological symbol of Samaria and so they read this statement moralistically, as if this were a commentary on her loose sexual proclivities. They even suggest that the woman was trying abruptly to change the subject from her questionable past to a debate about the proper place for worship. To read this story that way, however, is to miss its meaning totally. This is a symbolic conversation about how the unfaithful region of Samaria can be incorporated into the new understanding of Christianity that Jesus is believed to present and about how ancient religious divisions in the human family can be overcome in the new human consciousness that Jesus comes to bring.

"Sir," the Samaritan woman then says, "I perceive that you are a prophet," so tell me where (and probably how) people ought to worship. She is asking one she identifies as "a prophet" to settle the dispute as to whether true worship is to be identified with Mount Gerizim in Samaria or with the Temple in Jerusalem. Jesus asserts that God is beyond that sort of human limit. God is spirit—unbounded and all-permeating spirit—and those who worship this God must do so in spirit and in truth. Salvation comes from the Jews, he asserts; but he then immediately transcends the Jewish limits to embrace *all* people, including those who were the deepest objects of Jewish scorn, the Samaritans. This dialogue makes little sense so long as we assume that the Samaritan woman is a real person. She is not. In this narrative she is a symbol of Samaria itself. So Jesus is proclaiming that even those considered worthy of rejection by the Jews are to be included in the realm of God to which Jesus is the opening.

What then is this story saying about this woman's five husbands? The reference is to a passage in II Kings (17:24–34) in which we are told that the king of Assyria brought people from five countries and placed them in the cities of Samaria. Then the king commanded that a priest, then exiled in Assyria, be returned to Samaria to teach the new residents of the land the laws of the God of that land. The people of Samaria, however, were not faithful, but rather bonded with the false gods served by the people of the five resettled nations. These were the five husbands of the unfaithful Samaritans, symbolized by this Samaritan woman.

Jesus concludes this conversation by using for the first time in John's gospel the name of God, "I AM," revealed to Moses at the burning bush. This name rooted the God experience in the pre-Jerusalem, pre–house of David part of the chosen people's history. It had to include Samaritans since the name "I AM" itself located God in the being of humanity, not in the narrow cultic dimensions of human religion. Samaria was to be a part of the new Israel. No one was to be excluded. There was a new and different understanding of what it means to be human, and that was what Jesus came to reveal. This story is not about sexual immorality, then; it is about faithfulness to the God who draws us beyond human barriers, human divides and human prejudices. "Messiah," the woman says, "is coming and will show us all things." To this Jesus responds: "It is the 'I AM' who is speaking to you now." It is a transformative conversation.

At this moment the conversation is interrupted by the return of Jesus' disciples. They marvel, says the text, that Jesus is speaking to a woman. They have brought food for Jesus to eat. Jesus responds that he has food "of which you do not know." Living water will be accompanied by the bread of life. Because they are still bound by their literal mentality, this comment goes up and over the disciples' heads.

Meanwhile, the Samaritan woman, ecstatic over what she has heard, leaves her water pot to become an evangelist, just as John and James had earlier left their fishing nets to follow Jesus. The mission to the Samaritans is now in the hands of a woman, meaning that another barrier to oneness in the human family is being overcome. She goes to her village, relates her experience and raises with them the possibility that Jesus might be "the messiah." She is portrayed as having been quite successful; the Samaritans left their towns and came to Jesus. They asked Jesus to stay with them. He did for two days, and we are told that many believed "because of his word." When Jesus left them, he returned to Cana of Galilee, to the scene of the wedding where water was changed into wine. The story of the Samaritan woman by the well is thus wrapped in the parenthesis of two references to marriage.

The Samaritan woman becomes a herald of the new revelation. Later, Mary Magdalene will become a similar herald of the resurrection to the disciples. Jesus is a barrier-breaker. Before him falls the human division first between Jews and Samaritans and then between women and men. A vision of "the realm of God" begins to come into view.

CHAPTER 11

The Gentile Official's Son: The Meaning of God and Faith

Nicodemus, described as "a Pharisee and a ruler of the Jews," comes to Jesus by night and, unable to hear his message, disappears again into the shadows. The Samaritan woman by the well meets Jesus in the bright light of the noonday sun and becomes an evangelist bringing Samaritans into the covenant. Now the author of this gospel introduces another symbolic character. He too is unnamed, called only "an official" from Capernaum. Is he a Gentile? That is debated, but I am persuaded that he is. That designation certainly fits the storyline. This official has a son who is ill. The narrative is reminiscent of a story told in Matthew (8:5–10) and in Luke (7:1–10), where in both cases the official is "a centurion"—that is, a Roman soldier in charge of a unit of one hundred men—whose servant, not his son, is healed at a distance by Jesus. In those narratives Jesus comments that he has not found such faith in "all of Israel" as was shown by the centurion. There are minor differences in each of the narratives, but they all appear to reflect a common experience. It seems quite reasonable, therefore, in the light of these similar stories, to see this man as a Gentile. That assumption, furthermore, helps us to recognize how the author of the Fourth Gospel shapes this character in such a way as to serve his interpretive genius. John will use this Gentile official to address the huge tribal gulf that separates both physically and emotionally the Jew from the Gentile. Jesus, with his call to a new humanity, must confront and overcome this barrier.

John, however, works his other themes into this story and in the process has Jesus define both God and faith in new ways. All of that makes this "Gentile official" a pivotal figure in the Fourth Gospel.

In this narrative John once more makes a connection with the account of the wedding in Cana of Galilee. He does this by bringing Jesus back to the site of that wedding and by identifying it in the text as the place where "he made the water into wine" (John 4:46). At the end of this narrative he again relates this episode to the previous Cana in Galilee story by linking them numerically: The author asserts that "this was now the *second* sign that Jesus did when he had come from Judea to Galilee" (John 4:54).

Three things are accomplished in this story. First, in the Gentile identification of this official, we have another aspect of the theme of Jesus as a barrier-breaker, setting aside the defensive walls behind which we human beings hide and which serve to diminish our own humanity. It is behind our tribal fences that we human beings develop our life-strangling prejudices. One cannot be fully human while continuing to violate the humanity of another, which is what all prejudices encourage us to do.

Second, John develops in this story a radically new understanding of God, not as an external deity whose protection we seek and whose power we respect and even fear, but as a permeating presence that calls us beyond our limits.

Third, this author now moves to separate faith from the concept of assenting to certain formulas. Then he transforms believing from giving intellectual assent to a proposition into being a source of trust that invites the "person of faith" to walk into a new experience of reality. So this Gentile official fits quite nicely into John's storyline and John's theological understanding. We now enter this story by examining these three themes.

The separation of the Jew from the Gentile was, as all tribal boundaries are, a survival technique, which the Jewish people from the time of the exile built into a defining Jewish characteristic. While tribalism is an identifying characteristic of all human life and fuels every human rivalry, the Jewish exile in Babylon installed the separation of Jew from Gentile into the very core of each Jew's being. It is the nature of human life to feed our ever-present security needs by displaying fear in the presence of anyone who is "different." This fear grows out of not knowing how to interpret behavior that has not been vetted by the norms which govern tribal life and into which tribal members have been incorporated. That is why it is in the biological nature of human life for us to respond to the stranger with heightened suspicion. Strangers speak a language we do not understand, so we do not know how to process their words; and as a result we fear their motives. When we do not understand their words, our latent paranoia is fed and excited. Strangers who are not of our tribe also have different ethnic characteristics. Tribal thinking always defines the characteristics of one's own ethnicity as "normal," which immediately suggests that to be different is to be "abnormal." Strangers also worship in a different way and since the primary, primitive meaning of worship is to solicit divine protection for ourselves, worship that is different from our norms might turn out to put us at risk of losing the protection of our deity to the deity of another tribe, who might well be malevolent.

For all these reasons, xenophobia is a natural human survival technique that is present in all of us. We cannot lay it aside be-

cause it is part of what it means to be human. We can escape it
only by escaping the limits of our humanity. Making that escape
thus reflects a transformational moment, one in which we cross a
boundary and enter a new level of consciousness and begin to perceive the reality of human oneness. That is not easy, for survival
drives all life, and survival always demands barriers behind which
we can find security.

The history that produced the Jewish national identity was
filled with illustrations of this intense struggle for survival. The
Jewish nation was always on the edge of extinction and thus this
survival reality was imprinted on the Jewish character. The Jews
had been forced to endure and to survive as an underclass or
slave people in the land of Egypt. After a successful exodus from
slavery, they had to struggle to reclaim for themselves a pre-slave
history in a land which had been promised (their tribal mythology
had convinced them) to their ancestors by their tribal God. To
survive as a people they had to draw fierce lines of demarcation
that separated the Jew from the non-Jew. Later in their history,
when they were conquered by the Babylonians and exiled in a
forced relocation program to the land of Babylonia, they knew
that their only hope for a return to their native land lay in keeping
themselves separate from their conquerors. They accomplished
this, as we noted previously, by resurrecting three defining practices, which became the quintessential marks of Jewish identity:
the observance of the Sabbath, the requirement of a kosher diet
and the act of circumcision.

What drove the Jewish people to erect these extreme tribal
boundaries was the sense that they had a vocation to be the
people through whom God would bring a blessing to all the nations of the world and that only through their radical separation
could that vocation finally be accomplished. To make oneself
overtly different from all other people is not an easy vocation

for any person or group to live out. It invites ridicule, abuse and ghettoization and ultimately gives rise to a killing prejudice, all of which the Jewish people have experienced in the fierce anti-Semitism that has marked Western history and remains alive today. It also, however, accomplished their survival purpose, for can any of us recall another people who have maintained their national identity even with the loss of their nation from the maps of human history from 70 CE, when they were overrun by the armies of Rome, until 1948, when their homeland was re-established by the United Nations? Where today are the nation-states of such ancient peoples as the Edomites, the Moabites and the Philistines? Most tribes disappear from human history when their lands are conquered. The Jews, however, had such an indelible sense of both the realm of God and their intrinsic Jewishness that they kept their identity alive for more than eighteen hundred years without a nation-state, during which time they lived as strangers and exiles in someone else's country. Hardly ever were they welcomed and appreciated, but the survival of their national identity was accomplished. That is why the separating barrier between Jew and Gentile in the time of Jesus was so severe and so potent.

As John developed his Jesus story, he first brought Jesus into touch with a Jewish leader, Nicodemus, who was unable to receive his message; then he brought Jesus into a relationship with the Samaritans, who while sharing a common history with common patriarchal ancestors were nonetheless deeply alienated from other Jews. In that latter narrative, however, the historic limits of tribalism were transcended and the Samaritans found a oneness in an eye-opening vision of what it means to be human. Now in this episode (John 4:46–54) the author of John's gospel brings Jesus into dialogue with the enormous boundary that separated Jew from Gentile. That is what the character known as the "Gentile official" was meant to symbolize. It was not his status

as a Gentile, but a deep need arising out of his humanity, that led
him to step beyond the tribal barrier.

This Gentile official had a son who was ill; indeed he was at
the point of death. Jesus, although Jewish, had somehow come to
represent to the official a new kind of life force, a wholeness, even
a healing presence for which he yearned. People seeking cures for
an illness thought to be fatal will go to incredible lengths in their
search. Love drives us to climb life's most difficult mountains
and to overcome every obstacle in the search for life. This Gentile
official did not understand the source of the healing power he
attributed to Jesus, but he came to him as a kind of last hope to
avert a broken heart. Perhaps Jesus would turn out to be a source
of life and healing for his son. Throwing caution to the wind, he
crossed the tribal divide. The official came to Jesus, begging him
to come down to his house, to be present physically with his son
and thus perhaps to restore his son to life. Jesus responded with
what seems like a word of judgment. It was, at the very least, a
challenge to the official's hopes: "Unless you see signs and wonders you will not believe?" The official was not eager to engage in
debate, since his needs had already overwhelmed his tribal fears.
So he responded by repeating his desperate plea: "Sir, come down
before my child dies!"

The author of this gospel sees in Jesus the presence of the God
who is the source of life and healing, the giver of wholeness, and
he implies in this narrative that the Gentile official's question indicated that he had come to a similar conclusion. Where Jesus was,
God, understood in a dramatically different way, would have to
be. Jesus, John reports, recognizing this affirmation, responded
by saying, "Go, your son lives." There was no contact between
the sick child, for whom the supplication was made, and Jesus.
God was present in Jesus, but was not confined to his single life.
The presence of God could not be bound to a particular time

or space. God was (and is) a mystical presence permeating the world. Somehow this Gentile official grasped this reality. So this gospel states that he "believed" and returned to his home, where he learned that his son had begun to mend at the exact time, one o'clock, the seventh hour, when Jesus had said to him, "Your son will live."

How difficult it is for religious people to embrace an un-bounded God. We have through our history sought to define God as a particular being, albeit one possessing supernatural power. With God defined as a being, we then had to locate God in a place. Ultimately that place was thought to be somewhere above the sky in a three-tiered universe. Then we had to build for this God earthly dwelling places that we called "houses of worship."

Next, we began to assert that God's very words were cap-tured in the words of our sacred scriptures. Then we convinced ourselves that God's very nature could be defined in our creeds, doctrines and dogmas. We then built mythologies around each of these human creations, assuring ourselves that God was content to live within our developed theological and liturgical limits.

When these "sacred idols" began to be destroyed by the expan-sion of human knowledge, we acted as if God had died. The God who lived above the sky was rendered homeless when we began to embrace the infinity of space; yet we continued to address God as "our Father, who art in heaven." Next, the scriptures, which we once thought of as God's literal words, began to be understood as tribal tales and as human interpretations; but when we read them in public worship, we still asserted that "this is the word of the Lord." Then the creeds, the doctrines and the dogmas—which, we asserted, had captured God's revelation—began to be under-stood as political and cultural compromises; but we, in our fear, had in the past invested these human forms with such authority that those who questioned them were burned at the stake as heretics, and we claimed the word "orthodox" for our own human formulations.

That was when theism, the human word one adopted to refer to God as a being, began to die and we either had to become a-theists or search for another God definition.

In the Jewish mysticism in which the author of the Fourth Gospel was immersed, God had in the past been viewed after the analogy of the wind and our breath, both of which animated life, but neither of which was capable of being captured in any human form, or by any human analogy. The statement that there is no God above the sky does not mean that there is no God. The fact that God was perceived as present in Jesus of Nazareth does not mean that the God above the sky had become incarnate in Jesus of Nazareth, as later creeds would suggest. It rather means that the spiritual presence we call God permeates the universe, becoming audible from time to time in a particular person in whom "the word of God" is heard to be speaking, and visible in that life through whom "the will of God" is revealed. We Christians through the centuries attempted to define God in such a way that we could be certain that we possessed this divine presence in ways that we could control, but Jewish mysticism, like mysticism everywhere, could not tolerate any human limits.

God was not and is not bound to the life of Jesus! That is what John's gospel was trying to say in the story of the healing of the official's son. God is not a being present in one life at one time or in one place—not even in Jesus of Nazareth. Jesus spoke the word. The official's son began to heal. Life calls to life, love calls to love, being rises out of the Ground of Being, and in that understanding the separation of Jew from Gentile also quite clearly disappears.

Finally in this episode, revolving around the character of this Gentile official, whose creation was of literature and not history, we watch as faith is redefined. This official "believed the word Jesus spoke to him and went on his way" (John 4:50). Faith is not believing in creeds, doctrines, or dogmas; faith is trusting the divine presence to be in every moment, in every tomorrow. Faith is having the courage to walk into the unknown, to confront whatever life brings one's way without having our humanity destroyed in the process. There is no such thing as "*the* faith." No claim by anyone to possess the only way to God, to be the single infallible authority empowered to speak for God or to hold the only inerrant source of God's revelation is ever valid. Those things have been historically nothing more than human idols, designed to provide us with the religious security for which our hearts yearn. Faith does not, cannot and will not give us peace of mind, security and certainty. Faith gives us only the courage to put one foot in front of the other and to walk into tomorrow with integrity even though we know that in this world there is no peace of mind, no security and no safety. Faith calls us to recognize that we are all in this quest we call life and that our human defense barriers of tribe, race, ethnicity and even gender and sexual identity cannot finally separate us from one another. Faith calls us to understand that to be human is to be part of who and what God is and in the oneness of this God presence to find that our understanding of life is enhanced and all human barriers fall into insignificance. "If you have seen me," Jesus would later assert in this gospel, "you have seen God" (John 14:9).

This Gentile man found in the Jewish Jesus access to the oneness of life, to new aspects of our common humanity. He believed and that enabled him to enter a new dimension of reality. It was that reality which the author of this gospel believed broke into human awareness in and through the person of Jesus of Nazareth. It had nothing to do with religion; it had everything to do with life and being.

John will continue to tell his story of Jesus around characters that he created. That was why he opened his gospel with a poem that encompassed his vision of "the word"—operating through, but not bound by, the medium of what he called the flesh. In Jesus the word was made flesh and we beheld God's glory. As Irenaeus once asserted, "The glory of God is man [and woman] fully alive." To be fully alive is to give up defining barriers. That is what was revealed when the Gentile official came to the Jewish Jesus.

CHAPTER 12

The Man Crippled for Thirty-Eight Years

I suspect, as I hinted earlier, that the original order of John had chapter 6 follow chapter 4, and then came chapter 5. Rearranged in this manner the text certainly makes geographical sense, and that is convincing for many scholars.* Whether that is true or not, however, does not really change the impact of the story or the development of the primary Johannine characters, so I will follow the order as we have it and draw into our focus next the mythological character of the crippled man (John 5:1ff). The author sets the stage for this episode with great care, citing explicit details.

Jesus goes up to Jerusalem. In the Fourth Gospel, contrary to the pattern of the synoptics, Jesus goes up to Jerusalem on many occasions. What draws him this time is a feast of the Jews, one that since the Deuteronomic reforms of the seventh century BCE required a Jerusalem-only celebration. This gospel does not say what that festival is, probably because the author is blending two celebrations together and is content just to mention it to provide a background. Though hints of the conflict between the synagogue

---

* I think it is fair to say that most Johannine scholars think that chapters 5 and 6 ought to be flipped. C. H. Dodd is the major holdout.

and the Johannine community have been clear and present in this gospel before now, in this episode that conflict breaks out with a new intensity, and the ultimate result, which in the mind of the Fourth Gospel's author is revealed in how people would come to understand the death of Jesus, begins to come into view. Jesus' death will be interpreted by this gospel as light being extinguished by darkness in a world where God has been reduced to the status of one who is primarily the creator of religious rules, not one who will call us into radical humanity. For John the religious need to diminish and even to destroy life, a need that seems to be regularly present in religious history, is little more than an attack upon God, whom he perceives as the source of life. Since we have discovered John's way of making his point through the use of mythological people and circumstances, we are not surprised to see him present another of his unique characters, an unnamed crippled man in whom the human struggle to enter a new consciousness is real.

Jesus is in Jerusalem and he goes to a site known to be frequented by people in search of a cure. By a portal known as the Sheep's Gate is a pool that in the Hebrew language is called Bethzatha. Around this pool are five porticoes, inside which lie multitudes of invalids. John portrays these victims as "blind, lame and paralyzed." They are specimens of human life yearning for wholeness.

Folklore born in Jewish mythology had apparently developed around this pool. The waters of this pool were said to be miraculously troubled periodically and at those times to have therapeutic power. The popular conviction was that the first one who stepped into those troubled waters would experience healing. The fascination with healing miracles has a long history in human experience, as healing shrines like Lourdes and Fatima illustrate, and as the number of faith healers will testify. The wish is, I fear, sometimes the creator of the reality. The pool of Bethzatha had also achieved this popular reputation.

In this setting the author of this gospel brings one of the invalids front and center. The man's affliction has to do with his inability to walk. A detail as specific as the one stating that this crippled status has been endured for thirty-eight years is always suspicious. Is the number of years a historical memory or a symbolic truth? I am convinced it is symbolic, but its meaning has been lost in the sands of time. Perhaps it was related to the number of years in which the tensions had grown between the followers of Jesus and the synagogue authorities, which led to the expulsion of the Christians, occurring somewhere around the year 88 CE, although we cannot fasten on any event in 50 CE to be the starting point. The story does suggest, however, a significant time during which the followers of Jesus had endured a wounding persecution and a crippled state of life from the religious authorities, as they struggled in an ever-anticipatory way, always hoping against hope for the healing of the fracture. Some other details in this story seem to validate this hypothesis, but I do not believe it can be pressed too far. Just keep this possibility in mind as the story develops.

Jesus is once again endowed by the author with clairvoyant knowledge. He knows that this man has been trapped in that state of expectation for a long, long time (John 5:6). He speaks to the man directly: "Do you want to be healed?" The crippled man responds with an excuse: "Sir, I have no man to put me into the pool when the water is troubled, and while I am going, another steps down before me." Indecision is always someone else's fault. Stepping out of the familiar religious forms of yesterday and into the post-religious freedom of tomorrow is never easy. It takes courage and a willingness to think outside religious boundaries.

One does not easily admit either a lack of courage or the sin of indecisiveness.

Jesus cuts through these debilitating fears quite directly by saying: "Rise, take up your pallet and walk" (John 5:8). The command empowers the man, who immediately rises, takes up his bedding and walks. Then John notes that "that day was the Sabbath" (John 5:9). The boundaries of the conflict are now in place. New life and new wholeness are challenged by the religious rules of the past. That becomes the plight of this now whole, but formerly crippled man. Opening himself to wholeness, he trembles because he can no longer hide from his fears inside the excuses of his past. How often it is that after one does an audacious thing, one then trembles at one's own audacity!

Next, the synagogue's religious leaders observe that this formerly crippled man is carrying his bedding on the Sabbath day, an activity defined as work, and therefore an act violating the Sabbath day rules. Into the story come immediately those who see themselves as the arbiters of what is allowed. To the former crippled man they say: "It is the Sabbath. It is not lawful for you to carry your pallet." He responds by saying: "The one who healed me said to me: 'Take up your pallet and walk'" (John 5:11). It was a weak, but familiar response: I am not responsible; I was only following orders. This excuse has been used many times in human history. It is always the stance of one who has trouble grasping both life and the responsibility we each have for embracing life's realities.

"Who is this man [that healed you]?" the synagogue authorities ask him, smelling perhaps a more important target. If you will not be responsible for your own behavior, we will seek out the one who empowered you to break the law. "I do not know," replied the now-healed man. Indeed the story reveals the truth of that statement. He did not know the source of his new and ecstatic grasp of freedom. Jesus had withdrawn, the gospel writer insightfully notes.

Later, John says, Jesus found this man in the Temple and gave him one more chance to choose faith over fear, life over religion. "See, you are well," Jesus said. Don't sink back into your fears and your behaviors of the past. Those who cannot deal with wholeness and life, those who retreat once again to the security of clinging to their sweet sicknesses, frequently lack the courage to seek a second chance.

The formerly crippled man then went immediately to the synagogue leaders and identified Jesus as the source of his healing, and that finger-pointing led to a new persecution of Jesus. Wholeness, the religious authorities of that day were asserting, cannot be accomplished through the breaking of religious rules. This dialogue with the religious authorities then rose to a fevered pitch. No good work of God was to be allowed on the Sabbath! It was a stunning claim. Jesus responded with an equally stunning, if opposite, claim of his own. "My Father is working still," said Jesus, implying that the healing of the cripple meant that God was continuing to bring life and wholeness even on the Sabbath. The obvious implication was that God was clearly working through Jesus. The audacity of this claim by Jesus was confirmed when he added that, like God, "I am working" (John 5:17) even on the Sabbath.

Now the religious leaders had two charges. This man Jesus not only broke the Sabbath, but he also identified himself with God. He made himself "equal with God." The claim of oneness between Jesus and God comes front and center in this account. Jesus is part of who God is. The Johannine community will proclaim this in a number of ways and with intensifying symbols that will ultimately bring Jesus and God into a kind of mystical unity. At the same time the synagogue authorities will call that claim one of blasphemy, and they will assert that God can act only through proper religious channels and in accordance with proper religious rules. Increasingly the followers of Jesus inside the Johannine community will come to the conviction that God cannot be contained in forms created by human hands. Jesus' claim that God is working through him deeply startles the synagogue authorities. Jesus' sense of intimacy with God is more than they can bear. Jesus is saying that the oneness of the Father's love for the son is revealed in that the Father accomplishes the divine purpose through the son. Then the conversation turns to death. The Father raises the dead by giving them life, Jesus says. That is also the work of the son. The son is the source of both wholeness in this life and life beyond this life. The one who believes this does not fall under judgment, but has passed from death into life, from a limited consciousness to a participation in the universal consciousness that transcends every human limit and every boundary, even the boundary that separates this life from eternal life. It is a most provocative piece of dialogue.

Then the author has Jesus refer, albeit obliquely, to the final narrative in the Book of Signs, the story of the raising of Lazarus. "The hour is coming," Jesus says in this episode, "when the dead will hear the voice of God and those who hear it will live" (John 5:25). In the Lazarus story Jesus will call to the dead and say: "Lazarus come forth," and Lazarus, hearing his voice, will walk out of his grave and shed the garments of death. In that Lazarus narrative the decision to put Jesus to death will be made by the religious authorities. We will examine that story in detail later, but here it is clearly presaged and introduced. The identifying claim has been uttered: "The Father has life in himself," and he has "granted to the son also to have life in himself" (John 5:26).

I live, John has Jesus assert, inside the will of him who sent me. Some, like John the baptizer, saw this, and that is the witness he bore. Jesus says quite directly that his works bear witness to the same reality. Then Jesus is made to drive this point home relentlessly: "You, the religious authorities," he says, "search the scriptures" because you think that in them you have eternal life, but it is those scriptures that actually bear witness to me. Yet you refuse to come to me that you may have life. It is Moses who accuses you and in Moses (that is, in the Torah) that you set your hope.

One wonders if, in the mind of the author of this gospel, the healed crippled man was present to hear this dialogue. It doesn't matter since he is still the star of this drama. He experienced new life and wholeness, but it is clear that he did not grasp it and he did not enter it. He could not stand in this new life, this new freedom, this thing Paul had called "the glorious liberty of the children of God" (Rom. 8:21). He chose rather to seek the favor of the synagogue authorities, to trust in the security of his religious rules. He trembled on the edge of a new consciousness and then fell back into what he believed was the certainty of the past.

That is how the Fourth Gospel viewed the conflict between the synagogue and the now-excommunicated Johannine community. Many members of that community could not finally endure the split. They could not imagine that they could survive without clinging to the past. They had to worship in Jerusalem rather than "in spirit and in truth." Not all of the followers of Jesus could walk the walk into the new consciousness that John was outlining. They could not see the cross as the place where the glory of God was revealed. They could not embrace this new reality. They could not bear the anxiety of the uncertainty that maturity always requires. They wanted rules, scriptures that were authoritative, sacred traditions that were set and fixed. They actually wanted to hide in something less than life. They could not make the transition that following Jesus required.

This crippled man, who had found wholeness in Jesus, symbolized this. Despite his experience with new life, he was not able to live in that wholeness, so he drifted back into the symbols of his broken and crippled past. John sees what Jesus offers in a dramatically different way. It is a costly decision to choose life, but that is finally what the followers of Jesus must do. Choose life, grasp life, enter life and claim life. It requires a new vision, being born of the spirit, escaping the debates about religious superiority or the proper place or form in which to worship. Its claim opens one to frightening new dimensions of what it means to be human. That is what the Jesus of John's gospel will finally live out. In this episode and through the character of the one who endured the status of a cripple for thirty-eight years, John shows the contrast. When wholeness is offered and even entered, some will always find it too scary to continue the quest and so they will fall back into the patterns of the past.

John is painting a picture of new life being born. He is not writing about theology and religion; he is creating a vision of what expanded life might look like and what a new identity and a universal consciousness might symbolize. This gospel is about the ancient and time-bound Jewish understanding of God moving into the mystical experience of life unfettered by fear or the needs that human beings have for religious security. Not everyone can bear this vision, but those who can, Jesus suggests, will enter a new dimension of life which is eternal.

John's narrative moves on. The members of his community, primarily Jewish followers of Jesus, having been expelled from the religious life of the Jews, are now forced to redefine their experience without any appeal to their previous synagogue life. Religion has been transcended, though Christian history will reveal that Christianity will be forever the victim of religion, and that battle, which the Fourth Gospel chronicles in this episode, will have to be fought again and again.

CHAPTER 13

Andrew and Philip: The Red Sea and Manna

The first sign in the Book of Signs was the changing of water into wine. The second sign was the healing of the Gentile official's son. The third was the offer of new life to the man crippled for thirty-eight years. Now we come to the fourth and fifth signs, which are intimately related in this gospel. They are not unfamiliar stories to the readers of the earlier gospels. Indeed these two episodes appear to have been of significant importance to every part of the early Christian community. Every gospel has in its pages at least one account of the miraculous feeding of the multitude in the wilderness, and two of the gospels, Mark and Matthew, each have two versions of this story, one taking place on the Jewish side of the lake (with five loaves and two fish), after which twelve baskets of fragments are filled, and the second on the Gentile side of the lake (with seven loaves and a few fish), after which seven baskets of leftover fragments are filled. Connected with these feeding stories in each of the four gospels is a second miraculous-sounding event, namely Jesus' ability to walk on the water.

John will follow this pattern of connecting these two narratives by making the feeding of the multitude the fourth sign in his

Book of Signs, and the account of Jesus having the power to walk on water will be the fifth. To understand these two signs we must be able to see how they are connected.

Typical of the author of the Fourth Gospel, however, he will develop these narratives quite differently from the way the earlier gospels did, and in the process he will take the names of two disciples, who in the earlier traditions are *only* names, and he will clothe them with distinct personalities and then through them develop and connect these two signs. Let me first lift these two disciples, Andrew and Philip, out of the synoptic tradition and then show how John develops them to suit his own literary and theological purposes.

Mark had first introduced Andrew as the brother of Simon Peter some thirty years earlier. In that gospel both Andrew and Peter were identified as fishermen. According to Mark they were the first disciples to be chosen by Jesus and his invitation to them was to leave their fishing trade and become his followers (Mark 1:17). That is the entirety of the biographical material that we have about Andrew until the Fourth Gospel is written.

Philip gets even less notice in the earlier gospels. His sole mention is that of a name on the list of "the twelve" in Mark (3:13–19), Matthew (10:1–6) and Luke (6:12–16). On each of these three lists he is consistently in fifth place following Peter, James, John and Andrew. Beyond his name, however, there is not a single biographical note about Philip to be found anywhere in that earlier tradition, leaving the author of the Fourth Gospel with an open field for his rich imagination.

John begins by setting Andrew and Philip against the background of a liturgical observance in the synagogue. Both of these signs, the feeding of the multitude and the account of Jesus walking on the water, are to be built around the observance of the Passover.

Andrew in relation to Philip clearly plays the major role as John's chapters unfold, with Philip playing his sidekick. The fact that Andrew and Philip are the two disciples with Greek (not Hebrew) names may offer some insight into John's motives in developing the story the way he does and thus might provide a tantalizing clue, but there is no way to be certain, so I file this only as a possibility.

Chapter 6 opens with Jesus on the eastern side of the Sea of Galilee, a wilderness area. A great crowd, attracted by the previously described signs, has followed him. Jesus and his disciples climb into the hills. There they sit down and look at the multitude coming toward him. Turning to Philip, Jesus asks, "How are we to buy bread so that these people may eat?" It is a strange request. Jesus apparently assumes that he is responsible for feeding the people. That is hardly a literal expectation, but it does serve to set the stage for John to tell his story. Philip, recognizing the absurdity of this request, responds in a manner similar to the responses we have seen before in this gospel from literal-minded people. If one hears the question literally, one must respond with a literal answer. The question, John states editorially, is a test, designed to measure the level of Philip's understanding, for Jesus (we are told), believing himself to be the "bread of life," clearly knows what he is going to do. Philip, however, failing to comprehend, responds literally: "Two hundred denarii would not buy enough bread" for everyone to have even a taste.

Andrew then moves onto center stage with information that seems equally irrelevant. "There is a lad here," he says, "who has five barley loaves and two fish" (John 6:9). It is a tiny thing, a mere drop in the proverbial bucket of the need facing them. Jesus, however, takes this apparently insignificant gift and invites the people, said to number in the thousands, to sit down on the grass. He gives thanks and then begins to distribute the bread and the fish. The people eat "as much as they wanted" (John 6:11). Jesus then orders his disciples to "gather up the fragments that nothing be lost" (John 6:12). They do so, filling twelve baskets with fragments. When this feeding act is complete the people say, "This is indeed the prophet who is to come into the world" (John 6:14), a familiar Johannine reference to a promise of Moses. Then the text says that Jesus, perceiving that "they [are] about to come and take him by force to make him king" (John 6:15), withdraws to the hills by himself. That withdrawal sets the stage for him to come to the disciples later that night by walking on the water.

Surely we need to recognize first that this is not a description of a literal event that actually occurred in real time. To read this narrative literally is to misread John's intentions totally. I believe the same is true for the synoptics and their authors' intentions, though their language is not quite so clear. Let me be more specific. I am quite certain that there never was a time when Jesus multiplied the food supply and fed the hungry masses, nor did he ever walk on the water in some supernatural way! We penetrate the sense of this episode by examining first the meaning attributed to the disciple Andrew, then the meaning attributed to Philip, and finally what these stories would mean in the Hebrew tradition that gave the followers of Jesus the ears to hear what the gospel writers were communicating.

Andrew, as John portrays him, appears to be one of those people who has an identity only by referral to someone else. Recall the way this gospel introduces Andrew and Philip. Andrew, we are told, was a disciple of John the baptizer who, when he hears John's witness to Jesus, begins to follow Jesus. Jesus turns to him and says, "What do you seek?" Andrew answers: "Rabbi, where are you staying?" Jesus says: "Come and see." Andrew goes, he sees and he stays with Jesus that day. When that visit is over, we are told, Andrew goes immediately to find his brother Simon and to announce to him: "We have found the messiah." Simon then comes and Jesus looks at him and immediately gives him the nickname Peter, which means "Rock" (John 1:42).

Philip is introduced on the next day. Jesus finds Philip and invites him also to become a disciple. All we are told about Philip in this previous episode is that he hails from Bethsaida, the same town in which both Andrew and Peter live. Philip then goes and finds the one who is named Nathaniel and repeats to him the identification of Jesus previously used, as John continues to emphasize this point: Jesus is the one of whom Moses wrote in the law, the one pointed to by the prophets. When identifying him specifically, Philip refers to him as "Jesus of Nazareth, the son of Joseph" (1:45). It is a striking identification because there is no miraculous birth narrative in this gospel. Jesus is assumed to have been the child of Joseph.

So John portrays both Andrew and Philip as missionaries who respond to invitations to follow Jesus by bringing another person into discipleship. Andrew, however, is always deferential, content to play the role of the insignificant one. Andrew is the gatekeeper who opens the door to others and allows great things to happen. He seems to have no need for status, no need to accumulate recognition. I think of him as the patron saint of the ordinary people.

That theme is also operating when John has Andrew bring to Jesus the lad with the five loaves and two fish. A hungry multitude is before him and he confronts it with a boy's lunchbox! There is, however, no gift that, in the mind of this self-effacing man, is too small or too insignificant not to be used and even valued. So with Jesus now aware of this boy's gift, Andrew, having facilitated the connection, stands by and watches as the events unfold and the multitude is fed.

Behind this story clearly looms the figure of Moses. That is why John has so often repeated the designation of Jesus as the prophet promised by Moses. If he is going to be identified in this Moses role, then stories of Moses must be wrapped around him. Arguably, the two most dramatic Moses stories are the power seen in the feeding of the hungry multitude in the wilderness with heavenly bread called manna, which was rained down from the sky, and the power seen in the splitting of the Red Sea. Both of these stories were survival stories. God, through Moses, had saved the children of Israel from death by starvation with heavenly food and God, through Moses, had saved them from death at the hands of the Egyptians by delivering them through the watery grave in the midst of the sea. The sequence in the Hebrew scriptures was the Red Sea first, followed by the story of manna in the wilderness, but in those scriptures the Passover on the night of the exodus preceded the Red Sea. Since John will describe the feeding of the multitude as a Passover meal, he puts that story before the story of Jesus demonstrating his power over water, where Jesus does not split the lake to walk on dry land, but walks on the water to get to his followers and bring them to safety. The feeding of the multitude and Jesus walking on the water are always together, because both of these narratives are Moses stories and both are together in the story of the exodus.

Jesus, the prophet anticipated by Moses, is now revealed to possess the power that the God of Moses possessed. He can feed a hungry multitude in the wilderness with bread. He can transcend the barrier that water brings when it must be navigated. John then develops these images in his own distinctive way.

John's Jesus will make the claim that he is himself "the bread of life," which satisfies the deepest hunger in the human soul; in addition, by locating this feeding episode at the time of the Passover, John consciously identifies Jesus with the paschal lamb. He will make this identification overt later by refusing to view the Last Supper as a Passover meal, in contradistinction to the earlier gospels. He chooses, rather, to have the crucifixion of Jesus occur on the day of preparation for the Passover so that Jesus will be crucified at the exact moment that the paschal lamb is slaughtered. Recall that John the baptizer has already referred to Jesus earlier in John's gospel as the "lamb of God."

In both of these episodes John will have Jesus employ the name of God: I AM recalls once more a Moses connection (Exod. 3:1–14). John also tells these two stories as one continuous narrative.

After the multitude is fed Jesus begins to teach them about the meaning of the food they have just consumed. The food that Jesus brings is not to be confused with food that satisfies temporary hunger. It is, he says, the food which "endures to eternal life." To make sure John's readers get the point of this feeding story, John has Jesus relate it directly to Moses and the wilderness, but then he raises it to another level, a higher level. When one eats, he says, to satisfy physical hunger, the satisfaction is never permanent. One is always hungry again. Only the bread of God that gives life to the world will ultimately satisfy the deepest human hunger. The disciples listen, but they do not understand. Then Jesus says one of the most provocative things that John ever records him as saying: "You must," therefore, "eat my flesh" and "drink my blood."

The walls of literalism in their minds rise to block the insight. Eating flesh and drinking blood are not pleasant images. They are, in fact, rather repellent. John is saying to his readers that they must take Jesus' life into their life. Eating Jesus' flesh is the way he chooses to communicate that.

Suddenly John tells us that all of this talk about eating Jesus' flesh and drinking his blood took place "in the synagogue as he taught in Capernaum" (John 6:59). We readers thought that it had taken place in the wilderness or on a mountainside, but note that it was "in the synagogue."

By the time John wrote, Jesus' disciples had been cast out of the synagogue. So John was saying to them that Jesus must be to them both a new Moses and a new doorway into the meaning of God. What Jesus was to them was not just another (albeit different) path of religion. They were now out of the synagogue for good, but what Jesus was offering did not require a synagogue or the Torah. They needed to see Jesus ultimately, John tells us, as a part of who God is, "ascending to where he was before" (John 6:62). This is where even the twelve drew back, choosing to be with him no longer. The disciples seemed to prefer the religious security from which they had been expelled to the anxiety of walking to a new place in their own life of the spirit.

That is why when the disciples left Jesus and took to their boats to start across the Sea of Capernaum, which is also called the Sea of Galilee, John mentions that it was "dark." Darkness to this gospel writer is always a metaphor for being apart from Christ. The disciples were alone on the sea. The waves of water were rising. A strong wind was blowing. Rowing was hard. This was when Jesus was said to have come to them "walking on the sea." They were filled with fear as he approached, but he said to them: "I AM." That is not the way the text is translated, because even the translators did not understand the meaning of these words. The translators had Jesus say: "It is I," as if all the disciples needed was some sense of identification, but the Greek words in the original text are *ego eimi*—"I AM." Jesus was claiming the name of God. I am the life of God, he was saying, calling you into something new, something frightening and dangerous. I am the love of God calling you to move beyond your defensive barriers, your security walls and into a new understanding of what it means to be human. Eat my flesh—take my life into yours. Drink my blood—open your spirit to my spirit. Receive me from the water into your boat.

The signs of Moses—manna and the Red Sea—are wrapped around Jesus and transcended in Jesus. New doors are being opened. The Johannine community begins to see how deep the separation is between light and darkness, self-consciousness and universal consciousness, human life and eternal life. The drama is heightened; the pain of choice and separation is intense. These two signs are now complete, and John's story moves on. Questions not of Jesus' destiny but of his origins will now take center stage.

CHAPTER 14

The Brothers of Jesus:
A Debate on Origins

The identity debate continues, but the background setting has changed from the Passover to the Jewish festival called Sukkoth, Tabernacles, or Booths—the harvest celebration, the Jewish Thanksgiving, if you will. The story is now set in Jerusalem.

Certain features characterized the observance of Sukkoth. Prayers were an essential element—first prayers of thanksgiving and then prayers for the future abundance of water, that gift which appeared quite literally to come from heaven to make the produce of the earth possible. A second feature of Sukkoth involved the building of a temporary dwelling place, called a booth, which served to remind the Jewish people of the wilderness years when they wandered as homeless nomads. There was also a procession around the Temple, in which the worshippers would carry in their right hand a bundle of leafy branches called a *lulab*, made up of myrtle, willow and palm, waving the branches as they walked. In this procession they recited (or had read aloud to them) the words of Psalm 118, which contains these words that have become familiar to Christians in a very different context: "Save us [from the Hebrew word *hosanna*], we beseech thee, O

Lord" (Ps. 118:25), and "Blessed is the one [he] who comes [or enters] in the name of the Lord" (Ps. 118:26). In their left hand, these worshippers carried sweet-smelling spices—usually the leaves, fruit and zest of the citron tree, called in the Sukkoth liturgy an *ethrog* (sometimes spelled *etrog*)—which would be placed into their temporary shelter or booth, in which tradition required that they eat one meal.

Psalm 118 was clearly a favorite among the early followers of Jesus as they searched the Jewish scriptures for hints to illumine the Jesus story, which they would then wrap around his memory until people assumed that Jesus himself had actually used these texts or fulfilled them. Included in Psalm 118 is the verse: "The stone which the builders rejected has become the chief corner-stone" (Ps. 118:22). This was interpreted as a pointer to Jesus by no less a person than the author of Ephesians (Eph. 2:20). Long before John wrote his gospel, various parts of Psalm 118 had already been incorporated into Christian preaching. In the Christian observance of Palm Sunday, the waving of leafy branches was added to the triumphant march of Jesus from the Mount of Olives to the city of Jerusalem. Some scholars argue that they see in the temporary dwelling place employed in the Sukkoth celebration the seeds that later produced the story of the temporary tomb in which Jesus was supposed to have lain from the time of his burial on the evening of Good Friday until his resurrection at dawn on Easter day. They also suggest that the zest and fruit of the citron tree carried in the *ethrog* inspired the story of the women bringing spices to the tomb of Jesus at dawn on the first day of the week. Finally, some scholars maintain that the temporary dwelling place mentioned in Luke's resurrection story about Cleopas and his friend on the road to Emmaus at evening on the first day of the week was also borrowed from the Sukkoth liturgy (Luke 24:13–35). In this resurrection narrative, the meal shared among

Jesus, Cleopas and his companion might have been a reference to the ceremonial meal required by Sukkoth.

My point in introducing this chapter in this way is to demonstrate that the liturgy of Sukkoth had from the earliest times been transformed by the followers of Jesus into a "messianic" setting in which Jesus could be understood. We should therefore be aware that John may be using Sukkoth symbols in this story in order to continue developing his non-literal portrait of Jesus. Chapter 7 is no more history than the story of the feeding of the multitude or the account of Jesus walking on the water.

John once again opens the narrative by introducing characters around which he will create his storyline. In this episode it is the brothers of Jesus who carry the drama. The earliest Christian records are quite clear in the assertion that Jesus had brothers who were known to the disciples. These brothers are referred to in texts such as Galatians (1:19, 2:1–21), Mark (3:31–35, 6:1–4) and Acts (15:13).[*] In John's gospel, however, these brothers are asked to play a specific role in the development of John's story, a story that is not factual or historical. There is also a clear similarity between the role assigned to Jesus' mother earlier in this gospel and the role now assigned to Jesus' brothers.

The mother of Jesus at the wedding feast in Cana tries to force Jesus' hand. He rebukes her and says that the time is not right; his "hour has not come." In this episode in chapter 7, the brothers of Jesus also try to force his hand. "Leave here and go to Judea," they say, "that your disciples may see the works that you are doing. For no one works in secret if he seeks to be known openly.

---

[*] The text in Acts says only James. It is, however, the general consensus that this James is "the brother of the Lord." Supporting this conclusion is the fact that Paul, writing earlier in his letter to the Galatians, had referred to the "pillars" of the church and had named them "James, Cephas and John" (Gal. 2:9). From the context of Galatians (note Gal. 1:19), it is clear that this James, the pillar of the church in Jerusalem, is James the brother of the Lord.

If you do these things, show yourself to the world" (John 7:3–4). John then adds the editorial note that "even his brothers did not believe in him" (John 7:5). Jesus responds to this pressure from his brothers in the same way that he is reported to have responded to the pressure from his mother, with almost identical words: "My time [hour] has not yet come. . . . Go to the feast yourselves. I am not going. . . ." So he remained in Galilee (John 7:6–9).

In the wedding feast story we noted that even though Jesus rebuked his mother, he then did exactly what she had requested. So also in this story, while he publically refuses to do what his brothers are demanding, afterward he does go up to Jerusalem, and there John's story unfolds.

Jesus goes to Jerusalem "in secret." John describes the people as being in a high state of expectation and messianic fervor. They wonder if Jesus will appear. In the middle of this eight-day Sukkoth observance, John says that Jesus suddenly comes out of hiding, goes up to the Temple and teaches. The people marvel at his learning. Jesus tells them that his teaching is not his own; his is the voice of "the one who sent me." He speaks not on his own authority, nor does he seek his own glory. He seeks "only the glory of God."

Among the crowd are members of the synagogue, who try to dismiss him and his message by claiming as their possession both the law and Moses the law-giver. Jesus challenges this claim by saying: "You do not keep the law." The law says you shall not kill, but "you seek to kill me." The rhetoric heats up. "You have a demon!" they respond. "Who is seeking to kill you?" Then referring back to John's story in chapter 5, in which Jesus cured the crippled man on the Sabbath and by doing so incurred the wrath of the synagogue authorities, Jesus now confronts these same authorities with their misplaced religious priorities. "If on the Sabbath a man receives circumcision, then why are you angry with me because on the Sabbath I made a man's whole body well?" he asks (John 7:23). They do not yet embrace that his meaning has little to do with religion; rather, it is about life.

Not able to understand that, the synagogue members shift the debate to the religious claims they perceive Jesus to be making. Is he the messiah, the Christ? He speaks openly, and yet the authorities do not move to arrest him. Are they afraid? Do they know secretly that he *is* the Christ? They even console themselves by suggesting that according to the scriptures he does not qualify to be the messiah. The scriptures tell us, they say, that no one will know where the messiah is from, but we know this man's origins. Jesus disputes this, citing the claim that he was sent; he did not come on his own. He adds further that he knows the one who sent him. The people want to arrest him on the spot, but, John asserts, they do not do so because "his hour [has] not come." To stop this debate the chief priests and the Pharisees send officials to arrest Jesus, but they also fail to do so. Jesus then proclaims that he will be with them only a "little while longer" and asserts that where he is going no one will be able to follow. That statement is also heard literally by the crowd, and the enemies of Jesus begin to speculate on where it is that he might be going that they cannot go with him. They have no idea what Jesus' assertions means, but they speculate that he might go beyond the boundaries of the Jews. Is this the moment when he begins to achieve his purpose of breaking down every barrier that divides one human being from another? That seed is certainly planted, and the meaning of John's gospel comes further into focus.

Next the author of this gospel announces, "On the last day of the feast, Jesus stood up and proclaimed himself the source of living water." What does this message mean? Two concepts jump out. First, in Jewish thought water is usually a synonym for the Holy Spirit. Second, the words translated in this passage as "stood up" are the same words translated later to refer to the resurrection. The word "resurrection" comes literally from the verb to stand up! For some, these factors are all they need to proclaim Jesus "the prophet" of whom Moses spoke. Others declare him to be the "messiah." Still, to the literal minds in the crowd, nothing seems to add up. Jesus is from Galilee, after all. The Christ cannot come out of Galilee. He must be descended from David and he must hail from Bethlehem. The argument rages on, and still Jesus is not arrested. Why? The authorities answer their own question: because "no one ever spoke like that man" (John 7:46). A lynching mentality, however, is developing. This is the context in which Nicodemus, who is clearly one of Jesus' accusers, makes his second cameo appearance, arguing that the law prohibits Jesus from being executed without a trial. The crowd responds to Nicodemus, "Are you from Galilee too? Search the scriptures and you will see that no prophet is to arise from Galilee" (John 7:52).

Jesus, having earlier claimed to be both manna from God and the source of living water, now makes another "I AM" claim. "I am the light of the world" (John 8:12), he says, and before this light darkness fades. An argument ensues that reflects the memory of the Johannine community when they were excommunicated from the synagogue. It is quite juridical in nature and is typical of the arguments the synagogue authorities used to purge the disciples of Jesus. Jesus says again that where he is going, they cannot come. This time, however, the authorities speculate that he is going to kill himself (John 8:22). Jesus then returns to the language of human division that he used in chapter 3 with Nicodemus: "I am from above," he says, "you are from below." I am not of this world, you are of this world. I am spirit, you are flesh. They are stuck in the self-conscious mode of their humanity. Jesus is a doorway into a universal consciousness that no one can know until he or she steps into it. Only when you have lifted up the son of man, says Jesus, in a specific reference to the crucifixion, will you know who the messiah is and who God is—then "you will know I AM" (John 8:28). You must continue in my words if you want to be my disciples, he adds. You cannot deviate from the truth. It is the truth that will set you free.

The authorities deny that they are not themselves already free. Forgetting their days of slavery in Egypt, they declare that they have never been in bondage to anyone. They are the descendants of Abraham. You cannot give us freedom, they proclaim; it is our birthright. Jesus responds: I am speaking about a different kind of bondage, the bondage of self-centeredness, the bondage of being motivated by survival, the bondage of insecurity and fear, the bondage of the struggle to become, which prohibits each of us from the celebration of our being. He calls them to leave the bondage of assuming that in order to build themselves up, they must tear someone else down.

Jesus argues that their security claims are rooted not in their status as descendants of Abraham, but in their unwillingness to do what Abraham did. Abraham left the world he knew in Ur of the Chaldees to venture forth into the unknown world of becoming all that he could be. Abraham stepped out of the security of the known; he walked beyond the certainty of religion in order to enter the insecurity of expanding faith in a frightening world. You cannot hear me, Jesus concludes, because you cannot do what Abraham did, and that is the only way to know the God I came to reveal.

The debate descends, as all religious debates inevitably do, into name-calling, into claims and counterclaims with no common ground. Those who believe that they alone possess "the truth" have to destroy anyone who challenges their religious security. The typical response is to attack, and that is the script that the enemies of Jesus follow. "We were not born of fornication," they say (John 8:41), alluding obviously to rumors that he was. "You are a Samaritan," a half-breed! You have a demon! You cannot be of God! To this Jesus suggests that his "word" will lift them beyond every human limit, even the limit of death. They return fire. Who are you? "Abraham is dead; the prophets are dead." Are you greater than they, that your "word" can deliver us from death?

You do not understand, Jesus responds. Glory does not come by trying to accumulate power. Glory comes by having the freedom to give your life and love away. If you could but understand, then you would know that "your father Abraham rejoiced that he was to see my day" (John 8:56).

That is more than they can tolerate. "You are not yet fifty years old and have you seen Abraham?" To that Jesus is said to make the ultimate claim: "Before Abraham was, I AM!" I am part of the life of God. I am part of the love of God. I am part of the being of God. This God cannot be bound in time or space, by ethnicity or clan, by religion or ritual. God is beyond every human division. Even the close bonds of family and the laws of kinship cannot place a limit on the reality of God. Jesus' mother ushered in the burst of the first belief in him, according to the Cana in Galilee story, but she was not able to and did not share in that belief. Now Jesus' brothers try to force him into a revelation that they are incapable of understanding or embracing. Nicodemus, who represents the old order, also cannot make the transition, try as he might. If Jesus is right, the end of these people's religious meaning has arrived. The threat is, therefore, intense. The response of his enemies is typical: They "[take] up stones to throw at him" (John 8:59). Jesus hides himself and escapes by exiting the Temple.

No religious form, no holy place can contain what Jesus is, says John in this account. Jesus' meaning will be seen only when he is "lifted up," and when that time comes he will be in control. It will be in his total self-giving that the glory of God, the ultimate I AM, will finally be seen.

CHAPTER 15

The Man Born Blind: The Split from Judaism Is Complete

T he sixth sign features a character in John's drama who is not only mythological, but is also a corporate figure. He is not a real individual who lived in history, but a representative symbol. He stands for the members of the Johannine community, who saw themselves as having once lived in the darkness of not seeing, but having been changed when "the light of the world" permeated their darkness. That light brought to them a new perspective, which relativized everything that they had once assumed was "truth." This in turn increased their anxiety, making it necessary for them to choose whether they would embrace the light or deny it. Would they simply stave off the threat and then seek to rebuild their security walls and settle into the known routines of their past, or would they step into the light and walk with courage into the unknown, exposing themselves to the new realities that living in the light always brings? Those are the choices that new light, new perceptions and new insights always bring.

Any reading of this particular narrative on almost any level reveals at once that this story was never intended to be the description of an event that really happened in the life of Jesus. It was rather a code-like description of what the people who made up the Johannine community endured when they discovered that, for their part, they could no longer live inside the context of their traditional faith system. At the same time, the synagogue leaders had reached the conclusion that the synagogue could no longer tolerate the insights of these followers of Jesus, so they ousted the Johannine community. That expulsion from the life of the synagogue did not occur until some fifty-eight years after the crucifixion! This narrative seeks to describe the feelings of the excommunicated ones by telling this story as if it had happened in the life of one called "the man born blind." To assume that this story is a supernatural miracle attributed to Jesus is to misread the Fourth Gospel's meaning totally. So listen closely to the way that John binds together symbol and insight, memory and time.

The story actually begins in chapter 8, as Jesus is being buffeted by those the author describes simply as "the Jews." In this context, please note yet again (I repeat this because anti-Semitism is so deep in our history) that this was not an expression of anti-Semitism. Jesus was also a Jew, and so were his disciples. We can be sure that Jesus' Jewishness was clear in the mind of this author, for he wrote it into the story of the Samaritan woman by the well. Recall that she asks Jesus, "How is it that you, *a Jew,* ask a drink of me, a woman of Samaria" (John 4:9)? Later, Jesus states to this woman the conclusion of the Jews, a conclusion that he clearly acknowledges not only to be his own, but also to be true. "*Salvation,*" he says, "*is from the Jews.*" So whatever John meant by setting up "the Jews" as the enemy of Jesus, it was not an ethnic definition, but a theological one born out of the separation, indeed the *fracture,* that caused the synagogue authorities to define the followers of Jesus as no longer Jews and caused these followers to define themselves as the "new Israel," an Israel in which all limits were transcended. Jews who were able to see the meaning of Jesus were surely included in that new community; in fact, they were the core of the Jesus movement. Women were included, and so were both Samaritans and Gentiles.

The Jews believed that the "messiah" was to be the vehicle through which all nations would be blessed. The "messiah" was not necessarily an individual. Indeed through most of Jewish history "messiah" was conceived of as the defining symbol of the whole nation. When the messianic claim was attached to Jesus, and when that claim was interpreted to be a call to step beyond all ethnic boundaries, obviously some Jews, perhaps the great majority, could not navigate the transition. They could not give up that which had always defined them. As a result, even when the light appeared, John contends, they chose to live in darkness. When Jesus was portrayed in the previous chapter as exiting the Temple (John 8:59), the ultimate symbol of Judaism, to save his life from the agitated synagogue crowd intent on stoning him, he was leaving the limits that bound the faith of his fathers and mothers to the past. We need to remember that by the time this gospel was written, the Temple was no longer there. It had been destroyed by the Romans in 70 CE. Earlier in this gospel (John 2:13–22), Jesus had been made to identify his body with the Temple: "Destroy this Temple and in three days I will raise it up" (John 2:19). The function of the Temple, John argues, had now been taken over by the life of Jesus, whom the very defenders of the religious tradition of the past had crucified. God, however, had raised him up in glory. That is the remembered history against which John will now tell the story of the man born blind.

This episode begins with a question. The disciples ask Jesus: Who is to be blamed for this man having been born blind? The common theological wisdom of that day held that sickness and

tragedy were instruments of divine punishment. Religion had proclaimed that, with the all-powerful, supernatural God in charge,
there must be an explanation for human pain and tragedy that
protected the justice of God. So sickness meant that someone was
getting what was deserved. Since this particular man's status of
blindness had predated his birth, it was hard to see him as being
guilty of some overt act of wickedness and thus as deserving of
his blind status, so the disciples speculated that his blindness
must have been punishment inflicted on his parents. That idea
had appeared before in the Hebrew scriptures. The child born
of the adulterous relationship between David and Bathsheba had
died, the biblical narrative informs us, to punish his parents for
their sin (II Sam. 12:15ff). It was apparently more important to
protect the sense of God's justice than it was to leave God's love
uncompromised. Fear of divine retribution might help to control
human behavior, but the God who would punish the offspring for
the sins of the parents was clearly an ogre who did not know how
to forgive, not a deity that one would ever call "Abba, Father,"
whose nature was love and whose purpose was to enhance life. To
be born into the status of blindness was therefore to identify God
with darkness, with an inability to escape the boundaries of the
human understanding of justice.

Yet that retributive-punishment perspective is what the author
of the Fourth Gospel assumes to be the view of the defenders of
traditional Jewish religion. So John has Jesus respond to the disciples' query by saying that neither the man born blind nor his parents were at fault, but that this man's affliction was meant to be
used to make manifest a new understanding of God, a new vision
of what human life can be when born to a new consciousness. It is
Jesus' purpose to be the "light of the world" that is on trial here.
So Jesus, using the name "I AM" and claiming an identity with
God in the words "I am the light of the world," approaches the

symbolic old Israel, now portrayed as a man who was born blind. That is the focus of this sign.

Some of the details in this narrative bear a similarity to the healing story told in Mark of the bringing of sight to a blind man from Bethsaida (Mark 8:22–26). In both stories Jesus uses spittle. In Mark's story he places the spittle on the eyes of the blind man twice, bringing sight to him slowly, with restoration coming only after the second application. This Marcan story was also very probably intended by that author to be understood not as a simple miracle story, but as a parable about the conversion of Peter. Recall that Peter also hailed from Bethsaida and that Peter came to see the light of Jesus in stages. It is important also to note the placement of this story in Mark's gospel. It comes just before the account of Peter's confession of Jesus as messiah at Caesarea Philippi, a confession which indicated that Peter's understanding and therefore his conversion, was far from complete.

In John's story Jesus mixes spittle with clay, rubs it on the eyes of the man born blind, and then directs him to wash in the pool of Siloam. There may also be in this story an echo of Elisha curing Naaman of the symptoms of leprosy by having him bathe in the waters of the Jordan River (II Kings 5:2–14). In the midrashic tradition of the Jews, the details of healing stories are frequently recycled. It was another way that the biblical authors signaled that they were not literalists, but interpreters of a new God experience. John's symbolic story of the man born blind is right in line with this Jewish practice. This man was living in darkness, which was for John the status of his enemies and the enemies of his community— those he called "the Jews," by which he meant those descendants of Abraham who could not move out of the limits of darkness into the transforming light that he believed Jesus came to be and to provide.

Once restored by the light and blessed with the ability to see, this man born blind then set off a debate about his identity, which was reminiscent of the debate that John had just described in the previous chapter as already swirling around Jesus in regard to his origins.

The religious authorities first sought to determine whether this was a case of mistaken identity. Was this man really the formerly blind man who had once sat and begged in the city, or was he someone who just looked like that blind beggar? The now-seeing man maintained that his identity was real; he was in fact the blind beggar. Once again the religious establishment was offended because this healing had occurred on the Sabbath, diminishing, they felt, the power of their religious rules. The Pharisees vigorously interrogated the man. How did the man called Jesus do this wondrous thing? The formerly blind man related the details, only to have his explanation rejected once more. This action cannot be of God, the authorities said, since it violates the Sabbath law; God cannot and would not violate God's own law! So this Jesus, they concluded, must be a sinner. Others then entered the debate, drawn by the irrationality of this religious argument. If you say he is not of God, you must explain how he can accomplish this wonder, they said. The Pharisees dismissed this argument out of hand as a challenge to their authority and returned to the man born blind. "What do you say about this Jesus?" they enquired. "He is a prophet," came the man's first answer.

These gendarmes of religious purity were not content with that. So certain were they that he could not have been born blind that they proceeded to call his parents to interrogate them. This led only to more frustration, as this attempt to find an easy way to continue protecting the religious traditions was quickly dismissed by the blind man's parents. "This is our son," they said, "and he was born blind." We know that both of these things are true, they affirmed, but how he has regained his sight or who did it are questions that he alone is competent to answer.

John then adds a comment, noting that they gave this answer "for fear" of those who ran the synagogue, for these leaders had proclaimed that anyone who professed Jesus as the Christ was to be expelled from the synagogue. The tensions that marked the excommunication in the 80s and 90s of the first century are, in John's editorial comment, being read back into the life of the Jesus of history.

So the authorities renewed their interrogation of the man born blind, and in this debate the past and the present were collapsed into a single period of time. This debate opened with the authorities saying God alone could do these things, not this man Jesus, who by violating the Sabbath revealed that he was a sinner. The now-seeing man replied, "Whether he is a sinner or not I do not know." One thing I do know, he added: "I was blind, now I see" (John 9:25).

"How did he do it," the authorities asked, in obvious irritation at this challenge to their understanding of "truth." The now-seeing man replied: "I have told you once and you did not believe. Why do you want to hear it again?" Then he stepped up his defense by going on the offense: "Do you want to become his disciples?" Recoiling in denial at such a possibility, they proceeded to revile him, saying: "You are his disciple, but we are disciples of Moses" (John 9:27–28). "We know God has spoken to Moses," they added—that is the claim of the sacred scriptures—but we do not know the origins of this man. To this strange argument the formerly blind man said: "This is a marvel! You do not know where he comes from, but he has opened my eyes." If this man were not of God, he could not have done this wonder.

Recognizing that the facts were not sustaining their traditional view, the authorities resorted to anger and denunciation, as religious defenders of the faith are prone to do: "You were born in utter sin, and would you teach us?" And they cast him out of the synagogue (John 9:34). You cannot be right, they appeared to say. If you are right, then our religion is wrong. Every religious institution and every religious form in history has had at some point in its history to walk through this doorway.

Jesus, hearing that the formerly blind man had been expelled from the faith community in which that man had been raised, went to find him. The conversation once again was directed to the followers of Jesus who, at the time of the writing of this gospel, had endured a similar expulsion. John clarified the issues: "Do you believe in the son of man?" Jesus asked, using the most popular of the messianic titles. "Who is he, sir, that I may believe in him?" the man replied (John 9:35–36). "You have seen him, and it is he who speaks to you," Jesus responded. "Lord, I believe," the man said, and he "worshipped" Jesus. Since worship was reserved for God alone, the author of this gospel was asserting that God had been met, had been engaged and was indeed present in the life of this Jesus. Then John had Jesus explain that narrative: "For judgment, I came into this world that those who do not see may see and that those who see [or who claim to see] may become blind." Then it dawns on the established religious leaders what Jesus is saying: *They* are the ones who are blind. *They* were born blind. In Jesus God has offered them light and seeing. If they were really blind, they would be guiltless. Their guilt lies in the fact that they claim to see when they do not see.

The conflict between the Jewish Johannine community and the Jewish synagogue leaders was intense. It had to do with their response to the Jewish Jesus as the light of the world. If the Jewish traditionalists could not move out of the past and walk in the light that Jesus came to give, said John, they were choosing to live in darkness, to hide in the religious security of yesterday. That, John asserted, is to make a virtue out of closed minds. That is to pretend to be seeing when in fact one is still blind. That is to act as if the truth of God had been or could be captured in the religious forms of the past. That is to refuse to step into the new life being offered, the new consciousness that invites the world into a new and unlimited understanding of what life is all about. That is to refuse to step beyond human limits into the universal consciousness that Jesus opens for all to see and to enter. That is why it is necessary, John said, to understand that Jesus is "the way, the truth and the life." That is why Jesus can be made to claim that he is the doorway into eternity, the only pathway into God. Jesus, the fully human one, offers the only pathway to God because the pathway into divinity can be found only through the expansion and the transcendence of the limits of the human.

CHAPTER 16

Lazarus: Breaking
the Final Barrier

The Book of Signs is now drawing to a close. There have been seven separate episodes, seven signs, seven pointers to a meaning that the sign itself could never capture. Only people failing to grasp the purpose of the author of this book would call them miracle stories. They are narratives which lead to a new perspective, a new consciousness. They are not literal accounts of how a supernatural deity has invaded human history in order to change it miraculously. A sign, rather, permeates reality and interprets it.

Interwoven through these signs is a series of Johannine characters, most of whom we have already met. We now come to the final and most complex of these characters. His name is Lazarus. More than any other figure in the Fourth Gospel, Lazarus screams out the message that to read this book as if it were an account of literal history is to misunderstand it completely.

In the Lazarus story, told in John 11, every symbol employed by John reveals that Lazarus is not a person, but a sign and a symbol. We note first that Lazarus has not been mentioned in any pre-Johannine Christian source. A man this crucially important to the Jesus story, as John was developing it, would, if he were a real person, surely have made an impression on someone else in the sixty-five to seventy years of Christian history before the gospel of John was written.

Second, when Lazarus is finally introduced in this very late gospel, he is identified as the brother of Martha and Mary who live in Bethany, about two miles from Jerusalem. Martha and Mary are well known in earlier traditions, as reflected in Luke (10:38–42). There is, however, no suggestion in that previous source that these two sisters, who were apparently quite close to Jesus, had a brother.

Third, there is a deliberate quality about the way John develops his storyline. John tells us with great emphasis that Jesus, when first notified of Lazarus' sickness, refused to move until Lazarus was not only dead, but actually buried. By the time Jesus did arrive in Bethany, Lazarus had already been in his grave for four days and both Martha and Mary rebuked him for his tardiness. It had been so long that Martha did not want Jesus to remove the rock at the opening of the burial cave, because in the words of the King James Bible "already he stinketh" (John 11:39). The Revised Standard Version is a bit more sensitive, translating the phrase "by this time there will an odor."

Fourth, there is still a crowd of mourners present, including those the author calls "Jews from Jerusalem," a term that in John means the enemies of Jesus. This mighty act of raising one from the grave is to be viewed, says John, by friend and foe alike. In a fashion reminiscent of the other signs, the power being described is greatly expanded. Earlier we noted that Jesus did not just turn water into wine; he turned it into 150 gallons of wine. Jesus did not just heal a cripple; he healed a man who had been crippled for thirty-eight years. Jesus did not just bring sight to a blind man, but to a man who had been "born blind." Now Jesus is not just going to raise someone from the dead; he is going to raise a man who has been dead for four days and who remains bound in burial cloths and whose body is already in the process of decay.

Fifth, there is to be no doubt about the reality of death in this story. In the synoptic accounts of Jesus raising Jairus' daughter from the dead (Mark 5:22, 35–43, Matthew 9:18–26 and Luke 8:40–56), a hint is placed into that text that she was not really dead, but only sleeping. Very few people were around to verify her death, so some ambivalence was present. In the account of Jesus raising the widow's only son from the dead in the village of Nain, recorded only in Luke (7:11–17), the young man was on the funeral bier being carried to his grave, but he was not yet buried. We have all heard stories of mistaken diagnoses of death, in which the presumed-deceased person regains consciousness prior to his or her burial, so a sliver of doubt still remains in that Nain account. About the certainty of Lazarus' death, however, no doubt is to be allowed. This is going to be a powerful and dramatic sign acted out on a very public stage.

Sixth, the narrative is stretched out in a painfully long preamble. Jesus' emotions are portrayed. "Jesus wept" (John 11:35), says the text. His love for Lazarus and his sisters is told again and again. A long discussion between Jesus and Martha on the meaning of resurrection is recorded. The realities of the "general resurrection at the last day" are described, and these are contrasted with the raising of Lazarus that is about to occur. The public processional from their home to the place of Lazarus' grave is told in far more detail than necessary. Jesus has the time once more to utter another "I AM" claim: "I am the resurrection and the life" (John 11:25), adding that "he [or she] who believes in me, though he [or she] dies, yet shall he [or she] live, and whoever lives and believes in me shall never die" (John 11:26). Jesus then asks Martha whether she believes this. She responds with a three-part affirmation: You are the Christ, the son of God and the "one who is coming into the world."

Only then do we arrive at the dramatic climax of this narrative. Jesus walks toward the tomb of Lazarus and stops in front of it. The crowd behind him is silent. The great stone is removed. Death is being challenged quite directly. With a loud voice the person who has claimed to be one with the source of life calls to the deceased man locked inside the boundary of mortality: "Lazarus, come out." Lazarus obeys this command. He comes out, but not easily. He is still wrapped in the burial cloths. His hands are tied to his body and his legs are bound together. His face is wrapped with a burial cloth. If we pretend it was a literal event, then it must have been a strange sight—a mummy emerging from the tomb, walking in the baby steps required of one whose legs are tied together, without having arms free to use for balance. No faith healer has ever done that. Jesus concludes this episode by giving an order: "Unbind him, and let him go" (John 11:44).

Process the details of this story and the power of this drama for a moment. Imagine the crowd of friends and enemies, the gasps and wonder that would have marked such an event, if it had really happened in the life of the Jesus of history. Can anyone's mind stretch far enough to believe that no mention of this event would have found its way into any written material for three to four generations after its occurrence, until John tells the story near the turn of the first century? No, this is not and was not history.

Look first at the response to this episode that John describes quite fully. "Many of the Jerusalem Jews, who had come to be with Mary and had seen what Jesus did, now believed in him; but some of them went to the Pharisees and told them what Jesus had done" (John 11:45–46). This report to the authorities resulted in the chief priests and the Pharisees gathering the ruling council of the Jews together to condemn him. Finally, Caiaphas, the high priest, is allowed to interpret Jesus, quite unknowingly but prophetically, when he is made to say: "It is expedient for you that one man should die for the people." If we do not suppress this man, everyone will follow him and the Romans will destroy our nation; one man must therefore die lest the whole Jewish nation perish. John even adds that Caiaphas spoke not of his own accord, but *as one who prophesied the truth that Jesus should die for the nation* (John 11:51). Then John slips into his own mystical message. It was not to be "for the nation only, but to gather into one the children of God who are scattered abroad" (John 11:52). In his life and by means of his death, Jesus will bring about human oneness. John will spell this out in the passion narrative, but when he concludes the Book of Signs, he will make clear what he has discovered to be the purpose of Jesus' death: "And I, when I am lifted up from the earth, will draw all people to myself" (John 12:32).

Everyone in this episode is destined to play his or her role in this cosmic drama, for John tells us that "from that day on they took counsel on how to put him to death" (John 11:53). The final scene is set: "The Passover of the Jews was at hand" (John 11:55).

While the story of the raising of Lazarus from the dead was never told before this gospel's writing, we can still ask if there is any known source that John might have used to develop this character and this story. A search of the earlier gospels provides a possible clue. There is a character named Lazarus mentioned in a parable that only Luke records. It is known as the parable of Lazarus and the rich man, who is sometimes given the name Dives (Luke 16:19–31). In this parable Lazarus is a beggar who begs at the door of a rich man. The rich man has developed eyes that do not see the poor, since such people have no value to him.

In time, according to this parable, both Lazarus and the rich man die. Lazarus goes to a Jewish version of "eternal life": He rests in "the bosom of Abraham." It is an interesting image. I believe that if I were destined to spend eternity lying in someone's bosom, I would prefer it not to be Abraham's! The rich man, for his part, goes to an unspecified place of torment. In this parable there appears to be communication between the two realms of the afterlife, so the rich man in this parable speaks to Abraham: "Father Abraham," he says, "Have mercy on me!" This torment, this heat is more than I can bear. I need relief! Won't you "send Lazarus to dip the end of his finger in water and cool my tongue, for I am in anguish in this flame" (Luke 16:24). The rich man still sees the poor Lazarus as someone whose only purpose is to serve his needs—a thing to be used, not a person to be valued. Abraham replies, in effect, that justice is being done and Dives must accept this. You had a good life, Dives, and now you are in anguish. Lazarus, on the other hand, received evil things in his life and now he is being comforted. This rhetoric, hardly real in human experience, nonetheless speaks to one of life's deepest yearnings, the hope for fairness. Then Abraham speaks again and tells the rich man that one cannot get from where Lazarus is to where he is—"a great chasm has been fixed" that no one can navigate.

Dives accepts that this is impossible and then tries another tack. "Then, I beg you, Father Abraham, to send Lazarus to my father's house, for I have five brothers, so that they may be warned lest they also come to this place of torment" (Luke 16:27–28). Then Luke paints the scene in his striking parable that clearly is the link to John's story of the raising of Lazarus in the Fourth Gospel. Abraham says, "They have Moses and the prophets; let them hear them." Dives responds, "No, Father Abraham, but if someone goes to them from the dead, they will repent." Dismissing this hope, Abraham makes the point that the story of the raising of Lazarus is designed to demonstrate: "If they do not hear Moses and the prophets, neither will they be convinced if someone should rise from the dead" (Luke 16:31).

John, in his Lazarus account, is writing on several levels. First, he uses the story of the raising of Lazarus to demonstrate the truth of Abraham's words in Luke's parable. The result of this final sign in the Book of Signs is that even in the face of the raising of the four-days-dead Lazarus, the result is still predictable: The synagogue authorities are not moved to open themselves to new possibilities. From their perspective, the possibilities are terribly threatening. All of the things that have been holding the Jewish nation together in its tribal identity would be relativized if what John believes Jesus means is true. All of those things that keep the members of the human family separated from each other would disappear. Those things constitute only the limits on our humanity that bind our potential. Jesus thus represents an ultimate threat to our tribal and religious life. The insight Luke had developed in the parable of Lazarus and the rich man is that "they will not be convinced if someone should rise from the dead" (Luke 16:31). Now in the Fourth Gospel this parable is related, as if it were history, in order to demonstrate that what the parable suggests is true—and not just in a parable, but in life itself.

The second level at which John is writing is also obvious. It had now been sixty-five to seventy years since the final events in Jesus' life had occurred. He had been crucified. John's conviction and that of his fellow disciples was that in the moment of Easter the boundary of death had been transcended, life had expanded to incredible new dimensions and a new oneness was experienced as human lives stepped beyond self-consciousness into the universal consciousness of entering the eternal life of God. Did that life-changing moment bring faith? That is the question John is posing, and he answers it so clearly. No, he says, it brought persecution and expulsion from the synagogue community. Those who trusted in Moses did not understand that to which Moses pointed. They did not see in Jesus the prophet whom Moses had promised that God would someday raise up. They saw the law, the "word of God" that came through Moses, but they could not see the grace and truth that came through Jesus or hear the "word of God" that was in Jesus. It was this vision of resurrection that finally broke the synagogue in two. The enemies of Jesus were not able to believe even, as Luke's parable suggested, if one "rose from the dead." Their response to Lazarus was identical with their response to Jesus. On this note the Book of Signs begins to come to an end.

Between the end of the Book of Signs and the beginning of the Farewell Discourses, there is a transitional chapter, chapter 12, on which the story pivots. I do not want to ignore this chapter, but I also do not want to dwell on it.

It serves to set the stage. It begins with the words "six days before the Passover," and the tension starts to build from that moment on. It opens with the familiar story of Jesus being anointed by a woman in preparation for his eventual death and burial. The details are, however, strikingly different from similar narratives in the synoptic tradition. The anointing woman is quite "sensual." She anoints his feet with costly nard and uses her hair to wipe them. But this woman is not unknown; she is Mary, the sister of Martha, and this anointing takes place in her home in the presence of her family and of Jesus' disciples.

The text moves on to the Johannine account of the Palm Sunday procession, when Jesus begins his final journey. It is in this chapter that Jesus announces that "the hour has come." We have previously noted the catalyst. Some Greeks (that is, Gentiles) have come and asked to see Jesus, and they are ushered into his presence. The light of this Christ is to be universal: Jew and Greek together will share in it.

Jesus is then portrayed as embracing his death. He disappears momentarily as his death is contemplated. His followers will have the light only "a little longer," but they will not remain in darkness. Then the Farewell Discourses begin.

PART III

The Farewell Discourses and the High Priestly Prayer

CHAPTER 17

Peter and the
Commandment to Love

As this gospel turns toward its climax, a new mood appears that is both somber and clarifying. It begins with Jesus turning away from the crowds and toward his own disciples. This is a familiar setting since each of the synoptic gospels has recorded a similar transition. In those earlier gospels the Galilean phase of Jesus' public career is climaxed in the experience that came to be called the Transfiguration. In that episode Peter comes to a partial, not yet complete understanding of who Jesus is. Mark, Matthew and Luke then have Jesus begin his journey toward Jerusalem with his focus now completely on the disciples. That journey is said to take days, during which time Jesus instructs the disciples on issue after issue in episode after episode detailing the bulk of the teaching of Jesus. As they travel, a note of increasing and foreboding tension is struck. The background is clearly the impending crucifixion, but the idea that the disciples must begin to function in a new way in order to accomplish the fulfillment of Jesus' ministry is also present, as the disciples begin to embrace the reality that they must somehow accomplish the Christ purpose without him.

We noted earlier that the teaching of Jesus is quite different in the Fourth Gospel. John never portrays Jesus as teaching in parables or in short, easy-to-remember sayings. There is in John no version of Matthew's Sermon on the Mount (Matt. 5–7); there is no content-laden Sermon on the Plain, as Luke suggests (Luke 6:17–49). In the Book of Signs the teaching of Jesus is in dialogue around each sign itself. Think back on the dramatic conversations with Nicodemus, the Samaritan woman by the well and the man born blind. In the raising of Lazarus story we just looked at, we have the primary teaching of Jesus on the meaning of eternal life contained in a significant dialogue with Martha (John 11:17–27). When we arrive at chapters 13–16, the shift occurs from dialogue to monologue. Yes, the disciples provide the background, the foil for the teaching, but they are not seriously engaged in these conversations. This section is called the Farewell Discourses, and *discourses* they are.

In many sections of these discourses there is considerable repetition. They do not make for easy reading nor are they readily understandable. These documents pretend to describe Jesus preparing the disciples to live without him, but their content is actually aimed at the issues that the Johannine community was facing when this gospel was written, some sixty-five to seventy years after the crucifixion. This means that in these discourses the disciples themselves become symbols of the Johannine community of believers. They are portrayed as struggling with the reality of persecution. They are also experiencing the pain of separation, not only from Jesus by that point in history, but perhaps more poignantly from the synagogue from which they have so recently been excommunicated.

Some scholars have wanted to reorganize some of the confusing elements of chapters 13–16 to provide a new order, one that they assert was the original order. While fascinating, this idea is quite complicated and ultimately not germane to the scope of this book.*

These Farewell Discourses are set in the days preceding the Passover celebration. Jesus is with his disciples. John thus gives him a final opportunity to identify his mission and to interpret the divine love which John is sure dwells in him as the presence of God. This love is called *agape* in Paul and is defined as love without limit. (I call it wasteful love.) It is love that is selfless and thus produces and enhances life. John's Jesus wants to open the world to this love and thereby to invite his disciples into a new dimension of what it means to be human. That new humanity, John argues, is revealed immediately as soon as this divine love is grasped. This love renders the pressure of barriers in the community of the followers of Jesus to be scandalous. John's Jesus is determined to show this divine love revealing itself in the community, first in his passion, second in his death, and third in the Easter experience. John places all of these themes into a meal shared together with the disciples in the village of Bethany. It is not the Passover meal, as it was in the earlier gospels; it is rather a fellowship meal in anticipation of the coming Passover. Strangely enough, John never actually refers to the meal itself. Rather, fol-

---

* Rudolph Bultmann, the best-known and perhaps the greatest German New Testament scholar in the twentieth century, who spent most of his professional life teaching at the University of Marburg, has offered his version of this proposed new order. He argues that chapters 15–17, while being fully Johannine, nonetheless seem out of place. He suggests that if chapters 15–17 were attached to John 13:35 (leaving the prior text unchanged), it would form a whole and cohesive unit based on Jesus' command to love in John 13:34. Bultmann would then move the material in chapter 13 from verse 36 to the end of that chapter to a new place, letting it follow John 16:33. Chapter 17, the high priestly prayer, he would place after John 12:43 to mark an interval before the new action begins. That kind of reconstruction of the text itself is not of great interest to the audience for which I write, but I wanted my readers to be aware that such speculation is not uncommon in New Testament study. I am indeed fascinated by these possibilities. I will limit my work to the themes that are communicated through the text as we have it, but I do not mean thereby to vote against the order proposed by Professor Bultmann.

lowing his long-standing technique, he wraps his teaching around a character.

The focal character in the first discourse is both real and substantial in the memory of the community, but the material wrapped around him is clearly mythological. He is central to John's story, so he comes up in context after context. This character is none other than Simon Peter.

Peter is always portrayed in the gospels as a work in progress. This particular story comes in the context of the final separation. The satanic power of darkness has already entered into Judas Iscariot. Jesus, aware of this, rises from the table; whether the meal is just beginning, is at a midpoint or is completed is not stated, but there is a hint that it is still in progress, and Judas will, therefore, depart without participating in it. Jesus then acts out the role of the servant.

He lays aside his garments, which will shortly, John will reveal, be taken from him and divided among the soldiers who crucify him. Jesus then binds himself with a towel, as he will later be bound by nails and ropes on the cross. This towel presumably is now his only substantial covering. He pours water, the agent of cleansing, into a basin and begins to wash the feet of the disciples and to wipe them with the towel that was around him. In this dramatically written episode, which only John records, the strictures of life, the boundaries that establish status and power, are reversed; all human images of protective barriers that provide security are removed. Peter is the only one who seems to have the eyes to see this, however, and he recoils—perhaps in fear, perhaps in vulnerability, but surely with hostility.

"Lord, you do not wash my feet," he is recorded as saying. Peter is portrayed as one who knows the limits of his self-identity. He knows how to play the human game of status and survival. Do not force me into a place where I no longer know who I am, he seems to say.

Jesus responds, not in these words, but with this meaning: Peter, do not resist the freeing power of divine love, through which I am calling you into a new dimension of what it means to be human. Here status needs are not relevant. *Those* rules apply only in the world of consistent human yearning, the world of human becoming. I am a doorway for you into being itself. Come through me and you will become more fully human. I am inviting you into an experience that will make you whole. If I do not wash your feet, you cannot be part of the God I am revealing and of the humanity I am offering.

Peter responds to that understanding of this gracious act and its implicit invitation by saying: Why, then, Lord, do you wish to stop with just my feet—why not all of me? I do not want just partial access to the fullness of being, so bathe all of me.

Jesus counters by saying: You have already had a bath. I am adding only the final dimension that will make you whole. Not all will share in this revelation, for not all are clean. John then adds an explanatory note: "For he knew who was to betray him" (John 13:11). Judas Iscariot is back in the drama—the separation of his darkness from the light of Christ is now made clear. Evil cannot tolerate the light of Christ, nor can any darkness quench it. "The light shines in the darkness and the darkness has not overcome it" (John 1:5) is how this gospel sounded this theme in the prologue.

Jesus concludes this narrative by asking the disciples to reflect on the scene. I have served you, he says. I have taken the role of the servant. That is what love does. When my love lives in you, you will serve the world. You will give your love and your life to others. The status games that human beings play no longer work when the new awareness, the new consciousness is experienced. There are no master-servant relationships inside the embrace of divine love. You have been invited into a new order. You are welcomed to eat at my table as members of my family. Not everyone can make that transition. Please know that, so you will not be surprised when that transition confronts you.

Then, at this intense moment of oneness, Jesus informs them: "One of you is a traitor." The disciples stare at each other in wonder and ask: "Who could that be?" It is in this setting that John introduces his last mythological character, who will be the figure upon whom the final events in Jesus' life will turn. This character has no name. He is called "the disciple whom Jesus loved" or "the beloved disciple." He, alone of all the disciples, will be present at the cross. He will be present on Easter morning. He will run to the empty tomb and, when he enters that tomb, he will be the first to believe. He will make his final appearance in the epilogue, which is set back in Galilee well after the resurrection. There, in the role that he is constantly assigned, he will *recognize* Jesus. "It is the Lord," he will say to Peter. In the epilogue we will also be told that there was a debate about the death of this beloved disciple. We will examine each of the narratives regarding this enigmatic character in more detail when we come to the subsequent chapters in this book. For now, just note this character's introduction and watch him emerge in John's story. As he takes shape, keep asking yourself both what and who it is that this enigmatic and symbolic character represents.

In John's introduction of the "beloved disciple," we note that the man is (as he will always be) in a position of intimate closeness to Jesus. We are told that at the final meal he is "lying close to the breast of Jesus" (John 13:23). This means that Peter must go through him to get to Jesus. Ask him, says Peter, to "tell us who it is of whom he speaks"—in other words, who the traitor is. So this disciple turns and puts the question to Jesus: "Lord, who is it?" (John 13:25). Jesus responds that it is "he to whom I will give bread when I have dipped it." Then Jesus, in John's gospel only, dips the bread into the common dish in the middle of the table and hands it to Judas. Is this an expression of a Eucharist that Judas will refuse? Is Jesus offering the bread of life to Judas? Is he saying that no one is ever to be excluded from the invitation into life? Is he proclaiming that separation from the love of God will never come from God's side? Each of these possibilities would certainly fit with the interpretive portrait of Jesus that the Fourth Gospel is painting. So keep that theme in mind as the story unfolds.

For now Judas is unable to receive the bread. Jesus then is made to say to Judas: "What you are going to do, do quickly" (John 13:27). John adds that "no one at the table knew why he said this to him" (John 13:28). The disciples are pictured as offering some speculative theories, but the conclusion is that Judas has turned his back on the light. He goes out, and when he does, this gospel says, it is night (John 13:30).

John has already asserted that the role assigned to and played by Judas was so "that the scripture may be fulfilled" (John 13:18). To support this claim John points to Psalm 41:9, where a trusted "bosom friend"—one who "ate of my bread"—"has lifted his heel against me." The reference is to a story in the David cycle, in which a man named Ahithophel, who also ate at the table of the king, became a traitor. In order to understand this reference more fully, we need to be aware that the king was referred to as "the Lord's anointed," which is another way of saying "the Lord's Christ."

Judas' departure brings the first emphasis of this initial discourse to a conclusion. Next, John has Jesus say: "Now the son of man is glorified and in him God is glorified; if God is glorified in him, God will also glorify him in himself and glorify him at once" (John 13:31–32). It is a strange sentence, but what it is saying is that when Jesus reveals that he can give himself away totally, people will see God's glory in him and he will become part of who God is and God will become part of who he is. In Jesus' humanity—his full, unbroken humanity—the divine presence will be revealed. The human and the divine are not two separate realms. God is not external. God does not have to enter the world from some other realm. When a human life is open to all that humanity can be, humanity and divinity flow together as one. It was and is a radical insight, and one the consciousness of the mystic is destined to understand.

Jesus concludes this account by speaking of his final departure. "Where I am going you cannot come," he says enigmatically. The disciples think of his destination as a place. Peter returns to the conversation and says: "Lord, where are you going?" Give us the address! Jesus responds, You are not ready yet, Peter—perhaps someday. Peter, still not comprehending, asks, Why not now? Do you not know, Peter continues, that "I will lay down my life for you?" (John 13:37). Jesus says, "Will you?" You will first deny me. You still have a long way to go, Peter.

Through this exchange with Peter, Jesus has indicated the path his followers must walk if they wish to go where Jesus is going. It is not about geography. "A new commandment I give you, that you love one another; even as I have loved you, you also should love one another. By this all will know that you are my disciples, that you have love for one another" (John 13:34–35).

In the first epistle of John, thought by many scholars to be deeply related to the gospel of John, perhaps from the same pen that wrote part of the gospel itself, God is defined as love. Love is not an entity so much as it is a penetrating experience. "God is love," this epistle states. Might this author also mean that "love is God" flowing through human life? Love is seen in the ability to be free of survival-driven existence, free to give one's life away. Love embraces people just as they are. Love is not separate from God. One cannot say: "I love God," and hate one's brother or sister. No one can *create* love. One can only *receive* it, and when it has been received it must be immediately shared. Love cannot be stored. It cannot be saved for a rainy day. It cannot be used later like leftovers. Love that is not passed on dies. Love is the power that binds us to God and to one another. Love is the meaning of Jesus.

Love, says the Johannine Christ, is not only my commandment, but also the mark of my presence within my disciples. I dwell in the love of God; you dwell in my love. Oneness is achieved in our willingness and in our ability to love one another. God is experienced as present in us, in our freedom to escape our needs and to give ourselves away to one another.

The cross will be, John is beginning to reveal to us, the place where the love of God is most dramatically revealed. Peter brags that he is ready to die to protect Jesus, that he is ready to give his life away. Time will reveal that this is not yet so, that Peter does not yet see who Jesus is. So the intensity of this drama moves on.

CHAPTER 18

Not Atonement, but Glory!
John Clarifies Jesus' Death

A s we begin to immerse ourselves into the Farewell Discourses, it is important to keep in mind that the Jesus of history never said any of the words attributed to him in these discourses, nor did he utter any of the teachings found in them.

These discourses, rather, represent an interpretation of the meaning of the death of Jesus from a vantage point in history years after the time of the crucifixion. They are the product of a community that had undergone two deep and transformative divisions: the separation from the synagogue to which I have previously referred and the fracture within the Johannine community itself over how to understand the relationship between God and Jesus.

The second split caused some of Jesus' followers to feel so threatened that they began to find their way back to the synagogue. They could not journey to the new place to which this community was now walking. When this second separation was complete, the remaining members were free to move without impediment toward a new understanding of Jesus. This was, I believe, when the Christological debate began to take on universal and mystical connotations and the author of this gospel began to turn his writing in a very different direction.

There is in John no hint of what later came to be called the "doctrine of atonement." That doctrine was the emphasis marking the writings of Paul, especially the early Paul, and it found expression in the synoptic tradition, but is absent from the Fourth Gospel. Paul was obsessed with human evil. He felt himself captured by its power. In order to understand how very different John's interpretation is, we need to review how the doctrine of the atonement was formulated.

Paul portrays Jesus as the one who has the power to deliver human life from the depths of the sin by which it has been captured. When Paul relates the story of the crucifixion, he does so with the following words: "He died for our sins in accordance with the scriptures" (I Cor. 15:3). It is from this text that "Jesus died for my sins" was born. That expression was destined to become a mantra in Protestant and evangelical circles. This same theme is expressed by Roman Catholics when they refer to the Eucharist as "the sacrifice of the mass," an expression which means that the mass is a liturgical reenactment of the moment when "Jesus died for my sins." In both of these phrases the connection is expressed that the death of Jesus was the action that brought salvation or redemption to sinful human beings. God in the person of Jesus, and especially through his death, restored creation to its intended perfection. Jesus restored human life to oneness with God.

Primarily under the influence of a late-fourth-century theologian and bishop named Augustine, but continuing in history through Anselm in the twelfth century, to both Luther and Calvin in the sixteenth century, atonement theology has dominated Christian thought. Not having at that time the rudimentary critical study of the scriptures that is available to us today, these historical figures viewed the Bible from a very literal perspective.

They believed that it was a single volume, written under divine inspiration and therefore incapable of being inaccurate, so they merged the two creation stories with which the book of Genesis opens into a continuous account. This merger then formed the understanding of human life against which they told the story of Jesus. They did not know that these two stories (Gen. 1:1–2:4a and 2:4b–3:24) were written by two different authors separated in time by as many as four hundred years. The opening narrative (basically the story of the seven-day creation) is relatively late, probably a product of the late sixth century BCE, and somewhat more modern in its understanding. The second of these stories (basically the story of Adam, Eve, the Garden of Eden and the serpent) was a product of the tenth century BCE and was a far more primitive tale. The two narratives are factually quite contradictory in many details, though clearly neither of them was written to be read literally. In the story placed first in the Bible God created on the sixth day the "living creatures" to populate the earth. These creatures are described as "cattle and creeping things and beasts of the earth" (Gen. 1:24). In the later part of that same sixth day, God created human life, both male and female instantaneously and both in God's image. In its rather stiff and obviously patriarchal language, the text reads: "So God created man in his own image; male and female created he them. And God blessed them and God said to them: 'Be fruitful and multiply and subdue the earth'" (Gen. 1:27–28). This story ends with God pronouncing everything that God had made to be "good;" and because the divine work was now assumed to be both complete and perfect, God rested from the divine labors and established the Sabbath, the seventh day, as a day of rest for all of creation (Gen. 1:31, 2:1–3). From this narrative Augustine and his successors got the idea of the original perfection of God's creation, including the perfection of human beings.

In the second, but actually older story (Gen. 2:4b–3:24), God created the earth and the heavens first, but there was no plant or herb in the field, because God had not yet caused it to rain and "there was no man to till the ground" (Gen. 2:5). God, however, caused a mist to rise up from the earth to moisten the ground and from that moist ground or mud God formed one solitary man, breathing into his nostrils the profound breath of life. Then God planted a garden and into that garden God placed the man. The garden produced food quite naturally for the man. Around the garden flowed four rivers, two of which bore the names Tigris and Euphrates, which, if we want to be literal, would locate the Garden of Eden in modern-day Iraq. The man, according to this story, got lonely and God decided that it was "not good that the man should be alone" (Gen. 2:18), so to make a proper friend for Adam, God created each of the animals. None of them, however, satisfied the man's yearning for a proper companion. We have in the world today such a wide variety of sizes, shapes and species of animal life, the text assumes, because no matter how hard God tried, nothing seemed right to the man. Finally, in a second dramatic creative act, God put Adam to sleep, removed one of his ribs and from that rib fashioned the woman. So in this story the man was created first, then the animals and finally the woman. These two creation stories are not capable of being harmonized without distorting the texts significantly.

This second story then goes on to give an account of how evil entered God's perfect world and corrupted it. It came about through disobedience to a divine command given to the two human beings. As a condition for living in Eden, they had been ordered not to eat the fruit of the "tree of the knowledge of good and evil," located in the midst of the garden, but they succumbed to temptation and ate of that fruit. This overt act of disobedience resulted in both the man and the woman being expelled from the Garden of Eden and thus from the intimate presence of God. Human life, this story assumes, was from that moment on compelled to be lived "in sin." No longer could the man and the woman inhabit the Garden of Eden (even figuratively); human beings now had to live "east of Eden," to borrow a phrase from John Steinbeck.*

It was from this second story that Augustine and his successors got their understanding of "the fall," and with it the reality and the consequences of sin, by which they now defined human life. Augustine proceeded to put these two narratives together, whether they fitted or not. Then he used the resulting understanding to create the template against which traditional Christianity would ultimately tell the story of Jesus. There was an original goodness, that familiar narrative begins, followed by a fall into sin, which in turn necessitated a divine action of redemption in which God had to come to our aid. Salvation was accomplished, this storyline suggested, when God sent his son to save the world from the fall and to rescue human life from sin. That rescue demanded the death of the divine son as a "sin offering." In other words, Jesus had to pay the price that sin required. That is how this particular narrative portrayed the meaning of the crucifixion.

This same narrative was destined to become the framework in which Christianity itself would traditionally be understood. To the shed blood of Jesus on the cross great cleansing power was attributed. Some worshippers wanted to be bathed in this blood until their bodies were purged of evil and their sins were either covered or washed away. Other worshippers wanted to drink the blood of Jesus, offered as it was in "the sacrifice of the mass," in order to be purged internally, not just of the sins of the body, but of the sins of the mind and of the soul as well. This process of

---

* This phrase was used as the title of a book that he published in 1952. See bibliography for details.

atonement has throughout Christian history infiltrated everything Christians think and do. It is found in our doctrines, our dogmas, our creeds, our hymns, our prayers, our sermons and even in our consciousness.

Is this really what Paul meant when he said that Jesus "died for our sins in accordance with the scriptures"? I doubt it seriously. Though some of his words are read this way, I think he was referring rather to a Jewish liturgical practice that I will shortly describe. This atonement perspective is, however, how Paul was interpreted by a predominantly Gentile church, whose members were not only ignorant of Jewish liturgical understandings, but also quite prejudiced against learning anything Jewish.

There were three traditional Jewish images involving a lamb that was sacrificed from which Paul probably drew his primary understanding. Two of these were images taken from synagogue worship that required the death of a lamb: the Passover and Yom Kippur, the Day of Atonement. The third popular Jewish image of a lamb was found in the writings of a sixth-century-BCE prophet called II Isaiah (so named because his words were added to the scroll of Isaiah, forming chapters 40–55). The portrait drawn by this profound Jewish writer in this influential book came to be called "the servant" or "the suffering servant," and he was portrayed as a lamb, silent as he was led to his death. From the very beginning of the Christian movement, Jesus was seen and interpreted in terms of all three of these "lamb" images, familiar to Jewish worshippers.

The Passover lamb was identified with Jesus by Paul himself when he wrote, "For Christ, our paschal lamb, has been sacrificed" (I Cor. 5:7). In the Jewish tradition it was the sacrifice of the paschal lamb that was said to have had the power to banish death from among the Jewish people on the night of their escape from Egypt and slavery. The death of Jesus was said to have lifted human life beyond the boundary that death had previously imposed. It was because the death of Jesus was identified with the killing of the Passover lamb that (I am convinced) the gospel writers all told the story of the crucifixion against the background of the Passover celebration. That is not a connection of history, as we have for so long been taught, but an interpretive connection. Recall that the gospels were written at least forty years after the crucifixion, giving the interpreted story of that event plenty of time to be moved to the time of Passover so that the relationship between Jesus and the paschal lamb could not be missed.

The lamb of Yom Kippur is the second symbol in the background of Paul's image. This Jewish penitential observance occurred once each year on the tenth day of the month of Tishri. There tended to be two animals used in the observance of Yom Kippur. Both had to be physically perfect, having no scratches, blemishes or broken bones. In time these sacrificial animals also came to be thought of as morally perfect. Since animals live beneath the level of human freedom, they cannot choose to do evil. Hence these animals became the symbolic representations of the human yearning for perfection and wholeness. In the liturgy of Yom Kippur one of these creatures was slaughtered and offered to God as a sign of the human yearning to be at one with God. The blood from this sacrifice was then spread on the mercy seat of God, which was located in the "holy of holies" in the Temple, the place where God was thought to reside. Now, this Yom Kippur liturgy proclaimed, human beings even in their sinfulness could still come into the presence of God at least on this one day of the year, for now they could come through the cleansing blood of the perfect lamb of God. Their identification with the lamb's wholeness covered the reality of their own sense of separation and brokenness.

The second creature of Yom Kippur was then placed in the

midst of the worshippers, and the people, led by the high priest, began to confess their sins. The liturgical idea was that in the act of confessing, the sins of the people departed from the people and landed on the head and back of this "sin-bearing" creature. Then, with this creature symbolically laden with the confessed sins of the community, the people called for its death: It was now so evil that it was no longer fit to live. This creature was not slain, however, but was rather driven out into the wilderness, carrying symbolically the sins of the people with it and thus leaving the people cleansed and able at least for a day to be "at one" with God. This creature came to be called "the scapegoat."

There are many places in the gospel tradition where this Yom Kippur liturgy appears to have shaped the story of Jesus' death. John makes the identification of Jesus with the creatures of Yom Kippur overt. Only in the Fourth Gospel are we told that the legs of the two people crucified with Jesus were broken to hasten their deaths, but that Jesus, already dead, was to have none of his bones broken. The symbol of the lamb remained intact (John 19:32–33). Moreover, in the synoptic crucifixion stories as well as in John, Jesus was presented to the crowd and he listened to the people calling for his death as they had done for the sin-bearing creature in the liturgy of Yom Kippur. The cry of the crowd, "Crucify him, crucify him," was adapted from Yom Kippur to the crucifixion story these gospel writers were developing (Mark 15:13ff, Matthew 27:22ff, Luke 23:21ff and John 19:6ff). Finally, I am convinced that it becomes possible to read the story of Barabbas, introduced in all four gospels as part of the crucifixion, as a narrative shaped by the Yom Kippur liturgy. Barabbas is a name constructed from two Hebrew words: *bar,* which means "son," and *abba,* which means "father" or "God." So in all of these gospel accounts, there are two sons of God on trial, Jesus and Barabbas, just as there were two animals in the Yom Kippur liturgy. One is slaughtered; that is the story of the crucifixion. One is set free to bear the sins of the people away; that is the role assigned to Barabbas.

Finally, there is the story of "the servant" from II Isaiah. He too is likened to a lamb led to the slaughter, one that is silent in the face of his accusers (Isa. 53:7). This narrative was written when the Jewish exiles from Babylon were finally able to return to their homeland after some two or more generations of captivity. They came with great hopes of restoring their nation to its former grandeur, of rebuilding the walls around Jerusalem and ultimately of raising from the dust a new Temple in which God could once more dwell in their midst. Fueling their grandiose dreams was the opportunity to fulfill what they believed was their God-inspired and God-imposed vocation as a people. As we noted earlier, they were chosen to be "a blessing" to the nations of the world (Zech. 8:13). Previously they had always assumed that this vocation could be lived out in such a way as to bring honor and recognition to the Jewish people as well. This was to be the chosen people's crowning achievement for which the world would be deeply grateful. Upon their return from exile, however, those dreams were dashed by the reality of what they saw. The city of Jerusalem had been leveled to the ground. The Temple was a pile of rubble. The people who had moved into what the Jews assumed was *their* sacred land were not welcoming. The returning exiles saw no way that their national vocation could ever be fulfilled. They saw no possibility that the Jewish nation would ever again be significant among the peoples of the world. The realization dawned on these exiles that they were destined to live in weakness, not power; to bear pain, not glory; to be victims, not victors. Embracing this reality emotionally and rationally, the unknown prophet we call II Isaiah perceived a new image of how the Jewish people could live out their messianic purpose, how they could still be a blessing to the nations of the world. They were to turn their defeat and their weakness into an expression of their purpose. They were to allow themselves to be victimized by the world's hostility and in the process to transform that hostility into life and wholeness. They were to drain the world of its anger simply by absorbing it and then returning it as love. They were to accept their status as the despised, the rejected; a people of sorrows and acquainted with grief. They were to be wounded for the transgressions of the world, bruised for the iniquities of the world, and through their suffering, their stripes, the world would be made whole. The servant was to be the symbol, the dramatic presentation of this newly understood messianic vocation for the Jewish people. In their suffering they were to remain silent, not to open their mouths in protest. In this way the servant, another lamb of God, became "an offering for sin," and thus it was said of the Jews who would be faithful to this vocation that "many may be accounted righteous" (Isa. 53:11).

It is not difficult to understand why these ideas of Israel as "the suffering servant" proved not to be a popular vocation around which the Jewish nation might rally and to which they might feel called. In the first century, however, the death of Jesus was experienced and interpreted by the followers of Jesus in terms of his having lived out this vocation as "the suffering servant." Jesus absorbed the anger, the pain, the hostility and even the death that others poured out on him and by doing so he showed the world the meaning of love and even the glory of God. Paul seemed to lean most heavily on the Yom Kippur images, while John was clearly drawn to the servant images from II Isaiah.

John was surely aware that this understanding of the death of Jesus had moved the Jesus community in a very different direction. Messiah had come in Jesus, they believed, but the result was that he had been crucified. Yet in Jesus' ability to endure this experience without resisting, he had revealed a new dimension of human wholeness. Salvation, now perceived as a call into wholeness, had been accomplished, but only in those few who "believed"—that is, those who had stepped beyond their drive to survive and into a new sense of what it means to be human. When the synoptic gospels were written, following the destruction of Jerusalem and in the experience of Roman oppression of all things connected with Judaism, the Jewish disciples of Jesus also were forced to live under persecution. They had embraced at first the promise that this persecution would be short-lived and that soon Jesus would come again. On the occasion of this second coming, Jesus would establish the kingdom of God.

By the time the Fourth Gospel was written, however, that hope had wavered and even perished. Sixty-five to seventy years had now passed and Jesus had not yet reappeared. The persecution had not ended. The reign of evil had not been broken. So John changed the message and transformed the story of Jesus. He had not died to pay the price of sin. He had not promised to come again shortly to establish the kingdom of God. This kind of atonement was not in John's vocabulary. Instead, John said he had died to open human life to a new meaning, a new definition. His death was to be the moment of his glorification, the moment when God was fully revealed in him.

So John has Jesus lead his disciples to this new insight in the Farewell Discourses. In chapter 14 he does it by casting three of the disciples in the role of questioners, whose inquiries will allow Jesus to open their minds to this new meaning, this new understanding of his death.

First, Thomas is brought on stage and given a speaking role. Jesus explains his imminent departure by telling the disciples that they are not to be troubled, that he is going to prepare a place for them and that he will come again. He assures them that they already know the way. "We do not know the way," Thomas retorts, "for we do not know where you are going." You cannot know the way unless you know the destination (John 14:5). To this Jesus responds: You do not yet understand, Thomas: "I am the way, the truth and the life" (John 14:6). The journey is not an outward one, Thomas, but an inward one. God is not up there; God is in here. The only way into the reality of God is to live into the meaning of the Christ life, to discover the freedom to give yourself away. That, alone, is the pathway to the Father.

Philip is next to speak, interrupting the conversation. "Lord, show us the Father," he demands, "and then we will be satisfied" (John 14:8). Jesus responds, "Have I been so long with you and yet you do not know me, Philip?" (John 14:9). God is not an external being that you must locate and recognize in some place. Look at me, Philip! I am in the Father and the Father is in me. God works in me; God speaks through me. That is your destiny also. Indeed you will do even greater deeds than the ones I have done. The secret, however, is for you to keep the new commandment. You have to love, not for gain, but for love's sake. When I am gone, the spirit of truth will come to you. This will be God dwelling in you and you dwelling in God. "Yet a little while" (John 14:19), says Jesus, the first instance of a phrase that will occur time after time—it will be only "a little while" before I return and these things happen.

Then the third disciple speaks. This one is named Judas, but John hastens to tell us that this is not Judas Iscariot. "Lord," he asks: "how can you manifest yourself to us and not to the world?" (John 14:22). Jesus says: You must understand that this manifestation is an internal one, not an external one. The revelation of God comes with the ability to love beyond your limits. If you love me, you will keep my word to love one another and the Father will love you as the Father has loved me. Then the Father and the son will come to you and dwell in you. We will make our home in you—this is Jesus' summation.

Jesus concludes this part of the discourse by saying, "I have spoken to you while I am still with you" (John 14:25). He then tries to prepare his disciples for his absence. The Holy Spirit will come when I am gone, he says. The spirit will teach you all things and will bring to remembrance all that I have said. I leave you with peace. It is not the kind of peace the world seeks, but it is the kind of peace that will enable you to grasp the reality you will have to endure. Rejoice, because I go to the Father and only when I depart can the spirit come to you. Please recognize that the world has no power over me. The world cannot kill who I am. I am part of who God is and you will be also. I do what the Father commands because I love the Father. You do what I command because you love me. That is the pathway to understanding.

The first discourse is over and Jesus says the words mentioned previously: "Rise, let us go hence" (John 14:31). Similar words are found in the synoptic tradition when Jesus, after having wrestled with his destiny in prayer in the garden, returns to find his disciples sleeping. He has accepted his vocation to die. "Rise," Mark's gospel has him say, "let us be going" (Mark 14:41–42). John also now has him move toward that destiny, but in John's hands his destiny is also to become his glory. We listen to his words with a new set of ears.

The Analogy of the Vine: God Is Indwelling, Not External

As the Farewell Discourses continue, it is clear that the author is challenging the atonement framework in which the Jesus story had begun to be couched in his generation. That framework assumed a deep and significant division between the heavenly realm and the human realm. The Jewish mind was not yet fully dualistic, but the people of that day believed the two realms were connected only at God's initiative. God from heaven directed Noah to build the ark that would save humanity from the flood. God from heaven called Abraham to leave Ur of the Chaldees to form a new people (Gen. 12:1–9). God speaking from heaven commissioned Moses at a burning bush to be the liberator of God's chosen people (Exod. 3:1–22). Moses on one occasion (Exod. 33:17–22) sought to reverse the order of the divine initiative by requesting that he be allowed to proceed into a direct vision of God. That request was denied. When Moses continued to press the matter, however, God worked out a compromise. Moses could see God, but only the back of God as God disappeared around the side of a mountain.

I read that to indicate that it has been given to human beings only to see the past and to discover where God has been, never to see the future or where God is going. This external God called the prophets to speak the divine word in critical moments of Hebrew history (Isa. 6:1–5, Jer. 1:4–10, Ezek. 1:1–3, Hos. 1:1–5). The early biblical narrative is clear; it is not given to human life to discern the reality of God except as this reality is revealed by God. God could come to earth, but no human being could lift himself or herself to God.

Inevitably, when the Jesus story began to assume its mythological form this pattern was at its center. God was said to have revealed the divine nature in the person of Jesus, who had come to earth. As Christianity moved more and more into a Gentile-Greek world, dualism increasingly shaped the narrative. Once that idea of divine "invasion" was assumed, believers had to discover a reason that merited the coming of God into human history in a personal way. The solution was, as I noted in the previous chapter, to save human beings from their sins, which had separated them from God. The pattern was soon set in a very distinctive manner. The more depraved Christian leaders could portray human life to be, the greater was the grace and gift of God's saving rescue.

This developing pattern then had to explain just how it was that God had been able to enter the life of Jesus and thus to accomplish this act of salvation. How did heaven and earth come together? A number of understandings of how this was achieved appear in the New Testament itself, some of them quite surprising in the light of later theological understandings. First, there was the proclamation of what Jesus' followers believed was a very real experience: The holy God had been encountered in the human Jesus. The earliest affirmation of this experience offered by Paul was a simple statement: "In Christ, God was reconciling the world to himself" (II Cor. 5:19). When Paul, a few years later, tried to explain just how God and the human Jesus had come together, he suggested that God had "designated" Jesus to be the son of God in power according to the spirit of holiness "by his resurrection from the dead" (Rom. 1:1–4). That statement suggested that God had adopted Jesus into divinity at the time of the resurrection, a position that later in ecclesiastical history was rejected as heresy under the name Adoptionism.

By the early years of the eighth decade of the Common Era, a new understanding was developed when Mark, writing about the year 72 CE, portrayed Jesus as a fully human, adult male until the moment when he came to be baptized. As he emerged from the water, Mark says: "immediately he saw the heavens opened and the spirit descending on him like a dove, and a voice came from heaven, 'Thou art my beloved son; with thee I am well pleased'" (Mark 1:9–11). Jesus was, according to Mark, a human life that at baptism had now become "God-infused," as it were.

The next step in the development of this framework came in the gospel of Matthew, written in the early to mid 80s, and Luke, written in the late 80s and maybe even the early 90s. In these two gospels, expanding on Mark's original thesis, the Holy Spirit became, not the presence of God poured out on Jesus at baptism from heaven, but rather the father or male agent, if you will, in his biological conception. These gospels asserted that the divine and the human had actually come together in Jesus not at some later point in his life, but at the very moment of his conception. That was the context in which the story of the virgin birth entered the Christian tradition—a story, I suggest, of which neither Paul nor Mark had ever heard, and one that both of them would have found inconceivable!

With the divine invasion through Jesus now established in this growing tradition, the story of the cross was increasingly told as the ultimate point at which the God presence in Jesus assumed the pain and overcame the evil that was the presumed reality of the "fallen" human life. The background to the idea of a "sin offering" to overcome human evil was very primitive. It was grounded in the concept of animal sacrifice. In early human history animals were offered in worship to an angry deity to mollify this deity and, hopefully, to avoid punishment.

In a similar manner, the cross came to be thought of by Christians as the place where the price of human sinfulness was paid, the moral score settled, the power of death broken and a new relationship with God inaugurated.

The death of Jesus had not, however, brought about the expected end of history, nor had it inaugurated the kingdom of God on earth. The early Christians covered this disappointment by expanding their developing mythological interpretive framework to include the idea of a second coming for Jesus. The early Christians thus began to think of themselves as living between the first coming of Jesus, which culminated in the crucifixion, and the second coming of Jesus, which they were still anticipating. That is why they began to pray for that second coming in now-familiar words that they attributed to Jesus, "Thy kingdom come," and they described what the kingdom would look like in the next phrase, "Thy will be done on earth as it is in heaven."

As the years stretched out, however, the second coming of Jesus did not materialize. Jesus' followers, who had expected quite literally to see the return of Christ from heaven, began to die of old age, and this created a problem that Paul addressed in I Thessalonians, written in the early 50s. Later Luke suggested that perhaps the second coming they were expecting was not of the kingdom of God, but of the birth of the church, which had to precede the second coming of Jesus. So it was that in the writing of Luke's two-volume set that we know as Luke-Acts, this author described how the Jesus movement, which began in Galilee, made its way first to Jerusalem, the center of the Jewish world, and then to Rome, the center of the known world.

These aspects of the Jesus story were matters with which the author of the Fourth Gospel was familiar. He, however, as both a Palestinian Jew and a Jewish mystic, had a very different understanding of God and so he interpreted the God presence in Jesus in a very different way. That way is at the heart of this next segment of the Farewell Discourses.

Spatial and time images seemed to drop away from Jesus in the mind of John. Jesus lived in a more transcendent, mysterious world, it seemed. God was not an external "being" separated into a distant divine realm. As John saw it, when God at the beginning of creation said: "Let there be light" (Gen. 1:3), as the Jewish scriptures depicted the creative process, those divine words emerged out of God and enfolded, as light does, all that there was and is. Those who lived in this light lived in God. Jesus, according to John, was the "word of God" bringing that light to the world. Recall that there is no story of the birth of Jesus in the Fourth Gospel. Jesus was the life through whom and in whom God was being revealed. That is why John could portray Jesus and God as one. That is also why this author could place the very name of God into the mouth of Jesus again and again. For John there was no fall into sin and thus no time when the human and the divine were separated: One literally permeated the other. Since in John's mind God was not an external being, there was no division between God and life—at least no division with spatial, temporal or moral connotations. Jesus, therefore, did not "die for your sins." Neither was he the victim whom God punished so that God did not have to punish the deserving sinners, nor substitute the sacrificial animal for the sinner. Those were concepts that this author could not have comprehended.

God, for the Jewish mystic, was and is a permeating presence, not an external being. The death of Jesus, therefore, was not punishment; it was not paying the price which evil requires. It was rather the moment when the glory of God was ultimately revealed in the ability of Jesus to give his life away in love. The climax of Jesus' life on the cross was for John the ultimate revelation of the presence and meaning of God.

God was light, embracing all who could open their eyes to see. God was life, the same life which was flowing through the universe, but which came to self-consciousness only in human beings—indeed only in those who were willing to risk entering or being born into a new dimension of humanity. God, for John, was love, that life-giving power that embraces all those who are willing to accept the vulnerability that love always brings. This means that for John, Jesus was not one who had come and then departed and who would someday come again. Jesus was rather a God presence inviting all to enter who he was and is, to be born of the spirit—born, that is, to new dimensions of what it means to be human—and to participate thereby in the eternity of God. There is thus no idea in this gospel of a second coming of the person of Jesus. There is rather the new awakening to life, an awakening that makes it possible for those born into that spiritual dimension to be the bearers of the meaning of Christ and of the power of Christ in every generation. The second coming was thus nothing more or less than the coming, or perhaps even the dawning realization, of the ever-permeating spirit.

When we reach chapters 15 and 16 of John's discourses, the question-and-answer dialogue with various disciples is replaced by long Jesus monologues, but the struggle to allow this concept to be understood is still present. There is, moreover, an increasing sense of urgency. Time is growing short and the words of Jesus must be heard and embraced. If those words are not understood, the tension in which the Johannine community has been living will destroy them. The transforming meaning of Jesus is the burden this community has been called to bear. They have undergone great pain and stress, so their very survival depends on their ability to grasp this new meaning of Jesus, to step into it and to become part of a new reality. John now proceeds to paint a portrait of that relationship by developing some of his most memorable images.

One of the ancient analogies by which the prophets referred to the people of Israel was that they were "God's vineyard" (Isa. 5:1–10, Jer. 12:10, Ezek. 19:10). John now plucks that image out of his Jewish past and employs it to drive his message of mystical oneness home. Think of God as the vinedresser, he has Jesus begin. God wants the divine life to flow through the vine. So the vinedresser tends the vine, even pruning the vine to enable it to bear more fruit. Think of me, Jesus continues, as that vine. Just as the people of Israel thought of themselves as those whose vocation was to be the messianic people through whom all nations would be blessed, so now open your eyes, he continues, to see me as the symbol of that new Israel, the one in whom and through whom that vocation is now embodied. I am the focus of that messianic purpose. I am the human life in whom the life of God is present. I am the one through whom all the nations of the world will be blessed. Think of yourselves as the branches of the vine and see how we are all bound together in this divine purpose. God flows into me. I flow into you. Your vocation as a branch of the vine is to stay attached to the vine. A branch does not bear fruit unless it remains attached to the vine. You cannot fulfill your destiny alone. If you abide in me, I will abide in you. There is a new unity in that mutual abiding: If you abide in me, *my words* will abide in you; you too will become "the word of God incarnate," and in this new creation God will again be glorified. The Father loves me, and I love you. Love is the presence of God. Abide in this love. In love you escape the defense barriers behind which human beings hide seeking security. Love makes you vulnerable to hurt and fills you with fear, but love also opens you to new dimensions of living, new understandings of life. It is only in giving your life away in love that you can live fully. I will, therefore, be most fully alive when I am being crucified. To be able to escape the human drive for survival is to escape my own self-centeredness. Life is most perfectly possessed when one is free to lay one's life down in love. It is this kind of love in which you must abide, and when you do, my joy will be in you and your joy will be full. These words of Jesus offer a powerful mystical insight into the meaning of life.

Love, Jesus continues, is the secret to life; that is why my new commandment to you is so simple: You are to love one another as I have loved you. The greatest love is found when you are free to give your life away. That is also the doorway into a new consciousness. Walk through this door and you will no longer be disciples or followers or servants; you will be friends. We will share a mutuality of the divine mission to bring life—abundant life—to all.

The love of which I speak, says Jesus, will free you to bear hatred and abuse. Those who live in darkness will never appreciate your willingness to walk in the light. They will see your life as a judgment on their lives. They will see your love as a judgment on their defensiveness and insecurity. You will therefore be misunderstood. You should expect that. Every time there is a human breakthrough to a new dimension of consciousness, there is persecution from those who cannot take the step that leaders have taken. Many people will not be able to see that what you are offering is the fulfillment of their own expectations written in their own law. They will almost inevitably seek to turn their religious life into a new security system.

Now recognize, Jesus continues, that even if I go away, the meaning I came to bring will not disappear. What I have done is to open to you a new understanding of what it means to be human. Trust it. Now that it has been opened, it cannot be closed again. The spirit of truth, which proceeds from the Father, will come to stand where I have stood. This spirit, called the Counselor, will bear witness to me. You will recognize it and understand it because you have been with me from the beginning. As I abide in God, Jesus reminds them once more, so you must abide in me.

What Jesus is describing here is not redemption of the fallen, but transformation of the open. There is and will be no separation in our oneness. God is part of you; you are part of God. The same life and love that flow from God through the vine of Christ will flow into God's people, who are the branches. There is now a mystical and mutual indwelling that will create a new humanity. Mutual indwelling is not to be understood as an authority-subject, a master-slave or even a savior-sinner relationship. It is rather a startling new way by which we are to understand the divine. We have abandoned the God from above the sky. That God has now entered life. We met this God first in Jesus, and now the world will see that God in those who will someday call themselves the "body of Christ."

The Farewell Discourses now seem to shift from imagining Jesus speaking to his followers prior to his death, to Jesus speaking to the Johannine community in their own day—that is, at the time this gospel was actually being written, a time when the Johannine community was living in fear and facing persecution. The author of this gospel wanted that community to hear a word from Jesus that would put their current sufferings in the context of those new dimensions of God and the new understanding of the life of Jesus that he was developing. He wanted to place their trials into this sense of mystical oneness.

One can easily imagine in listening to these words something of the pain with which this community was dealing. "They will put you out of the synagogues," John has Jesus say. That indeed had happened. The time will come, Jesus continued, when whoever kills you will think he is offering service to God (John 16:2). I suspect that had also happened. Don't cling to me, he reiterated, just remember what I have told you. You must not be dependent on me. You must rise to a new level of responsibility, a new maturity. It is to your advantage that I go away. God cannot be limited to one mediator. All of you are lives in whom and through whom God can live and work. I was the doorway into this new experience, but once you've walked through the doorway you know that beyond the door there is a limitless spirit that you can and will engage. (John calls this new aspect of God the Advocate, even the Paraclete.) This spirit will open new doors and lead you into all truth. You do not need to ask anyone questions. Trust what you know; trust who you are; live into your new being. All that the Father has is mine. All that God is, I am. Now I give it to you. You can now be the way and the truth. You can be the door. You can be the bread of life, living water, a good shepherd and even the source of resurrection. Grasp the spirit and share it. Be who you are and in the process free others to be who they are. Don't see human limitations. Don't concern yourself with the circumstances of your life, no matter how bitter they might be. As I am glorified by being lifted up on the cross, you too will be glorified by your ability to mediate the meaning of my life to the world, not in spite of your sufferings, but because of your sufferings.

We need to recognize that these are words that the author of the Fourth Gospel is directing to those living near the end of the first century of the Common Era. That being so, John adds a telling paragraph that contains enormous, even boring repetition. Jesus says, "A *little while* and you will see me no more; *again a little while* and you will see me again" (John 16:16). The phrase "a little while" is then repeated seven times! What is being communicated here? What is the meaning of *a little while?* The time between the crucifixion and the second coming is by now no longer "a little while." That gap has extended to some sixty-five to seventy years. If a generation is twenty years, that time constitutes three-plus generations. As we saw earlier, the original hope and expectation was that the second coming would occur in the lifetime of those who had heard Jesus' words from his lips. Most of them by now had died. The reference "a little while," then, has to be something other than that.

The disciples ask: What do you mean "a little while"? What is "a little while"? They repeat the phrase as if processing it internally. The phrase "a little while" is then related to Jesus going to the Father (John 16:17). "What do you mean?" they ask. We do not know what "a little while" means. They will soon learn that according to John the second coming is not the end of the world. It is, rather, something that will come only "a little while" after the crucifixion. We will discover what it is only when the gospel reaches its climax.

Finally, Jesus breaks into this circular conversation and describes what they already know their experience to have been: "You will weep and lament, but the world will rejoice; you will be sorrowful, but your sorrow will turn into joy" (John 16:20). Next he uses the analogy of childbirth. The time of labor is painful and stress-filled, but when the labor of childbirth (he calls it travail) is over and the woman is delivered, then the anguish fades in her memory and is replaced by the joy that new life has entered the world. So endure the present, he says, in the knowledge that the future is secure.

The theme of the gospel is then once more repeated: "I came from the Father as the revealing word, and have come into the world; again I am leaving the world and going to the Father" (John 16:28). That sounds clear. *That* should make them understand.

The disciples respond as if on cue. "Ah, now you are speaking plainly. Now we know that you know all things and need none to question you. By this we believe that you came from God" (John 16:29–30). "Do you *now* believe?" Jesus asks, as he recalls their shameful and disappointing behavior. Then why did you scatter when I was arrested, leaving me alone and fleeing to your own homes? Why did you deny? None of those things matters, he assures them; if God is in me, then I am never alone. That is what you must learn. God is known when those who can open their eyes to see do so and when those who have the courage to live into this new experience of human life, this new sense of freedom, can take the next step. In that moment you will learn that nothing can destroy you. So Jesus concludes, "In this world you shall have tribulation, but be of good cheer. I have overcome the world" (John 16:33). As my most shaping theological teacher, Paul Tillich, has said, you must have the "courage to be," which comes when you know that your being is rooted in the Ground of Being.*

These Farewell Discourses have now ended. The climax draws near.

---

* From *The New Being* by Paul Tillich. See bibliography for details.

CHAPTER 20

The Prayer of Jesus:
Gethsemane Transformed

John's Jesus now proceeds to offer a prayer before he approaches the climax of his life. In the Farewell Discourses Jesus tried to communicate through the medium of words. In the passion narrative he now will seek to communicate with the example of his life. This prayer divides the discourses from the passion story and, like most things in the Fourth Gospel, uses words and images that will cast this prayer in very different terms, with vastly different meanings, from anything that has appeared in the synoptics.

In those earlier gospels, prior to his arrest Jesus was said to have offered a prayer in a place called Gethsemane, a name, which in Hebrew is related to an "olive oil press." The words of the prayer varied slightly in those earlier gospels, but the message was essentially the same. Mark records the words this way: "Abba, Father, all things are possible to thee; remove this cup from me; yet not what I will, but what thou wilt" (Mark 14:36). Matthew makes no change of any significance to these words. Luke adds (in some but not all of the ancient manuscripts) a few new details, such as an angel who appears to him from heaven to strengthen him in his resolve (Luke 22:43) and a description that conveys Jesus' intense agony: Luke tells us that as Jesus prayed more earnestly, "his sweat became like great drops of blood falling down upon the ground" (Luke 22:43).

Even before the Farewell Discourses began, John had dismissed the Gethsemane prayers of earlier gospels. Those words simply do not fit John's understanding of Jesus, his passion or his death. Shall he say: "Remove this cup from me"? No, John has Jesus conclude: "It was for this purpose that I was born. When I am lifted up, I will draw all men [and women] to myself" (John 12:32). John then adds to this interpretation by explaining: "He said this to show by what death he was to die" (John 12:33). The cross is to be Jesus' revelatory throne!

With that preamble to the crucifixion laid and with that understanding of what the death of Jesus signifies, it is quite obvious that John's version of Jesus' prayer will have to be very different from the synoptic writers' understanding. At least one major Johannine scholar believes this prayer is the key to understanding the entire gospel,* and indeed it is.

Look first at the way the prayer is introduced: It begins with Jesus announcing that "the hour has come" (John 17:1), familiar words in John's drama describing a compelling destiny that draws Jesus inexorably into the meaning that "his hour" will reveal. The time has arrived for which "the word of God" was born. The cross becomes visible, not as the place of execution, but as the throne on which Jesus will be lifted up from the earth to become the ultimate meaning of divine revelation. "Father, the hour has come. Glorify the son that the son may glorify thee" (John 17:1). The "high priestly prayer"† then proceeds in three parts. The

---

* I refer to Ernst Käsemann, whose book *The Testament of Jesus* has as its subtitle *A Study of the Gospel of John in the Light of Chapter 17*. See bibliography for details.

† This prayer was given this name because throughout Christian history it has been treated as a prayer for the Church of the Ages in which Jesus would presumably be enshrined as its high priest.

first is a prayer that Jesus utters for himself, the second is a prayer he prays for the disciples and the third is a prayer that is offered for those throughout history who will believe because of the witness of the disciples. The primary request in this prayer is that unity be achieved among believers. The desired outcome is not *ecclesiastical* unity, however, as has so often been concluded. That usage is always in the service of institutional power. Nor is it *content* or *doctrinal* unity, as various councils of the church have so often implied and sought to impose. It is not a unity imposed on any basis from outside in the service of any agenda. No, the unity of which this prayer speaks is the oneness of the human with the divine that has been the constant theme of this gospel. It is the unity of the vine with the branches. That unity is found in understanding God, not as an external being, but as the essence of life. John even makes Jesus use the third-person name and title for himself to make his point: Unity comes in knowing "the only true God and Jesus Christ whom thou hast sent" (John 17:3). The word of God comes from God, reveals the meaning of God and returns to God. It is a mystical experience of oneness—not a oneness in which individuality is lost, but a oneness in which individuality is affirmed, security is surrendered and a new being is entered.

Jesus then turns the focus of his prayer to his disciples. He begins by recalling episodes he has shared with them in the course of his life. "I have manifested your name," he says to God, "to those you gave me out of the world." In the idiom of the Hebrew world, the "name" of God equals the essence of God, as we saw earlier in the "I AM" discussion. That is why we pray, "Hallowed be thy name." What John's Jesus is saying is this: I have made known the divine being. I have given to my disciples "the word," the revelation of who God is, the revelation that you, God, have given me. The disciples would understand that the word of God is the revelation of the being of God. The call of Jesus is into a new being, then, in which a new dimension of life is entered and through which a transcendent unity is experienced.

"Now I am no more in this world," John has Jesus say, revealing that he is not composing these words in the pre-crucifixion span of time, but in the time for which this book was written. In that later time the Johannine community is in the world. So he prays for them: "Holy Father, keep them in thy name" (John 17:11). I have opened a door for them into the essence of God, he says. Keep them in that essence. That was my role while I was with them, but now I am leaving them and their joy needs to be fulfilled in their own new life. They have been lifted beyond the barriers behind which human beings hide in survival mode. They now see with new eyes, they love with new hearts and they have come to a new understanding of what it means to be human. They are, therefore, different, and the world will always hate that which it presumes to be different. Light is fearsome to those who hide in darkness. Love is threatening to those whose defenses cannot be penetrated.

"I do not pray," Jesus continues, "that thou shouldst take them out of this world, but that thou shouldst keep them from the evil one" (John 17:15). Believing, Jesus is trying to explain, does not mean that pain and danger will not be endured. It means that one has the strength of being to walk through that pain and danger without falling apart. It means that nothing that is outside any one of us can finally destroy us. We are connected to that which is ultimately real and ultimately eternal.

"Sanctify them," make them holy, make them whole, Jesus continues (John 17:17). Free them to be all that they are capable of being. That is how they will know the revelation of God, the truth of the "word" and the essence of the life of Jesus. God sent me into the world as the bearer of this "word of God," he says.

Now, just as I was once sent, it is my turn to send them. I have been consecrated, made whole and holy and set free to give my life away. I pray that they too may be consecrated, made whole and holy and be set free to give their lives away.

Then this prayer turns ultimately to the future, to those who will "believe in me through their word" and through the followers' lives as disciples. "That they may all be one" is his prayer, "even as thou, Father, art in me and I in thee, that they may be one in us" (John 17:21). Unity, the inner connectedness of life and love, brings together God and the human, the Ground of Being and being. Again and again the Fourth Gospel drives home its point. God is not an external, distant entity; God is a life we enter, a love we share, the ground in which we are rooted. The call of Christ is not into religion, but into a new mystical oneness. The death of Jesus will not be the end of his life; it will be the moment when the meaning of God is ultimately revealed, the moment in which Jesus will be glorified, because the world will see God in him when he is on the cross. There Jesus will reveal God as the portrait of expanded life, limitless love and enhanced being. It is an invitation to walk through the door of Christ ("I am the door," John 10:9), to follow the way of Christ ("I am the way," John 14:6) and to enter into the expanded life of Christ ("I am the resurrection," John 11:25).

The final part of this prayer asks that those who become followers may be with Christ "where I am to behold my glory" (John 17:24). This is not a request to go to a place where one can be reassured by seeing what eyes cannot normally see. It is instead a request that the life of God, found in the person of the Christ, can be seen in the followers of Jesus and that we too may reveal the glory of God. It is a prayer that the essence of love may be "in them as I am in them." The good news of the gospel, as John understands it, is not that you—a wretched, miserable, fallen sinner—have been rescued from your fate and saved from your deserved punishment by the invasive power of a supernatural, heroic God who came to your aid. Nowhere does John give credibility to the dreadful, guilt-producing and guilt-filled mantra that "Jesus died for my sins." There is rather an incredible new insight into the meaning of life. We are not fallen; we are simply incomplete. We do not need to be rescued, but to experience the power of an all-embracing love. Our call is not to be forgiven or even to be redeemed; it is to step beyond our limits into a new understanding of what it means to be human. It is to move from a status of self-consciousness to a realization that we share in a universal consciousness. John's rendition of Jesus' message is that the essence of life is discovered when one is free to give life away, that love is known in the act of loving and that the call of human life is to be all that each of us can be and then to be an agent of empowering others to be all that *they* can be.

That is the meaning to which the signs in John's gospel point. That is the message spoken over and over in the Farewell Discourses. That is the essence of this prayer, which John has created to place upon the lips of Jesus.

PART IV

The Passion Narrative: From Darkness to Light, From Death to Life

CHAPTER 21

A Brief Introduction to the Climax of This Gospel

Readers of the Fourth Gospel must always be aware of the fact that it was written on two levels. One level tried to recall the original Jesus. A long time had passed between the crucifixion and the writing of this text, so that task of recollection was not easy. The second level sought to understand Jesus as he was filtered through the Johannine community, a group that inevitably interpreted Jesus through the lens of the traumas which engulfed them in their own time near the end of the first century.

Most people try to read this gospel on only the first level, when in fact the text reveals in almost every verse that it is referring to the second level. In the passion and crucifixion of Jesus, it is not the historical memory of Jesus that is front and center; rather, the current life experience of the community is the prism through which the story is told.

By the time the Fourth Gospel was written, the Johannine community had faced, in order, three defining realities. We have previously gone into great detail about each of these realities, but because they are so crucial to understanding the climax of this gospel, let me recall them here quite briefly.

The Christian faith was born as a movement within the synagogue. The followers of Jesus were known as "the followers of the
way," a distinct subgroup, but there was no sense in which this
movement wanted to be separate from Judaism. Obviously any
new insight or movement within a particular faith challenges the
religious status quo and produces tension. That was not the *purpose* of this movement, however: The followers of Jesus wanted
only to expand Judaism to include Jesus, just as Judaism had been
expanded many times in the past to include such figures as Isaiah,
Hosea, Amos, Micah and other prophetic voices. That is why in
the earliest phase of Christianity the followers of Jesus kept trying
to relate Jesus to Jewish heroes of the past, such as Abraham,
Moses and Elijah.

The tensions between the old tradition and this new possibility
were not always comfortable, but they were at least tolerable until
external circumstances made the price of any tension more costly
and more threatening. That was the situation until 66 CE, when
the outbreak of the Jewish-Roman war in Galilee did in fact make
the price of any tension more costly and more threatening. When the
war expanded to Judea, the city of Jerusalem and its Temple were
destroyed by the Roman army in 70 CE. At that moment, and as a
direct result of that destruction, Judaism entered a struggle for survival. By the time hostilities ceased at Masada in 73 CE, Judaism had
lost its national home, its holy city, its Temple and its priesthood.
It could no longer tolerate any revisionist movement that sapped its
energy and challenged its boundaries, and so the Johannine community was forced to flee Jerusalem. Though we cannot be certain
of their final destination, a strong tradition locates that community
in the city of Ephesus, where they existed once again uncomfortably
within the synagogue. The tensions increased between the orthodox
leadership and this challenging revisionist movement until finally,
somewhere around the year 88 CE, the orthodox leaders of the

synagogue expelled the followers of Jesus. A movement that had sought to define itself as an expansion of Judaism now found itself completely outside that framework. The second stage of life of the Johannine community was about to begin.

The Johannine community was now in a new situation. The question became: How could they continue to relate themselves and this Jesus to the Hebrew scriptures, with their messianic expectations, if they were no longer to be a part of Judaism? They now settled into the post-Judaism phase of life, marked as it was with a deep and abiding hostility toward the synagogue leaders who had excommunicated them. This was when the phrase "the Jews" entered the Johannine writings as a symbol for the enemies of the followers of Jesus. This negativity grew to be a constant expression in the Johannine community as they sought how to define themselves not as an extension of Judaism anymore, but as quite separate from the Judaism from which they had been expelled. This set the framework for the third stage in the transition of the Johannine community.

In this new context the tensions became internal. As people sought to redefine themselves outside the context of Judaism, they wrestled with how far they could go in speaking about the Jesus experience as a God experience without making discipleship something that many of their own members, who had been raised in Judaism, found impossible to affirm. These formerly Jewish disciples might be able to see Jesus as the fulfillment of Jewish expectations, but could they go to the place where God and Jesus were so closely identified that they could hear Jesus make the claim of oneness with the Father? Could they be comfortable with the suggestion that Jesus might have applied the divine name of "I AM" to himself?

As they sought to come to a common mind on these issues, another split occurred in their community: Some who could not make this developing transition broke away and returned to the synagogue. To the Johannine community, those who did so were seen as traitors. Still others wavered between the two camps as doubters, as those who might abandon Jesus, might deny him, as those who were always on the verge of falling away before finally finding the courage to move into a new place and to embrace a new vision. Of course there were also some at the core of this community who were always faithful to their developing vision. They came to be known as the ideal disciples, even the beloved disciples. In the passion story, the Fourth Gospel appears to develop characters who symbolize each of these historical responses.

Finally, the hostility of the world had to be embraced and endured. This struggling Johannine community was separated from its Jewish roots and torn internally in its attempt to see Jesus as the determinative life for their vision of the future. Now, looking outward, they found themselves facing the Roman Empire. The human symbol of this world, the person who was the highest Roman official in Judea—Pilate—became the "face" of that world. When Jesus confronts Pilate in the passion story as told by John, there are many themes being addressed, from the meaning of truth to the meaning of kingship, but we need to be aware that everything in this gospel's long confrontation between Jesus and Pilate refers to real issues in the life of the Johannine community many years after the crucifixion. This passion story is not history and must not be read as such. It is not a record of the final events in the life of Jesus, so much as it is an attempt to make sense out of the life that the members of this community were living near the end of the first century.

As we embark on a study of the climax of this gospel, the warning of the previous chapters remains intact: This passion narrative is not a literal story; it is, rather, the painting of an interpretive portrait by a devoted artist. If one reads John's narrative of the cross literally, it will never be understood. Thus warned anew, we plunge into John's story of the crucifixion, the resurrection, the gift of the spirit and the consequences of these acts as John understood them—namely new life, new consciousness, and a new doorway into the mystery of God. In this passion narrative John lays out clearly his purpose in composing this "new" gospel. It is to bring us into a dimension of life that we have never known before. It is to bind together the former Jewish expectations with a new sense of God as mystical oneness. It is as if John were saying: For those who have eyes to see and ears to hear, let them see and let them hear.

CHAPTER 22

Judas: The Figure
of Darkness

All of the preliminary preparation is complete. Jesus is now ready for the great climax, and he is portrayed in this gospel as fully in charge, never shrinking from his destiny, always moving forward toward that ultimate revelatory moment. In the high priestly prayer just concluded, he noted that he had "kept" those whom the Father had given to him. He prayed for their "oneness." He then spoke of how he had guarded them so that none of them was lost except "the son of perdition, that the scripture might be fulfilled" (John 17:12). The story of the passion opens with an intense light thrown on that "son of perdition," the one who was permanently lost.

Judas Iscariot was introduced into the Fourth Gospel for the first time at the conclusion of the story of the feeding of the multitude (John 6:71). There is in John no list of the twelve disciples in which he might have been mentioned earlier in the narrative. John's introduction of Judas is a bit strange since Judas, in this passage, is identified as "the son of Simon Iscariot," as if "Iscariot" were a family surname. Surnames were not used in that time, however. One tended to be identified as the son of a father—for example, Jesus, son of Joseph. If the introduction was not as the son of a father, one would be identified by his place of residence, as in "Jesus of Nazareth," or "Paul of Tarsus." Simon was a common name in the first-century Jewish world, and yet there are some commentators who think that every reference in all of the gospels to one named Simon—whether it be Simon Iscariot, the father of Judas (John 6:71); Simon of Cyrene, who carried the cross in the synoptic tradition (Mark 15:21, Matt. 27:32, Luke 23:26); or Simeon the high priest in Luke (2:25ff), who saw in the Christ child "the salvation" he had been promised he would see before his death—was an oblique reference to some aspect of the character of the Simon who was called Peter. This is too complex a theory (and probably too far out) to present or to defend in this study, but I file it here just to have my readers embrace again the reality that this gospel should never be approached or read simplistically.

The word "Iscariot" is today believed to be a description of Judas' character, a title that got attached to him in the synoptic tradition and that, in time through common usage, came to be thought of as part of his name. It is believed to have been derived from the word *sicarius,* which means "political assassin." For John to introduce Judas as the one who was lost and then to assert that his lostness was predestined in order that "the scriptures might be fulfilled" suggests the possibility that Judas was far more a symbol than he was a person of history—a symbol who, over time, was literalized by people who did not understand the way these characters were drawn into the community's memory of Jesus.

Another fact which suggests the possibility that the designated traitor was originally a literary creation and not a figure of history is that we can find no reference to Judas Iscariot in any written Christian source prior to his introduction in Mark's gospel in the early years of the eighth decade. In Mark, Judas receives his first mention when Jesus chooses his disciples on a retreat into the hills of Galilee. He is twelfth on the list and is called "Judas Iscariot," with the added wording "who also betrayed him" (Mark 3:19). I grant there are not many written pre-Marcan sources through which to search, but there are some, and each of them strengthens my argument. Some scholars, for example, would date the so-called Q document prior to the writing of the gospel of Mark.* That is not a dating theory with which I would concur, but that debate is not germane to this discussion. Even if an early date for the Q document could be established beyond reasonable doubt, there is in that document no reference to Judas Iscariot. The same argument can be used for the non-canonical gospel of Thomas. Some also date this work prior to Mark, but even if that dating is correct, there are no references to Judas Iscariot within its verses.

With the writings of Paul, however, we have a very different story. Paul is universally believed to have experienced his conversion, become the great Christian missionary, written all of his authentic epistles and been martyred prior to the writing of the first of the gospels. If Judas Iscariot had been part of the early memory of the Christian community, it is hard to conceive of this detail not having been a part of Paul's memory. Paul does tell us in Galatians (1:18) that just three years after his conversion, he went up to Jerusalem to visit Peter, whom he referred to by his Aramaic nickname, Cephas.† He says he saw none of the other disciples "except James the Lord's brother" (Gal. 1:19). If the treacherous act of Judas had been a literal part of history, is it possible that a

---

* Robert Funk, the founder of the Jesus Seminar, tended in this direction. The Q document is the hypothesized source of those sayings of Jesus that form the similar but non-Marcan passages that appear in both Matthew and Luke. The similarity of such passages led to the supposition that both of these authors had access to a now-lost collection of sayings, which was given the name Q from the German word *Quelle*, which means "source."

† Cephas comes from the Aramaic word "Kepha," which means "rock." As a nickname it might be similar to "Rocky." "Rock" in Greek was "petras," from which the familiar name of "Peter" is derived.

trauma of such magnitude would never have come into the conversation? I find that inconceivable.

This conclusion is reinforced when we discover the fact that Paul does refer to Jesus being "handed over" (I Cor. 11:23), which is the earliest meaning of the Greek word *paredidoto,* which came to be translated "betrayed." This word comes in one of only two places in the Pauline corpus where the apostle says that he is passing on a "received" part of the tradition. He writes, "For I received from the Lord what I also delivered to you, that the Lord Jesus on the night when he was betrayed [or handed over] took bread, and when he had given thanks, he broke it and said, 'This is my body which is broken* for you. Do this in remembrance of me'" (I Cor. 11:23, 24). This account of the institution of the Christian liturgical meal is the context in which Paul's sole use of the word "betrayed" appears.

Please note three things about this meal that Paul describes ever so briefly, but nonetheless as "received," handed-down tradition. First, there is no reference to it being a Passover meal. That tradition would be added later by the synoptic gospel writers and then altered still later by John so as *not* to be a Passover meal in the Fourth Gospel. Second, there is no reference here or anywhere in the writings of Paul as to who it was who did the handing over or the betraying, and likewise nothing about the person to whom Jesus was betrayed. Third, there is not even a hint that this handing over or betrayal was done by the hands of one of the twelve. Paul appears to know that there was a betrayal, but he is not aware of any details. This lack of knowledge of the identity of the traitor and particularly of the possibility that one of the twelve was the culprit, is strengthened just four chapters later in the same epistle. Here Paul is talking about the Easter event, and this is the

---

* The word "broken" does not occur in many of the early manuscripts.

only other time that he prefaces his words by saying, "I delivered to you as of first importance what I also received" (I Cor. 15:3). After discussing the crucifixion, he describes the Easter event this way: "On the third day" after the crucifixion, Jesus "was raised." We note first that he refers to this by using a passive verb—that is, Jesus "was raised." Then he says that Jesus "appeared first to Cephas [Peter]" and then to "the twelve" (I Cor. 15:4, 5). "*The twelve,*" please note, is still intact in Paul's mind three days after the crucifixion. *Judas must still be with them!* That would be inconceivable if the traitor had been one of the twelve. The figure of Judas is now wobbling visibly, especially if he was indeed supposed to have been a person of history.

Once that possibility is opened up, other factors become obvious. Judas' name is the name of the Jewish nation, Judah. The difference between Judah and Judas is only in the Greek spelling of the latter. By the first century Judah was not a nation so much as it was a province of a nation, and it was by then called Judea. The word "Jew" meant a citizen of Judah/Judea. "The Jews," the citizens of Judea, we noted earlier, become in the Fourth Gospel the name of the enemies of the Christian movement. John uses the phrase "the Jews" in his gospel to stand for the hierarchical religious leaders of the Temple and synagogue, who have by this time excommunicated the followers of Jesus from the life of the synagogue. The split with (and then within) the Johannine community was so severe that John no longer defines himself as a Jew, which he surely was ethnically, instead reserving the word for the enemies of Jesus. To give the ultimate anti-hero of the Christian story the same name as the nation that was persecuting the followers of Jesus when the gospels were written is simply too convenient a technique not to be questioned.

When one adds to this the fact that the details that are woven into the New Testament's biography of Judas appear to have been lifted out of other traitor stories in the Hebrew scriptures, the case is strengthened that Judas is a mythological, literary creation, not a person of history. John does not include all of the details from the synoptic gospels in his narrative. There is in the Fourth Gospel, for example, no reference to "thirty pieces of silver." That detail, added by Matthew only, seems to reflect a reference to the prophet Zechariah, in which the shepherd king is bought off for "thirty shekels of silver" (Zech. 11:12). Matthew alone puts into his Judas story the account of the traitor hanging himself, which appears to be drawn from the story of Ahithophel, who betrayed King David, and when that betrayal backfired went out and hanged himself (II Sam. 17:23). It was also Ahithophel about whom the psalmist wrote, stating that his treachery was more abhorrent because he had eaten at the king's table and, despite that, still raised his hand in treachery against the king (Ps. 41:9). This Ahithophel narrative appears to be the background for the story, which the gospels, including John, do relate, about Jesus identifying the traitor as one who "breaks bread with me at this table." Only in the Fourth Gospel, however, is the bread handed specifically to Judas (John 13:26). Judas looks like a compilation of the traitor stories in the Jewish scriptures.

These are the various things that make me suspicious of the historicity of Judas. This lack of historicity, as we have noted many times, does not impact John's story, however; indeed he employs non-historical characters constantly to develop his narrative. Judas Iscariot, I believe, was one more of these and for us to read his story as if literal history were being described is to misread the Fourth Gospel in a dramatic way. So focus now on the ways the character of Judas is employed in this final gospel.

In John's narrative in which Jesus' feet are washed at the home of Mary and Martha in Bethany, just six days before the Passover, Judas Iscariot is described as a thief (John 12:1–8). He objects to the extravagance of the use of "pure nard" in the act of anointing Jesus' feet. Judas argues that this act represents frivolous waste and points out that the nard would have brought a large price (three hundred dinarii, the going daily wage for three hundred days)—money that could have been used to care for the poor. Judas is moving away from the light into darkness. Jesus responds by affirming the foot-washing and anointing act in anticipation of his death and burial.

The next time Judas appears in the Fourth Gospel is when he is handed the bread from the table in a gesture that identifies him as the traitor and that finally separates him from the Johannine community. Judas, John tells us, receives the morsel and "Satan entered into him" (John 13:27). Then Jesus says: "What you are going to do, do quickly." Judas departs immediately into the darkness. John then notes in his text that "it was night" (John 13:30). The prologue is recalled: "He came to his own and his own received him not." Jesus came, John is saying, to bring life and light. That life cannot be extinguished; it will shine in a darkness that will not be able to overcome it (John 1:4–5). Judas is the symbol of those who prefer death to life and darkness to light. He is portrayed as one who cannot make the transition from death and darkness into life and light. As such, he stands for those in his day and ours who are blind, for those who cannot or will not enter the Christ experience, for those who try to snuff out the light that opens a doorway into a whole new understanding of life.

In Judas' final appearance in John's gospel, he sets the stage for the story of the passion. He comes to what John describes as a familiar place, one where Jesus has frequently met with his disciples. Judas is accompanied by people with torches and lanterns in a vain attempt to push back the darkness that is enveloping him. He is accompanied by two distinct groups of people. First, there are with him "some officers from the chief priests and Pharisees."

Judas in this gospel ultimately represents them all. He is, however, also accompanied by Roman soldiers. That is an addition that only John makes. The opposition of the Jews to Jesus will soon be portrayed in this gospel as the opposition of the world to the Jesus movement. So the Roman soldiers are introduced here to prepare for the final confrontation between Jesus and Pontius Pilate, an episode that will dominate John's passion account.

Jesus is portrayed as completely aware of all that is to befall him. So he comes forward and confronts Judas and this band. The other disciples stay behind in the shadows. Note well and listen carefully to the conversation. Jesus speaks: "Whom do you seek?" They respond, "Jesus of Nazareth." Jesus states: "I AM." Yes, I know that most versions translate that as "I am he," but the Greek is *ego eimi,* "I AM," and what is intended here is that Jesus be made to utter and to claim for himself the divine name. He is not giving us some version of "That is who I am; you have found your man." The response of the arresting party makes that very obvious: When Jesus utters the divine name as if it were his own, the arresting party, this gospel tells us, "drew back and fell to the ground" (John 18:6). The interrogation is then repeated almost verbatim to make sure the point is made. Jesus again says: "Whom do you seek?" They again respond: "Jesus of Nazareth." Jesus once more identifies himself with the words "I AM." Then he goes on to say: "If you seek me, let these go," referring the disciples. This, John says, was to fulfill Jesus' own words, uttered in the high priestly prayer, that he would lose none of those whom the Father had given him except the one, the son of perdition, who could not make the journey with him.

So the arrest is made. The soldiers seize Jesus, bind him and lead him away to Annas, the father-in-law of Caiaphas, who is described by John as "the high priest that year." Caiaphas in turn is identified as the one who had said, "It was expedient that one man should die for the people" (John 18:14).

Judas Iscariot then disappears from the drama. He confronted the light and was repelled by it. He preferred to live in the security of his darkness, where he could be comfortable in the familiar and was not required to risk venturing beyond his limits. When the light came too close, Judas set about trying to snuff it out. He wanted the light to disappear. Judas is thus a symbol of all those who could not and cannot walk into the light.

One author of a book on this gospel, John Sanford, a Jungian analyst,* sees Judas in Jungian terms as the shadow side of Jesus. Human wholeness in Carl Jung's thinking is not possible unless one's shadow is embraced. Shadows cannot be repressed or cut off. Sanford argues that the drama of the cross is an internal drama as much as it is an external one. He suggests that all of the characters in the passion narrative have counterparts in the human psyche. Judas is the one who finally says no to all of the possibilities that Jesus represents, while Jesus is able to embrace the entire human experience, including darkness and death, just as fully as he embraces light and life. Sanford portrays the cross as representing the fact that in Jesus light and life triumph over darkness and death. In John's story of the cross there is no external darkness at noon on the day of the crucifixion (as in the other gospels), because that external darkness has been incorporated into the life of Jesus. Judas thus disappears from the drama because he has been "absorbed" by Jesus. Light doesn't destroy darkness; it shines within it and the darkness cannot extinguish it.

Darkness is not darkness until it is confronted by light. Death is not death until it is confronted by life. One does not know who one is until one is confronted with who one can be. Jesus will not reject his own darkness. Rather, he will shine within it, but there will always be those who cannot make the journey into light.

---

* He makes this case in *Mystical Christianity: A Psychological Commentary on the Gospel of John.* See bibliography for details.

Through this imagery of dark and light, John presents Jesus as inviting others to step beyond all security, to embrace darkness and to transcend it, and to enter a new consciousness that relativizes all values by which life has previously been lived. That is the road to life, to mystical oneness, to wholeness. It is always scary. Judas symbolizes the world that cannot transcend the human quest for security, that cannot embrace the glorious liberty of the children of God (Rom. 8:2), that cannot step into the dimensions of a new humanity. Judas is lost. The Judah citizens he represents, who believe they have captured the holy in the forms of their religious life and practice, are lost. Those who seek to stay out of the threatening light that has entered the world in Jesus are lost. Judas Iscariot is their name. That is how the Fourth Gospel deals with Judas.

The drama at the cross is intense. All one can ever do is to open the door, reveal the light, invite a response. No one can push another into the light. Judas makes that choice real. He cannot escape his own security prison.

Someone must. When Judas fails, the Fourth Gospel portrays another—one who is very much like Judas—and moves this second figure to center stage as the passion drama continues.

CHAPTER 23

Peter: The Struggle Within the Soul

In at least one sense the Fourth Gospel can be read as the story of the inner struggle and ultimately the conversion of one named Simon, nicknamed Peter. Again and again, this gospel circles back to this pivotal figure. We watched him come close to leaving Jesus in the episode of the feeding of the multitude. We looked at his dis-ease when Jesus assumed the mantle of the servant and tried to wash his feet. Now Peter is portrayed as a major figure in the drama of the passion. He will also be central when this gospel writer begins to tell the story of the resurrection. So, following this author's lead, we too will now circle back to Peter as we enter the story of the passion.

All of the characters in this gospel appear to have been assigned symbolic roles. I think it is fair to say that Judas, as we saw in the previous chapter, stands for those who cannot move from darkness to light, from death to life. If that is so, then Simon Peter must surely symbolize those in whom the struggle between darkness and light is the most intense, and in whom the ultimate outcome is in doubt until the very end. Let me open this second of what will ultimately be three chapters in this book on Peter and review briefly the biographical details that John has already presented.

Recall that Simon Peter is first introduced in this gospel simply as "the brother of Andrew," who acts as his gatekeeper. Andrew's first response to his experience of Jesus is to find his brother, announce to him that in Jesus the messiah has appeared and then bring him to Jesus (John 1:40–43). The resulting confrontation of Jesus with Simon Peter gives us a glimpse of what lies ahead, but it also makes it clear that John is not writing history. "So you are Simon," Jesus says, "but your destiny is to become as firm as a rock" (hence, as we saw earlier, the nickname "Rock," or Peter). I am not so interested in who you are now, says Jesus in effect, but in what you are destined to become: a rocklike person of resolution and strength.

That transition, however, would not come easily. John was signaling in this exchange that the struggle to be born into a new consciousness, a new being, a new source of what it means to be fully human, would be fought out most extensively in the soul of Simon Peter. At the same time, we the readers must recognize that Peter's struggle is in fact every person's struggle. He had been born of the flesh years before. His ability to be born of the spirit would test everything his life seemed to mean and it would be an intensely difficult labor.

As the gospel begins, "the disciples," a term in which Peter, as the quintessential disciple, is always assumed to be included, had accompanied Jesus to the wedding feast in Cana of Galilee. It was there for the first time that "his disciples believed in him" (John 2:11). What did they believe? For starters, the waters of Jewish purification had been transformed into wine, the spiritual beverage that gives life. In addition, they were with him when the Temple was cleansed, and they "remembered" the scripture that suggested, "Zeal for thy house has consumed me" (Ps. 69:9). Jesus then likened his body to that Temple and said that if it were destroyed, he would raise it up in three days. "The disciples believed the scriptures," we are told. Later, they were shocked that he was talking to a woman, a Samaritan woman at that, and slowly it began to dawn on them that such barriers as ethnicity, gender and religion had to fall away before the presence of this Jesus (John 4:27). In the experience narrated at the feeding of the multitude (John 6:1–21), the disciples tried to embrace the concept that Jesus was to his day what the heavenly bread called manna was to their ancestors. Manna gave the Israelites life. Jesus' body would also give this generation life, but that meaning of Jesus' body had to be internalized. "Unless you eat the flesh of the son of man and drink his blood, you have no life in you" (John 6:53), Jesus told them. It was a strange saying. For one thing, it was cast in the third person, not the first person. Worse yet, it sounded repellently like cannibalism. The disciples said: "This is a hard saying; who can listen to it?" (John 6:60). Jesus spoke to their musings: You do not yet understand, he said. I know a dimension of life that you have not yet entered. "It is the spirit that gives life," not the flesh. I am talking of spirit and life. Not to believe is to betray. Not to see is to be like Judas. You must journey into this new dimension. The Father must call you and the Father must open your eyes to enable you to see.

The disciples drew back at this message, no longer willing to accompany Jesus. To the one who is the composite of "the disciples," Peter, Jesus now issues the challenge: "Do you also wish to go away?" It is the first of many moments in which a decision has to be made and Peter passes this early test, but just barely. "Lord, to whom shall we go?" he responds. "You have the words of eternal life" (John 6:68). Peter then goes on to say: "We have believed and have come to know that you are the holy one of God" (John 6:69). Was God thought of as a being? That is the way John is traditionally read, but if this book is one shaped by Jewish mysticism, as I am now convinced it is, this statement can also be a reference to a new dimension of life, something beyond the boundaries of our fear, where self-consciousness passes into universal consciousness and in which oneness is experienced. The boundary between being self-conscious and entering a universal consciousness is both genuine and real. Jesus could not be contained inside the boundary of mere self-consciousness and neither ultimately could the disciples, nor their composite representative, Peter, if he came to embrace what Jesus meant.

This was followed with the story of Jesus walking on water. Matthew has one unusual note in his version of this story. Peter, seeing Jesus on the water, says: "Master, if it is you, bid me to come to you." Jesus invites him to come, but after initial success fear grips him and he begins to sink and has to be rescued (Matt. 14:28ff). That is typical of the New Testament's memory of Peter and, while John does not record that episode, it fits his description of Peter. He is impulsive, he is fearful and struggles inwardly to come to a new self-understanding. In the story of Jesus walking on the water, John has Jesus invite the disciples and most especially Peter, to cease living on the surface of life. Come to me, he says: taste and see. The internal debate raging inside Peter could be processed only with external words. That is always the way it has to be. Peter still has to learn this.

The disciples, including Peter, next see the man born blind and ask what this blindness means. Who caused it? "Who sinned?" is the way they ask the question. Was it something his parents did? Was it something he did? No, says Jesus, once again driving them beyond shallow literalism to the heart of the meaning of life; this blindness is to enable you to see God as light in this blind man. "I am light," he continues, once again using God's "I AM" name; you must leave your darkness to come to where I am. I am the door through which you must walk. I am the good shepherd who calls you. I and the Father are one.

Jesus' words keep cascading against the defenses of the disciples. The inner conflict is intense, but they do not turn away.

In the final sign portrayed in John (which we looked at earlier from a different perspective), the disciples are portrayed as seeing life come out of death in the story of the raising of Lazarus (John 11:1ff). Some of the authorities, as a direct result of Lazarus' restoration, move to kill Jesus. The threat to their worldview and to their security is just too great. Judas is still in the group at this time. The disciples are portrayed as still squirming, still fighting, still doubting. Jesus lays down the final challenge: "I am resurrection," he says; "I am life." The world cannot see. They have turned away. They will kill the bringer of life and light. The disciples will linger a while longer in the frightening land of indecision.

Then Jesus speaks intensely only to the disciples in the Farewell Discourses. The battle goes on in that section to enable them to choose light over darkness, life over death, expanded humanity over the fearful and warped life that hides behind the defensive walls of human insecurity. Eventually Peter moves out of the disciple band and stands alone and individualized in the center of these discourses. This is when the offer for Jesus to become his servant and to wash his feet occurs (John 13:1ff). Peter, as we saw in our earlier discussion of that scene, is caught in emotions he cannot fathom. Then Jesus is portrayed as speaking to him again, calling him beyond his ego, his pretenses, and offering him the freedom to give his life away. God is to be found in the human capacity to give, the human capacity to love. Peter is unable to hear. You will understand this someday, Peter, says Jesus. That day will come, we discover, when he stares at the picture of vulnerability and powerlessness hanging on the cross.

Peter is not yet ready to go there. He trembles on the edge for a very long time in this gospel, but he always finally seems to make the right decision; he never closes the door on this new possibility. On the other hand, neither is he yet willing to embrace it *fully*. The Farewell Discourses continue. The revealer continues to hold the vision before the disciples. "I am the way," he says: come and dwell in me. "I am the life," he says: come and live in me. "I am the truth": come and partake of me. "I am the vine": come and abide in me.

All of this dialogue depicts little more than the drama that unfolds inside the life of Peter, who—like all of us—must die to what he is before he can become what he is capable of being. Peter is Everyman and Everywoman. His struggle is our struggle. Now, John says to us, his readers, we are ready to watch the story of the cross as it plays out inside Peter.

Jesus is arrested in the garden. He goes to his captors willingly and asks that his disciples be set free. Peter, however, does not choose to depart or to flee. Instead, he is pictured as being drawn like a magnet to the power that Jesus seems to reveal. He draws his sword to defend Jesus and strikes the slave of the high priest, cutting off the man's ear. He will be true to his word. He will die for Jesus. Jesus orders him to put his sword away. Life is never found in a physical struggle to preserve it (John 18:9–11).

Next, through the influence of another disciple (who is not named), Peter gains access to the court of the high priest (John 18:15ff). There Peter is routed by a maid. "Are you not also one of this man's disciples?" she asks. "I am not," Peter responds. Survival has trumped loyalty! Peter then watches Jesus be struck by an officer of the high priest for what the officer deemed to have been an insubordinate response. The pain must have been felt as if it were his own. The scene then shifts back to where Peter is warming himself by the fire. Someone in the crowd picks up the maid's attack: "Are you not one of his disciples?" (John 18:25). "I am not," Peter responds a second time. The inescapable daggers of human words are all around him. Still another picks up the accusation that is relentless when one seeks to cover one's soul with lies. "Did I not see you in the garden with him?" (John 18:26), this new voice inquires. Peter denies again. Bravado is demolished. The crow of the cock is heard. They take Jesus away. Peter enters the dark night of his soul.

Peter wants to *become*. He does not know how to be, how to live fully. Peter also wants to survive. That is the deepest drive present in *every* living thing. In self-conscious human life, the drive to survive locks each of us into the prison of self-centeredness. If survival is our highest value, we organize our lives to meet that ultimate need and we will do anything it takes to accomplish that final goal. We brag to hide our fear. We lie to cover our inadequacy. We push others down to elevate ourselves. We give to no one except insofar as our giving serves our survival needs. We love no one more than we love ourselves. Our life is bound by our security walls, by our defense barriers. To lay those barriers down is to shake with survival-driven anxiety. We must hide to avoid the vulnerability that love requires. We must cultivate an image, a public persona, but we never find the courage to be who we are. That is what is going on in Peter. That is also the nature of every human life. That is who I am, that is who you are— survival-driven creatures, unable to enter into the fullness of our humanity.

The story of the cross is the story of Peter confronting the "word of God." It is the word which says that we are part of that which is limitless. It is the word which invites us to come to him and to find rest from the struggle of becoming. It is the word which says we are part of who God is and God is part of who we are. It is the word which proclaims that the life of God is found in our living, the love of God is found in our loving and the being of God is found in our being. John in this gospel is asserting that this word is made flesh in Jesus of Nazareth. This does not mean that the external theistic deity comes out of the sky and enters the human Jesus in some incarnational way. It means rather that Jesus reveals in his life the freedom to live and in that living not to be at the mercy of every distorting force in life. It means that in Jesus there is a refusal to hide personal identity inside the security of tribal identity. It means that each of us can step outside the prejudices of our cultural roots, which serve to give us a sense of superiority that we think gives us a survival edge. It means that we can refuse to live inside the boundaries of a religious system that tells us that if we practice the things which our religion requires, we can win the favor of the one who has the power to guarantee our survival. It means that the drive to survive can no longer distort our humanity, nor can it compromise our existence. It means that the life of God lives in us. It means that the love of God flows through us. It means that no one is placed beyond the boundaries of that love. It means that, like Jesus, we are free to give our life away and that *this* is what the experience of God is ultimately all about. That is John's understanding of the mystical reality that is met in Jesus.

Peter wrestles with this. He fights, he denies, he flees, but he does not remain in the darkness as Judas did. He finally escapes. He moves ultimately beyond the human to see the meaning of Jesus, where the human and the divine are seen to flow together into oneness.

In the epilogue of this gospel, to which I shall turn in the final chapter, Peter is portrayed as finally making the transition, when he is called to be the giver of life and to feed the sheep of God.

The passion narrative now moves to its final dialogue. Jesus, the "word of God," confronts Pilate, the symbol of yesterday's worldly power. In this episode, John pens the most poignant dialogue in the entire gospel.

CHAPTER 24

Pilate: The Conflict Between Survival and Truth

We know very little historically about the low-level Roman official who was assigned to be the procurator of the province of Judea in the year 26 CE. We know that he fulfilled that role for approximately ten years, until 36 CE, when he was recalled by Rome for his inability to keep the peace. Because he was in power when the crucifixion of Jesus occurred, he has entered immortality in history as few political figures have ever done. He is recalled by name every time a Christian community anywhere in the world recites its creed.

Keep in mind, however, as we seek to enter the Fourth Gospel's unique understanding of the passion of Jesus, that Pilate had departed from the land of the Jews about two generations before his name was first mentioned in any Christian written source of which we are aware. That first notice of Pilate is found in the gospel of Mark, written, many scholars believe, in the city of Rome about forty-two years after the crucifixion. In that original reference, Mark's readers are told that "the chief priests, with the elders and scribes and the whole council [of the Jews], held a consultation, and they bound Jesus and delivered him to Pilate"

(Mark 15:1). About twenty years later, in a note that appears in the gospel of Luke, we are informed that Pilate had another name. It was Pontius (Luke 3:1). That single Lucan reference is the only place in the entire Bible where the name Pontius is added to the name Pilate. It is familiar to us, we need to recognize, not from scripture, but from the fact that it was this full name that Christians inserted first into their baptismal formulas, which evolved into what is now called the Apostles' Creed, a late-second-century or early-third-century creation, and which was confirmed by the Council of Nicaea in 325 CE and thus included in the Nicene Creed, produced at that time.

Luke's context for introducing the full name is that he is going to tell of the significance of Jesus for the whole world, so he begins his story by making his readers aware of the power figures who occupied the world stage in Jesus' day: "In the fifteenth year of the reign of Tiberius Caesar, Pontius Pilate being governor of Judea and Herod being tetrarch of Galilee, and his [i.e., Herod's] brother Philip tetrarch of the regions of Ituraea and Trachonitis, and Lysanias tetrarch of Abilene, in the high priesthood of Annas and Caiaphas, the word of God came to John, the son of Zechariah, in the wilderness" (Luke 3:1–2). Luke, as an historian, needs to cover all the bases!

The role assigned to Pilate in Mark's story of the crucifixion is relatively brief. Pilate appears and disappears in only fifteen verses (Mark 15:1–15). His purpose, according to Mark, is to make possible the execution of Jesus, since the Jews, as a conquered province, do not have the legal authority to put anyone to death. Mark in these fifteen verses portrays Pilate somewhat sympathetically as one who is trying to find a way to release Jesus. Pilate offers to follow what Mark asserts is an established custom: to release a prisoner at the season of Passover as a token of goodwill to the conquered province.* Pilate, however, ultimately "delivers Jesus to be crucified." His is a cameo appearance at best.

Matthew, the next gospel to be written (ca. 82–85), adds a few notes to the growing Pilate story. After telling of Judas Iscariot's repentance and of his attempt to return the money given him for the betrayal, Matthew relates an incident about Pilate's wife, who appears to have had a bad dream about Pilate's prisoner, in which some mysterious aspects of Jesus' power were revealed. With Pilate in the seat of judgment, she sends him a warning message: "Have nothing to do with that righteous man" (Matt. 27:19). That is clearly not a remembrance of history; rather, it attests to the fact that the Pilate myth is growing.

When Luke, the third gospel writer (ca. 88–93),† tells his story of Pilate, he heightens the narrative still more. Luke details the charges of the Jewish authorities that caused them to take Jesus to Pilate seeking a summary execution. Jesus was, they said, "perverting the nation, forbidding tribute to Caesar and saying that he himself is a king" (Luke 23:2). These charges are much more political than any mentioned before. Luke adds one additional wrinkle in his chronicle of Pilate's well-publicized attempt in the gospels to escape condemning Jesus to death. Discovering that Jesus is a Galilean, Luke says that Pilate shipped him off to Herod, who just happened to be in Jerusalem for the Passover. Only in Luke is there this additional interrogation of Jesus. It was a hostile interrogation, Luke says, for Herod treated Jesus "with

---

* There is no record that I could locate of such a custom ever being practiced, much less practiced with such regularity that it became a tradition. It appears to be a detail created to enable the Barabbas story to be developed.

† Marcus Borg, a man whose work I admire greatly, has in his latest book adopted a second-century date for the Luke-Acts corpus—around the year 140 CE, he suggests. Burton Mack, another formidable New Testament scholar, made the same claim some twenty-five years ago. I am not persuaded by the arguments of either of them, and few in the world of New Testament scholarship have, at least as yet, saluted this flag that they have run up the flagpole. See bibliography for details on both.

contempt and mocked him"; then Herod placed on the body of Jesus "gorgeous apparel" before he returned him to Pilate.

Pilate is clearly being developed in the synoptic gospels as a sympathetic figure, seeking to escape from the task of pronouncing the death sentence. All of his efforts, however, ended in failure. Surely there was a growing tendency in the Christian community to paint Pilate as something other than the villain. Something like a historical whitewash was at work. When we recall that these gospels were written generations after the events they purport to be describing, we are driven to seek the operative agenda that was at work embellishing the reputation of Pilate.

With that question stated, but not yet answered, we turn to John's gospel and examine how this author continues and even enhances this revisionist view of the historical memory of Pilate. For that is exactly what he does. John will shape the figure of Pilate to suit his personal, literary and mythological needs. The long, beautifully drawn, intense dialogue between Pilate and his condemned prisoner, Jesus, is crucial to John's understanding of the crucifixion. As we look at this dialogue, we need to remind ourselves over and over that this is not the recollection of a confrontation that actually happened in history. This is a literary composition, deliberately designed to move the Fourth Gospel's story of Jesus to its grand climax. It is also designed to say to the early Christians, for whom this gospel was written, that in their conflict with the power of Rome in their generation, they must be open to the possibility that the Romans seemed to come closer to understanding Jesus than did the Jews. Indeed, winning the approval of the Roman Empire might well have been one of John's goals. In some strange ways, his text suggests, Rome itself perceived Jesus' power even though neither the Empire nor its representative was able to act upon it. There is also a clear need operating in this gospel to victimize the orthodox Jews.

This long Pilate-Jesus dialogue, which the author of the Fourth Gospel has obviously created, is one more step in his masterful portrayal of the revealer of God working against the power of religion as well as the power of the government.

So we set the context for this dramatic confrontation: Judas has betrayed, Peter has denied and the religious authorities, personified by Caiaphas, have judged Jesus worthy of death. They deliver Jesus, bound, to Pilate. These Jewish accusers, however, balk at the entrance to the Roman praetorium. They refuse to enter this Gentile center of power, for it is to them unclean territory. If they do not keep themselves from this Gentile pollution, they will not be able to eat the Passover. The defining and routine rituals of religion are to be observed, and yet these accusers place themselves in the position of trusting a moral code that allows the death penalty to be carried out against religious troublemakers. Here the values of religion are deeply compromised.

Pilate, responsive to their purity concerns, agrees to go outside and to conduct his interrogation in public (John 18:28ff). "What accusation do you bring against this man?" he asks them. They respond, seeking to justify their action, but without answering Pilate's question: "If this man were not an evildoer, we would not have handed him over."

Pilate responds: "Take him yourselves and judge him by your own law." Those in the Jewish crowd have misrepresented Jesus' crimes, as he sees it. If Jesus is just a religious "evildoer," a burdensome troublemaker, as they have suggested, then *they* can punish him under the authority of the Torah. Pilate has thus removed their pious facade.

This is to these religious leaders, however, a capital case—one for which the death penalty must be applied—and the conquered nation must thus receive the cooperation of its conquerors to punish one of their own. They need the Roman government to carry out their religious desires. John is saying that "the Jews" (a title, we need always to remember, that he uses for those who oppose Jesus) have come to the limit of their power. Ultimately, before this trial is over, Rome will also have come to its limit, for Jesus is standing before Pilate because "God so loved the world," of which Pilate is now the representative.

So this conversation forces a new level of honesty into the public arena and Caiaphas or his spokesman responds: "It is not lawful for us to put any man to death." John adds an interpretive note here, for in John's mind Jesus must be "lifted up" to "draw the world to himself." That lifting up must occur on the cross, so Roman execution alone fulfills that expectation. Stoning at the hands of a religious mob is not in John's plan for the "glorification" of Jesus.

Pilate then breaks off the dialogue and enters the praetorium. He calls Jesus to himself and a one-on-one conversation begins. Jesus is apparently unbothered by the fact that he has entered an unclean Gentile realm. "In him was life," the life of God, and this "life was the light of men [and women]," as we heard in John's prologue. The light shines in the darkness and the darkness has not (cannot and will not) overcome it. So no darkness and no unclean pollution can affect him.

Pilate now speaks directly to Jesus: "Are you the king of the Jews?"

Jesus answers: "Do you say that of your own accord or did others say it to you about me?" Jesus was asking: Are you a seeker or do you pretend to be my judge?

Pilate, not eager to be perceived as concerned about religious issues that are separating the Jews from each other, responds: "Am I a Jew? Your own nation and the chief priests have handed you over to me. What have you done?"

Jesus answers: "My kingship is not of this world." If it were, he implies, my servants would fight that I might not be handed over to the Jews. I am operating in another realm. I am struggling not to survive, but to open life to new realities that are beyond religion and are even beyond the power struggles of the political world, over which you preside.

Pilate is portrayed as listening closely and trying to discern the meaning implied. He is still a seeker. He is looking beyond the limits of his words. So Pilate responds: "So are you a king?"

Jesus answers: "You say that I am a king. For this I was born and for this I have come into the world, to bear witness to the truth." When you know the truth, Jesus said previously, "the truth will set you free" (John 8:32). Jesus is offering Pilate a glimpse into his being.

Pilate, a symbol of the world, then asks the question the world always raises: "What is truth?"

The dialogue ends on that stark note and Pilate is portrayed as leaving Jesus and going out once again to face Jesus' religious accusers. His conclusion startles Jesus' critics: "I find no crime in him," he says. Then he offers them all, himself included, a way out of this rising tension. "You have a custom that I should release one man for you at the Passover. Will you have me now release for you the king of the Jews?" It is a provocative offer. Does Pilate see into the meaning of Jesus' kingship? It is, however, also like waving a red flag in the face of Jesus' accusers. To admit the kingship of Jesus would bring their religious defenses crumbling down. Their religious system, like all religious systems, was created to win divine favor from an external deity. The kingdom about which Jesus was speaking invites them into another realm of life—born of the spirit—in which there are no religious boundaries, not even a boundary between God and human life. Threatened deeply, they have to play the traditional human survival card. So they cry out: "Not this man, but Barabbas."

This is the first mention in John's gospel of Barabbas and it indicates to me that John as well as his readers were probably familiar with the synoptic tradition. Pilate, still squirming, decides that he will seek a lesser penalty, one that hopefully will satisfy Jesus' accusers. He delivers Jesus to be scourged. The soldiers then plait a crown of thorns and place it on his head. They put on his back a purple robe, the color of royalty. They mock him, bowing and saying to him: "Hail, King of the Jews!" They strike him with their hands. This is a king to be ridiculed, to be abused, a king with no power.

Then, with Jesus beaten and wearing symbols of kingly power clearly designed to indicate his powerlessness—a crown made not of gold and jewels but of sticks and thorns—he is led out to the crowd. "Behold," Pilate says, pointing to Jesus, "I am bringing him out to you, that you may know that I find no fault in him." As Jesus comes into full view, Pilate then announces, "Here is the man." Jesus is presented to the Jewish crowd as a human life thought to be claiming enormous power, but actually powerless, for he is now totally in the control of the state, its soldiers and its rulers. The values of the world in which both Pilate and the religious leaders are clearly invested are obvious. When the chief priests and the Temple officers see Jesus, they cry out: "Crucify him, crucify him!"

Pilate hurls their cry back at them, as he did earlier, again forcing those religious officials to recognize their own powerlessness. "Take him yourselves and crucify him, for I find no crime in him."

To this charge his religious accusers appeal to their law, the Torah, which was called by them "the word of God." "We have a law, and by that law he ought to die," they say—and finally the real issue that separates the followers of Jesus from the synagogue worshippers is articulated: Jesus' real crime is that he had "made himself the son of God." He had identified himself with "the great I AM." He had claimed that the "word of God" was spoken through him and that the "will of God" was lived out in his life. He had ascribed to his human life things that no human life (in their minds) could be or could ever seek to be. The divine could not wash the feet of the human. The divine could not be powerless. The divine could not forgive those who put one to death. Human life could not see or tolerate that kind of God presence. Jesus, his accusers say, had claimed a different kind of oneness with God that was inappropriate to their understanding of the nature of humanity.

That accusation is enough to get Pilate's attention. Earthly power cannot tolerate divine intervention. Neither can religious power. So Pilate returns to Jesus and a second round of interrogation begins (John 19:8ff). For the readers of this gospel it has a familiar ring. Pilate now joins with so many in seeking out Jesus' origins.

"Where are you from?" Pilate asks. Jesus is silent, giving no answer.

"You do not speak to me?" Pilate prods. You do not recognize my power, my authority? "Do you not know," he challenges, "that I have the power to release you and the power to crucify you?" It is a typical claim of the world. The power to decide who lives and who dies is the ultimate power of the state. It is, however, not in touch with the meaning that Jesus has come to reveal. So Jesus responds: "You would have no power over me unless it had been given you from above; therefore he who delivered me to you has the greater sin."

This is an interesting shift. In the mind of the author of the Fourth Gospel, the ultimate blame for the death of Jesus is to be placed on the religious authorities of his nation. Pilate is simply their tool. The world has been enlisted on the side of religion. The state is now the instrument of divine punishment.

To put this placing of blame in context, we need to know that it was widely believed among the followers of Jesus at this time that the Roman destruction of Jerusalem in 70 CE was direct punishment for the Jewish refusal to receive Jesus. At the actual moment of the writing of this gospel, the Jewish nation was itself broken, destroyed and powerless, but the Christians were also oppressed by the world. There was hope for the world, but no hope remained in John's mind for the religious authorities of Judaism. The message of the Christ must transcend both religion and the power of the state, so those two entities are now aligned in degrees of guilt as the drama rolls on.

Pilate once more seeks to release Jesus. This time, however, the religious authorities play on Pilate's own survival fears. "If you release this man, you are not Caesar's friend; everyone who makes himself a king sets himself against Caesar." It is the ultimate power play. The religious authorities claim the Roman government as their ally in the struggle against Jesus and Pilate now has to decide on which of these two sides he stands. The stakes are now rooted in the instinctual human drive to survive.

John writes, "When Pilate heard these words he brought Jesus out and sat down on the judgment seat at a place called the pavement." It was, says the Fourth Gospel, "the day of the preparation for the Passover"—that is, the day on which the paschal lamb is slaughtered and its blood sprinkled on the doorposts of Jewish homes to break or to hurl back the power of death. Jesus is to be the new paschal lamb who will hurl away death, the ultimate limit on our humanity, thus breaking the boundary that separates us from the eternity of God.

Pilate then says to Jesus' accusers: "Here is your king." They respond: "Away with him, away with him; crucify him!"

Pilate, tightening the noose, answers with a question: "Shall I crucify your king?" Then John places the ultimate words of religious idolatry on the lips of the chief priests: "We have no king but Caesar." The final denial has been spoken. "He came to his own and his own received him not" (John 1:11). The role that the Jewish nation was to play in bringing to earth the kingdom of God has been denied. The right of God to rule the world has been dismissed. The messianic claim has been renounced. God could never again be seen in the power symbols of either religion or politics, in church or state. Something quite different was to be revealed in Jesus of Nazareth. Pilate was the final foil through whom the revelation of Jesus would be received. Jesus' revelation would carry him and his disciples beyond the scope of religion and beyond the realm of the world's most powerful symbol of authority. They would be born to a new dimension of human life. The doorway into that new dimension would be opened in the death of Jesus, accused by entrenched religion, executed at the hands of the state.

Pilate has played his role on this central stage, and now he disappears. It will be in the revelation of life in the midst of death that the symbolic true believer, the one who understands the meaning of Jesus' life, will finally be recognized in this gospel. He is called the "beloved disciple," and to his story we turn next as the drama of the passion of Jesus continues.

CHAPTER 25

At the Cross: The Mother of Jesus and the Beloved Disciple

In the second half of John 19, the pace of the crucifixion drama gathers speed. Contrary to the earlier synoptic tradition, John portrays Jesus as bearing his own cross. John's Jesus will be in control of every aspect of what John understands to be his ultimate revelation. The procession moves to a hill called "the place of the skull," Golgotha in Hebrew. "There," John says with strikingly spare detail, "they crucified him" (John 19:18).

By the time John wrote, the other two victims who were said to have been crucified with Jesus were solidly in the tradition, though I suspect they were originally created to fulfill the expectation of the prophet Isaiah, who had written that the "servant" was to be "numbered with the transgressors" (Isa. 53:12). The prophetic role of Pilate in declaring Jesus to be the king of the Jews was not to be lost. Pilate had written a title and ordered it to be appended to the instrument of execution. It read, "Jesus of Nazareth, the King of the Jews." One suspects that if there is any shred of history to this detail of John's story, and most scholars do not believe there is, it was designed to be an act of mockery. This king was powerless. A cross is hardly a throne, and no crown is ever made of thorns. Yet in John's mind something far deeper was being revealed in that title and crown. Having escaped the survival syndrome that marks all living things, here was a human life living out a new human destiny. As such he would be shown to be illustrative of the inverted order of values that will prevail when the kingdom of God dawns. Here was a life designed to reveal what it means to be born of the spirit. Here was a life in which strength could be found in weakness and life could be entered through death.

The author of this gospel was an artist, a portrait painter, and the portrait he was painting was filled with the symbols of this new kind of "kingdom" power. As we saw in the previous chapter, John presented Jesus' critics as having abdicated their last claim to being a messianic people. "We have no king but Caesar," they were made to shout to Caesar's representative, Pilate. No matter how distorted Pilate's vision of Jesus was, he was left in John's story to be the only one who would proclaim Jesus' kingship. "Behold your king," Pilate said to the crowd, as he presented Jesus beaten, bleeding and on his way to the cross.

Now at the scene of the execution Pilate's designation was to be broadcast through that sign he had ordered to be attached to the cross. In this scene, weakness is the doorway into strength and love is the ultimate revelation of the self-giver. The sign on that cross also served to lift the meaning of Jesus to universality, for it was written in Latin (the language of the imperial government), in Greek (the language of the culture) and in Hebrew (the language in which this life had been raised and through which it was now to be interpreted).

This title created offense among Jesus' critics, and an effort was made to revise it, to "subjectify" it. One must not say "the king of the Jews," for that is a statement claiming objective reality. It should be changed to read, "This man *said,* 'I am the king of the Jews'" (John 19:21)—that would make it nothing more than the delusional rantings of a pathological victim. Pilate was firm: "What I have written, I have written" (John 19:22). It was important to the author of this gospel that the representative of the power of Rome recognize, even inadequately, the profound truth that John was seeking to convey: Jesus' kingdom is not of this world, but it is real. It is transformative.

John then repeats a detail, which Mark, incorporating a verse from Psalm 22, had earlier written into the story of the cross. The soldiers divide Jesus' clothing among themselves, but then John develops the details of this story in his own way. If Jesus' tunic were to be torn into equal pieces, whatever value it had would be lost. John says that its future owner is to be determined by a roll of the dice, thus newly aligning Jesus with the servant portrait to which Psalm 22 pointed. John quotes that text to make sure the reader knows the source of these words: "They divide my clothes among themselves and for my clothing they cast lots" (Ps. 22:5). Jesus is now stripped of every vestige of a defensive shell. He has no dignity; he owns no clothing and no property. He possesses nothing behind which to hide his vulnerability. Is this the end of Jesus' life or is this now the door, the way, through which a new meaning of life itself is destined to be revealed? That is the question John's portrait of Jesus is being painted to answer. Remember that John's assertion is that the crucifixion will be the moment of Jesus' "glorification," and that it is only by being lifted up that he will draw the world to himself.

Against this background, John reintroduces two symbolic figures through whom he is going to reveal the meaning of the cross. One is Jesus' mother, in her first appearance in this narrative since the wedding feast at Cana of Galilee. There, we were told, she was taught that it was not her role to force Jesus to act before his "hour had come." Yet he did act in that first of John's signs, and because he did the waters of purification pointed to and became the wine of the spirit. Signs, however, only *point* to meanings that they cannot finally enfold. The mother of Jesus had produced the son she could never keep inside her bounds. Even at that early moment in John's story the mother of Jesus looked more like a symbol than a person. (As I have already indicated, it is my conclusion that most of John's characters are symbols rather than historical people.*)

Now we watch as John places the mother of Jesus quite literally at the foot of the cross. That is also a unique Johannine twist. There is no reference in any other gospel to the presence of the mother of Jesus at the place of his execution. All of those great and magnificent pietàs carved or those portraits painted of the mother of Jesus holding her limp and dead son after he was taken from the cross are based solely on this single text. This detail is not history. It should be noted that it is the tenth decade of Christian history before the mother of Jesus and the cross are brought together in any Christian literature and when that juxtaposition finally occurs it serves a major Johannine motif. Christian piety and Christian art have through the centuries focused their devotional life so totally on this scene of the mother of Jesus at the cross that to point out the facts of biblical history almost seems like an act of irreverence. When we look, however, at the portrait of the mother of Jesus in the other gospels, we see why it took her so long to be placed in this role in the powerful Johannine interpretive story. She is not a major figure in any of the gospel portraits of Jesus.

---

* The literature on the mother of Jesus is massive, but much of it is devotional and therefore not of great historical significance. The best book that I have read which separates fact from fiction and reality from legend was written by a Roman Catholic laywoman named Marina Warner. It is entitled *Alone of All Her Sex*. See bibliography for details.

Her rise to prominence in the Christian tradition was very slow, far slower than most people realize. Only in later centuries does she begin increasingly to dominate Christian piety and even doctrinal development. So embrace the biblical fact that it is some sixty-five to seventy years after the crucifixion that she is finally portrayed as being at the foot of the cross—and that only in the Fourth Gospel. What is the purpose then, we must ask, for this placement? What does this woman symbolize? If John is consistent in his interpretation of the life of Jesus, then one must search for truth beyond literal descriptions, for meaning that is not history but that interprets history, for that is John's style.

The case for seeing this episode as symbolic rather than historical is greatly strengthened by the fact that Jesus' mother makes her appearance at the foot of the cross in the company of another figure, one who, as we have previously indicated, is mentioned and developed only in the gospel of John. He, like the mother of Jesus, is also nameless and enigmatic. He is called the "beloved disciple" or the "disciple whom Jesus loved," and John will portray him as the first disciple to believe.

This person's identification has been debated throughout Christian history. The majority tradition had been to assume that the "beloved disciple" is John, the son of Zebedee, but no one today, outside fundamentalist circles, still tries to make that case. Others have proposed Thomas as the "beloved disciple," as well as John Mark, Mary Magdalene, James the brother of Jesus and even Lazarus. I have already indicated (when we looked at this disciple's entrance into the tradition in John 13) that I do not regard this figure as a person of history at all, but as the final great literary creation of this author. He is the crescendo character in a line that has produced a series of remarkably drawn figures. We have examined these characters in detail as we have journeyed together through this gospel. It is because I have come to recognize that the "beloved disciple" is so crucial to John's development of the Jewish mystical theme that I spent so much time on his rise and development earlier in this book. John will now build on that prior development, and the next step is clearly this appearance at the foot of the cross. The "beloved disciple" will make two other appearances before this book is concluded. I will get to them at the time they arise.

Does John give us any clue about this figure's identity? I think he does, but that clue is quite hidden. It is found in this figure's primary identification. He is said to be beloved of Jesus. Is there any character in John's gospel about whom it has been said that he is particularly loved by Jesus? Yes, there is! He is, however, a character in the Book of Signs, a man whose historicity we have already dismissed. Let me take you, briefly, back into that narrative, but this time I ask you to note carefully its words.

Observe first that it is only after the story of the raising of Lazarus that the description "the disciple whom Jesus loved" is first used. With that in mind, now look closely at the language that John uses about Lazarus. That story opens with Mary and Martha sending a message to Jesus about the sickness of their brother, Lazarus. The literal message in the text says, "Lord, he *whom you love* is ill" (John 11:3). Two verses later the author of this gospel writes, "Now Jesus *loved* Martha and her sister *and Lazarus*." Recall the strange quality of the details in that story. Jesus does not go at once. He first says that Lazarus is asleep. Then later he says that Lazarus is dead and he is glad he was not there so that the disciples "may believe" (John 11:15). When Jesus finally arrives at Bethany, where Lazarus was said to live, speaking to his sisters Mary and Martha he says, "Your brother will live again," and then he says of himself, "I am the resurrection and the life" (John 11:21–27). Next, Jesus is portrayed as weeping (John 11:35). "The Jews"—that is, those who were opposed to Jesus—interpret this weeping by saying, "See how he *loved* him" (John 11:36). It is apparent in this story that the author is deliberately making the point that Lazarus is "the beloved" of Jesus. Lazarus is, however, clearly not a figure of history. Is this not the Fourth Gospel writer's clue as to the identity of the "beloved disciple"? Lazarus, who has passed from death to life, is referred to in this story again and again as the one "whom Jesus loved." Given that fact, it begins to make sense that the "beloved disciple" is seated by John next to Jesus, "leaning on his breast" at the supper in which the traitor is identified, and that he is now placed by John at the foot of the cross. The "beloved disciple" is the one, alone of all the disciples, who follows him to his death. Who then, if not a historical figure, is the "disciple whom Jesus loved"? What does he mean? Whom does he symbolize?

He is a mythological character, a symbol of those who see, of those who respond and of those who are transformed. He is the archetype of the Jesus movement. He represents the ones who are born of the spirit, the ones who are able to taste and experience, to share in the new life that Jesus came to bring. He is the "Lazarus" who has passed from death into life. The one who knows that to be in Christ is to have the life of God flow through him as the life of the vine flows through the branches. He is the symbol of the new creation, the first citizen of the new Israel, the representative of the first fruits of the kingdom of God. He is the one who sees, who believes and who understands. He is the ultimate representative of the Johannine community of believers, who have been excommunicated from the synagogue and then purged of those, like Judas, who cannot go all the way into the life that Jesus represents. He is the one who confronts those, like Peter, who waver and doubt, and he is the one who finally enables Peter (and those like him) to walk with his doubts and fears into the presence of all that Jesus means. He is the one at the Last Supper through whom Peter has to go to get to Jesus when the traitor is identified. Perhaps he is also Peter's assurance that the traitor is not Peter himself. Perhaps John also intends it to be understood that the "beloved disciple" is the one who opens the door so the wavering Peter can get into the courtyard of the high priest.

The "beloved disciple" will be the one who accompanies Peter to the tomb and then stands aside and makes way for Peter to enter before he does. Once inside the tomb, however, he will be the first to believe. Finally, he will be the one who identifies the risen Christ to Peter by the lake, the same risen Christ that Peter will finally see in the breaking of the bread on that lakeside. That experience, still to come in our investigation, is what finally will enable Peter, according at least to the author of the epilogue, to be fully restored and thus fully able to walk into the transformative Jesus experience.

The "beloved disciple" is thus the ultimate definition of a follower of Jesus. Judas, another of John's symbols, cannot see and remains in the darkness; he leaves the disciples and goes out, and it is "night." Peter embodies the intense struggle of faith, resisting until the meaning of Jesus eventually dawns and he is finally able to step into the new life of resurrection. Pilate is the symbol of earthly power, the one who sees the kingship of Jesus, but only within limits, in vague outlines. He speaks a truth that he cannot finally embrace and becomes a symbol of the world against which the followers of Jesus must forever struggle. Finally, the "beloved disciple" is the symbol of what it means to journey beyond life's defensive boundaries into the mystery of new life, new consciousness, that is to be found in the Christ experience.

So John has this symbol, the "beloved disciple," take his place at the cross, at the moment when this gospel asserts that the meaning of Jesus is finally revealed, at the moment of Jesus' glorification. He is the symbol of those who can make the transition and step into the meaning of eternity.

Who is he standing with in this dramatic scene at the foot of the cross? It is the mother of Jesus, who is also herself a symbol—a symbol of Judaism, the people of God. The Jewish people, who received the law, who raised up the prophets and who have now produced that "prophet of whom Moses spoke." They have, however, had great trouble receiving what was their own great gift to the world. So John has Jesus on the cross commend his mother, Judaism, to the care of the "beloved disciple," the one who embodies the future fulfillment of the Jesus movement. You cannot forget your past, John is saying to the community of the followers of Jesus, who have been expelled from the synagogue. You must accept and cherish the womb that bore you. You must embrace Judaism, your mother, and incorporate her into your own life. The tension that John's community has experienced, their distress over their excommunication, their hostility toward the Jews, the chief priests and the Pharisees— all this must finally be overcome. "Woman, behold your son." Judaism, behold your child, the Jesus movement. Then he says to that anonymous symbolic disciple, "Behold your mother" (John 19:27). From that day forward, this gospel writer says, "the disciple took her to his own home."

The work of the Christ is almost over. Reconciliation of the deepest divisions in human life is being accomplished. The oneness of God is to be displayed in the oneness of the people of God. Death comes in response to the separation that is rooted in the struggle to survive, but life is born in the freedom to overcome one's fears and to give one's life away. John is not writing a literal narrative; he is creating a mystical portrait of oneness, of new life, of a transition into a new being, a new consciousness. In the narrative in which the mother is commended to the care of the "beloved disciple," the barriers separating the human family are portrayed as falling away. A literal reading of this text will never lead the reader into new life. The vision that comes through seeing this text as a portrayal of the depths of Jewish mysticism will. The conclusion to Jesus' life, his task and his ministry is almost here. The meaning of that life, however, will live on and on.

CHAPTER 26

It Is Finished: Water and Blood Flow Together

Two things alone remained for the author of the Fourth Gospel to complete before his story of the passion was finished. He wanted people within the Jewish tradition to see that Jesus was the fulfillment of their own sacred scriptures, and he also wanted to open the possibility of new life for *all* to share—Gentiles as well as Jews.

As an early step toward establishing the inclusiveness of new life in the Christ, Jesus had called his disciples into the reality of new life. His symbolic faithful one, the "beloved disciple," had passed the test: He had been present at the foot of the cross and he would later be present at the entrance to the tomb. He would understand and believe. He had now been charged to carry the one who symbolized Judaism, the mother of Christianity, with him into the future. The synagogue and the Temple leaders had purged themselves of the revisionist followers of Jesus, but the followers of Jesus were to see themselves as the next phase, the universal phase, of the Jewish story. It would be their responsibility not to reject or to destroy their mother, but to transcend her limits. The people of Israel had survived through a difficult history by erecting defensive barriers behind which they could

accomplish survival as a people. Their history had been replete
with chapters in which that survival was in doubt, sometimes
hanging by a thread. They had endured slavery in Egypt, years
of wandering in the wilderness, the endless struggle to secure a
small parcel of ground not much bigger than the state of New
Jersey as their home. They had known war and defeat, exile and
homelessness. They had cultivated symbols of difference in the
service of survival. Their customs were designed to keep them
apart from other nations. They would fit into no other people's
way of life because they refused to work every seventh day. They
would not share a meal with anyone who was not part of their
tribe, for they believed that they had a sacred obligation to eat a
special diet—"kosher," they called it—and to eat food prepared
only in a kosher kitchen. They went so far as to cut their Jewish
identity into the bodies of their males, in the practice of circumcision, so that intermarriage and the possible loss of identity for the
offspring of that union would be difficult to impossible.

All of these practices they grounded in what they called "the
law," found in their sacred scriptures. They read the Torah and
their other holy writings in worship every Sabbath to each succes-
sive generation. They ordered their common life with a series of
festivals and fast days that marked the great events of their national
existence and that were celebrated in set liturgical patterns both
inside and outside the synagogue. Those holy days had names that
every Jew knew: Passover, Shavuot, Rosh Hashanah, Yom Kippur,
Sukkoth (or Tabernacle) and Dedication (or Hanukkah), just to
reference the major ones. They believed that in their scriptures,
including both the Torah and their other writings, they could hear
the "word of God." This word, however, seemed to come to a halt
at the boundaries of their tribe and at the limits of their faith.

The author of the Fourth Gospel would never want to abandon
the faith of his fathers and mothers, but he did want to transcend

its limits, to transform its pillars of exclusion into a radical inclusiveness. He wanted to open the treasures of Jewish life for all to share as they journeyed into a new understanding of what it means to be human.

That is why John perceived Jesus as a new "word of God," a new Torah spoken to the world. That is why Jesus was portrayed in his gospel as a divine gift, one who came from God and was destined to complete the circle and thus return to God. That is why the task of searching the Jewish scriptures to find pointers therein that would illumine the Jewish people's understanding of Jesus had such a powerful attraction. That is why the writer of the Fourth Gospel told of the sign in Cana, where the Jewish water for purification was turned into an abundance of the wine of new life. That is why this writer identified the body of Jesus with the Temple. Both Jesus and the Temple were thought to be places in which the holy God was experienced as present, and both, if destroyed, could be raised to new life, even in just three days. That is why John identified the flesh of Jesus with heavenly manna on which the people could feed and in that act of eating make themselves one with God. That is why the boundaries that separated Jew from Samaritan and Jew from Gentile faded. That is why true worship could not be limited to either Mount Gerizim in Samaria or the Temple in Jerusalem, for the God who is spirit must be worshipped everywhere in spirit and in truth. That is why the crucifixion of Jesus, like the slaughter of the paschal lamb, could hurl back the ultimate human boundary of death and call all people into new life. That is why the "beloved disciple" had to embrace and take to himself the "mother of Jesus," the faith of the people of God, and to make her forever a part of what the Jesus movement would become. The "word of God" in Jesus was destined not to destroy Judaism but to open it to possibilities that were grander and more inclusive than a national life, based on the deep-seated human desire to survive, could ever be or even imagine being. That is also why the crucifixion of Jesus was his moment of glorification, for in that ultimate act of self-giving he had escaped that human drive to survive.

To John the cross was a portrait of one who could live without boundaries, of one who could love without limits and of one who, in the moment of dying, could exhibit the courage to be all that he was meant to be. Embracing yesterday's understanding of God, expanding it beyond all previous imaginings, transcending all religious limits and offering that new understanding to the world was the messianic role that John argues was lived out on the cross. The first gospel writer, Mark, had also glimpsed this truth, and that is why he put a Roman soldier at the foot of the cross and made him the interpreter of the meaning of Jesus. This soldier, by Jewish standards an unclean Gentile, saw in the person on the cross one who could lay his life down, give it away, even while loving those who violently took it from him. Looking upon that limp and dead body, the soldier said: *That* is who God is. His words are usually rendered: "Truly this man was the son of God," as if that soldier had just completed a course in Nicene Theology 101, but that came three hundred years later. This soldier was speaking of his own transformative experience. God is present in our willingness to give ourselves away, to escape the driving power of survival which wraps us in self-centeredness, for we judge all people, all actions and all things by the effect they have on our survival. The call of Jesus was to life—new life, abundant life. It was a call to enter the ultimate life of God. So at the cross John has the "beloved disciple" embrace Jesus' mother, the symbol of the past, incorporate her into himself, the symbol of the future, and transcend all her limits. The task of the faithful followers of Jesus was and is to seek to lead the world into a new universalism, a new understanding of what it means to be born into the life of the spirit.

John now wanted to complete his story by demonstrating that the sacred scriptures of the Jewish people pointed to and found their fulfillment in the life of this Jesus. It was a theme he had initiated early. To Nathaniel in chapter 1, Jesus had been introduced as the one of whom "Moses in the law and also the prophets wrote" (John 1:45), but when Nathaniel came to Jesus he was told: "You will see heaven open and the angels of God ascending and descending on the son of man" (John 1:51). These references, which echoed words from Deuteronomy (18:15) and Genesis (28:12), were designed to proclaim that the sacred writings of the Jews had found their fulfillment in Jesus. Jesus, John was arguing, did not come to create a new religion, but to transform their religion of the past by transcending its boundaries and removing its limits. Part of the work of the Holy Spirit was, therefore, to "open the scriptures," or to recall to people's memories the scriptures (John 2:22). When Jesus invited his audience by saying: "If anyone thirsts, let him [or her] come to me and drink" (John 7:37), it was, said this gospel writer, to understand the words that the prophet Isaiah had written hundreds of years before, in which living water was a synonym for the life of the spirit (Isa. 44:3, 55:1, 58:11).

Throughout John's gospel a debate is carried on as to the "origins of Jesus." The appeal in this debate over and over is to the Jewish scriptures (John 7:42 and John 10:35). The story of the traitor is said to be in fulfillment of the scriptures (John 13:18 referring to Ps. 41:9). Even the betrayal was to fulfill the scriptures (John 17:12). The abandonment by the disciples of Jesus when he was arrested was in fulfillment of the scriptures (John 16:32 referring to Zech. 13:7). The details around the crucifixion were in fulfillment of the scriptures (John 19:24 referring to Ps. 22:18).

With this being John's constant theme, it is not surprising that this gospel now closes its story of the cross with two actions which were not reported on in earlier writings, but which allow this author once more to show how Jesus incorporates the Jewish past and carries it with him into a universal future. After Jesus' directions to the "beloved disciple" and to his mother have set the stage, John has Jesus say only two further "words" before "he bowed his head and gave up his spirit" (John 19:30). Both of these "words" were designed to announce the fulfillment of the messianic role revealed in the scriptures that John believed had occurred in the life of Jesus.

The first word is "I thirst" (John 19:28). It is a startling reminder that Jesus is human and that his suffering is real. This is no "docetic"* act of pretending to be human. It is, however, all pre-programmed in the scriptures, for in response to this cry the soldiers put a sponge filled with vinegar on a hyssop branch and lift it to his mouth. No, that did not literally happen, but the word and response were designed to relate Jesus to a reference found in Psalm 69:21: "For my thirst they gave me vinegar to drink." This text could now be said to have found fulfillment in Jesus. Then Jesus uttered what John called his final cry: "It is finished" (John 19:30). It was not a cry of despair, but of triumph. It fulfills the promise articulated in the prayer of chapter 17: "I glorified thee on earth, having completed the work thou gavest me to do" (John 17:4). The new creation is now accomplished. A door has been opened into a new meaning of life, a new humanity, a new being. I have shown them the way to new life, says Jesus. I have revealed God's glory, the glory which calls us to live fully, to love wastefully and to be all that each of us can be. As we saw earlier, there is no atonement here; there is just expanded humanity—humanity

---

* The word "docetic" refers to an interpretation of Jesus that was dismissed as heresy in the early church. That interpretation, called Docetism, suggested that Jesus was not really human; he just appeared to be human. John counters that interpretation in such phrases as the invitation to "eat my flesh and drink my blood" and in this text, which makes real the human suffering that Jesus endured.

that enters into the life of God and shares in the eternity of God.

John is, however, not quite ready to close his story of the cross. He must emphasize once more that Jesus is the new paschal lamb, whose death, like the death of the original paschal lamb, will banish death itself. So John reminds us that the day of the crucifixion was the day of preparation for the Passover (John 19:31–37). Jesus is killed on the cross in John's gospel at the exact time that the lamb is slaughtered for the Passover feast. That lamb has to be a physically perfect specimen, for it represents the human yearning for perfection. The lamb, therefore, must have no broken bones, scratches or blemishes. So John tells us that the authorities come to Golgotha to hasten the deaths of the victims. The Sabbath would commence at sunset and no dead bodies on crosses are to be allowed to defile the Sabbath. To speed death the soldiers break the legs of the two victims crucified on each side of Jesus. Coming to Jesus, however, they find him already dead. No bones are therefore broken. The symbol of the lamb remains intact. This act also "fulfilled the scriptures," citing words that we can trace to Exodus 12:46, Numbers 9:12 and Psalm 34:20.

One additional word from a prophet remains to be employed in this interpretive process. John has a soldier hurl a spear into the side of Jesus, recalling words from the prophet Zechariah,* who wrote: "They looked upon him whom they pierced and they mourned for him as one mourns for an only son" (Zech. 12:10). Then John files one final symbol in his deeply symbolic, non-

---

* The correct reference here should be II Zechariah, for this book, like the book of Isaiah, is the work of more than one hand. Chapters 1–8 reflect a time in Jewish history at least a century prior to that which is reflected in chapters 9–14. It is chapters 9–14 that are regularly referred to by the authors of the gospels. This text in John is illustrative of that. There are scholars who believe that what we now call the book of Malachi is really III Zechariah, which at some point got separated. This, they suggest, accounts both for the continuity in themes and for the fact that Malachi is not the name of the author. Malachi is a Hebrew word which means "my messenger." The author is actually nameless, a voice crying in the wilderness.

literal work. From this spear wound, he says, there came forth "blood and water." This is a reference once more to the wedding feast in Cana, perhaps now impacted by the Christian Eucharist. The blood is the wine of the Eucharist. The water is the water of baptism. Jewish purification rites conducted with water are background to baptism. The wine of the banquet, which was to mark the arrival of the kingdom of God, is now the wine of the Eucharist in which the life of Jesus is believed, quite literally, to enter the life of the believer. We are the branches living on the life of the vine through which the divine life flows into each of us. Jesus opens the door to mystical oneness. His death is the ultimate revelation of life.

Now the time has come to remove the body for burial (John 19:38–42). Two people, we noted earlier, carry out the preparations: Joseph of Arimathea, a figure introduced in the synoptic gospels only at the time of the burial, and Nicodemus. Joseph is like Nicodemus, who came to Jesus only by night. Joseph, too, is impressed by Jesus, but not willing to be public about his discipleship "for fear of the Jews," who had banished the disciples from the synagogue. These two, nonetheless, are allowed to preside over his burial. Neither of them will appear in the stories of the resurrection. The burial is elaborate. A hundred pounds of myrrh and aloes, an extravagant amount for a burial, is used. The body is bound, like that of Lazarus, in linen cloths. It is placed into a new tomb in the midst of an unnamed garden. The meaning of this life is now enclosed by a tomb. The world waits. The meaning of life transformed is about to dawn.

PART V

Resurrection: Mystical Oneness Revealed

CHAPTER 27

Introducing John's Story of Easter

I f, as I have suggested, the author of the Fourth Gospel viewed the crucifixion as the moment of Jesus' glorification, how did he view the experience that came to be called "resurrection"? That is now our question, and the process required to probe the data we have available to us for an answer takes us not only into the heart of the Christian story, but also deeply into the faith crisis of our time in the twenty-first century.

If "resurrection" means resuscitation of a deceased body back into the physical world of time and space, it stretches credibility beyond the breaking point. Such an understanding would violate everything we modern people know about how the world operates. It would require not just one mighty miracle, for which some fundamentalists argue as they try to narrow the battlefield upon which literalism must fight, but it would also require hundreds of millions of tiny miracles. We would have to believe, for example, that time itself could be reversed. We would have to develop a definition of God that would fit into no frame of reference that human beings today either acknowledge or are able to understand. To reverse the death process in any literal and physiological sense would require the restarting of the heart, the reconnection of every artery, vein and capillary, the reversal of the inevitable decay process, the reconstitution of the cells of the brain, the restoration of the gastrointestinal processes, the reactivation of the larynx, the vocal cords and even the skeletal system. It would require that the deceased one, now resuscitated, would be able to fit into all previous relationships as if there had been no interruption. In Jesus' case, it would mean that feet pinned to a cross by spikes could walk as if no injury had occurred.

Some of these aspects are in fact hinted at and claimed in the later gospels as the resurrected Jesus is portrayed increasingly as a physical phenomenon. It is a fact that the later the descriptions of the resurrection, the more supernatural and miraculous are the details. In Luke's gospel the risen Jesus can walk, talk, eat, interpret scripture and even offer his flesh for examination. He can rise physically into the air of a three-tiered universe in order to return to the God who lives above the sky. That, however, is not the understanding of resurrection in the earlier Christian writings.

Paul, for example, argues for a transformation: "We shall all be changed, in a moment, in the twinkling of an eye" (I Cor. 15:51–52). Paul even talks about and tries to describe the transformative process. The dead shall be raised "imperishable," since "flesh and blood cannot inherit the kingdom of God" (I Cor. 15:50). That which is "mortal" must "put on immortality" (I Cor. 15:54). Paul tries to stretch his vocabulary, as people always do when they seek to move beyond the categories of time and space in which human life is lived, and so he speaks of a "spiritual body" (I Cor. 15:44). He then develops the analogy of a planted seed that must die before the new life of a plant can emerge out of it.

Paul is quite clear that God has raised Jesus to new life, but nowhere does that mean resuscitation back into the life of this world. Jesus was raised into the life of God and made universally available. He was not resuscitated to walk again the dark streets of Jerusalem or the dusty trails of Galilee. We noted earlier that Paul uses the passive, not the active, verb form to describe the resurrection. Jesus *was raised*; Jesus does not *rise* (see, for example, Rom. 4:24, 6:4, 6:9, 7:4, 8:11, 8:34, 10:9, 15:28). The action of resurrection belongs to God, not to Jesus.

Most top New Testament scholars do not believe that Paul is the actual author of the epistle we call Colossians, but there is general agreement among them that this epistle is Pauline in its character, probably penned by one who had been influenced by Paul. There is universal agreement, however, that the epistle to the Colossians was written long before Luke's gospel or the book of Acts, when the ascension of Jesus as a physical act entered the tradition. Yet Colossians says, "If, then, you have been raised with Christ, seek those things that are above, where Christ is seated at the right hand of God" (Col. 3:1). It is clear that Paul and his immediate disciples, who were the earliest writers in the New Testament, did not view the Easter experience as a physical resuscitation of a deceased body. It is also clear that Paul believed that Jesus had broken the power of death and that God had raised him to a new dimension of both life and being.

In the epistle to the Romans, about which no one doubts the authenticity of Pauline authorship, we find these words: "Christ, being raised from the dead, will never die again; death no longer has dominion over him. . . . The life he lives he lives to God" (Rom. 6:9–10). When Paul wrote that the raised Christ "will never die again," he was asserting the obvious. This was not the account of someone restored to physical life in this world. Bodies that have been resuscitated to this world must eventually die again. Paul was clearly talking about something other than a deceased body walking out of a grave in an act of supernatural restoration to life. Those Christians who insist that one must believe in the "physical bodily resurrection of Jesus" in order to be a Christian are profoundly uninformed about both the scriptures and the ways the world operates.

It is also important to notice that in the writings of Paul those whose eyes have been opened to see the raised Christ are enumerated (I Cor. 15:5–8). They are: Cephas (Peter), the twelve, five hundred brethren, James, the apostles and Paul. It is also important to note that no description of that experience on the part of any on this list is offered. Furthermore, we need to be aware that Paul never speaks anywhere of a Damascus road conversion experience, though that experience is often discussed in Christian circles today. He never mentions his supposed blindness, the carefully crafted conversation he was supposed to have had with Jesus during that conversion experience, or the role that Ananias played either in the restoration of his sight or in his baptism. Those things remained for Luke to relate to us some thirty years after Paul's death. So whatever it was that Paul "saw," it was not the physical Jesus. Even if the Damascus road experience was assumed to be literal history, the date of Paul's conversion is generally thought to be no earlier than one year and no later than six years after the crucifixion.

It is a profoundly important insight into the nature of the original Easter experience to recognize that in the writings of Mark, the first gospel written, there is no account of anyone seeing the resurrected Jesus. Mark tells us only of the women coming to the tomb at dawn on the first day of the week. What they see, he says, is only a "young man . . . dressed in a white robe" (Mark 16:5). This young man is not an angel. He will become an angel about a decade later when Matthew heightens the story and describes this young man as having the appearance of lightning, with his raiment as white as snow (Matt. 28:3). About a decade after Matthew, Luke will turn this messenger into *two* angels (Luke 24:4), who are in "dazzling apparel," as the story continues to grow.

The young man in a white robe in Mark directs the women to

inform Jesus' disciples that Jesus "has been raised" and that he is "going before you to Galilee" (Mark 16:7). The women do not see Jesus; he simply does not appear. Instead, Mark tells us, they "fled from the tomb trembling and astonished, and they said nothing to anyone, for they were afraid" (Mark 16:8). That is where Mark's gospel ends. So troubling an ending and so lacking in assurance were these original words of Mark that early Christian writers wrote new endings to Mark's gospel.* They could not believe that Mark meant to end his text in this enigmatic and unconvincing way. The fact is, however, that he did.

We see just how the story grows when we recognize that Matthew, with Mark as one of his major sources, changes the story in Mark to provide these women with an appearance of Jesus while they were still in the garden on that first Easter morning. Then, to cover all his bases, Matthew proceeds to give his readers the details of the Galilean appearance story to which Mark's messenger had only alluded. The appearance took place on top of a mountain, he says, and there "the disciples worshipped him" (Matt. 28:16, 17). The implication in this latter story is that Jesus appeared to the disciples not in the flesh, but out of God, or out of heaven. He had already been transformed and he was clothed with the authority of "the son of man." In this story the raised Jesus spoke for the first time and gave the great commission: "Go . . . make disciples of all nations, baptize, for 'I am with you always to the close of the age'" (Matt. 28:20). Note well that, as in Mark, none of the details of this second, Matthean story of the resurrection indicate a physically resuscitated body.

Luke comes next in the historical order of gospel writing. He is the primary one who transforms the resurrected Jesus into a very corporeal being, one who was restored to a physical, earthly

---

* These endings still appear in the King James Version of the Bible, but later, more scholarly versions, such as the RSV and the NRSV, have removed them to footnotes.

life that ultimately, since he cannot die again, must somehow be extricated from this world. To accomplish that, Luke develops the story of the ascension (Luke 24:50–52 and Acts 1). I suppose literalizing tendencies were inevitable as decades passed after the crucifixion, but ultimate truth is never well served by literal words developed by limited human minds. The author of the Fourth Gospel was surely aware of that fact, and so when he comes, in the latter years of the tenth decade to relate the Easter story, he makes that very clear. His passion against literalism, which we have noted over and over, is not going to be compromised by his telling of the meaning of Easter. He will, however, walk a fine line in this narrative.

We turn to the twentieth and final chapter of John's gospel (assuming, as most scholars do, that the epilogue of John 21 was not part of the original text). Here in John 20 we discover four distinct resurrection stories. They have been clumsily linked in order to be read as a continuous narrative, probably to serve a liturgical purpose in corporate worship.* A closer reading of this chapter will, however, reveal that these four resurrection stories were originally separate parts of the tradition.

The opening story is that of a woman alone at the tomb. Her name is Mary Magdalene. Her story is interrupted by the narrative of Peter and the "disciple whom Jesus loved" coming to the tomb, but when that story is removed, the account of Magdalene at the tomb has a wholeness and an integrity which cry out that the text originally stood alone. So John's first resurrection vignette is chapter 20, verses 1 and 11–18. It develops, as we shall see later, a particular theme; that is, it looks at the resurrection

---

* Early in Christian history, an octave of eight days was placed around major liturgical celebrations like Easter. An octave would include two Sundays and would require two resurrection narratives. Matthew and Luke both have two Easter stories. John has four episodes, but they can be read as two and two. I suspect that that is how all of these accounts developed.

through a special lens. I will view this Magdalene story as if it were an uninterrupted whole, making it the first of John's four resurrection vignettes.

The second story (John 20:2–10) reveals once more the particular dynamic between Peter and the one John calls the "beloved disciple." It is filled with symbols, but it too reveals themes that have already been introduced in the body of this gospel. It also looks at the resurrection through a very different understanding. This story also appears originally to have stood alone. This becomes clear when we get to the third story, which involves the other disciples, and we discover that they are totally unaware of this previous experience, in which two of their number have already been to the tomb. That is another part of the data that convinces most Johannine scholars that these resurrection stories in John 20 were originally quite separate and quite distinct, with each designed to look at Easter from a quite different perspective.

The third Johannine resurrection story (John 20:19–25) is set at evening on the day of the resurrection, probably at the time of the evening meal, when the disciples have already secured the house for the night. Here Jesus is said to have appeared despite the locked doors and closed windows, so the implication is of non-physicality. He offers them his peace, described earlier as different from what they have known of peace before. It is "not as the world gives" (John 14:27), Jesus says, and then he breathes on them the gift of the spirit. The phrase "a little while" that we noted earlier in its frequent repetition in the Farewell Discourses now comes back into play and becomes understandable. It is important to note, however, that there is no hint in this particular narrative that anyone is missing, which means that the fourth and final resurrection story in this gospel—which mentions Thomas' absence—was originally quite independent of this third one.

When that final story is related (John 20:26–31), the author seeks to hook these last two narratives together with the words "eight days later." The content of this fourth story is the tale of Thomas' doubt. If the four Johannine resurrection stories are treated independently, as I plan to do, we will see old Johannine themes repeated and new Johannine insights into the meaning of Jesus revealed.

John will, in three of them, either display characters that he has created himself through whom he will relate his message, or take characters known to him out of the tradition and develop them in new and mythological ways in order to carry his meaning. In the first narrative the primary character is one called Mary Magdalene. Only in John's gospel does Magdalene assume any aspect or sense of a personality or the flesh-and-blood content of a living character.

In the second episode John combines the familiar character named Peter with his own mythological creation known as "the disciple whom Jesus loved" in order to reveal the struggle the early disciples endured, before they broke through their darkness and entered into the light, before they experienced the new birth of the spirit about which Jesus spoke in the narrative about Nicodemus (John 3).

In the third episode the characters are deemphasized, but the story is built around a final sign that will in some sense hark back to and perhaps complete the Book of Signs. This sign is the one that separates the old covenant from the new one, light from darkness, life from death and the new creation from the old. It is a fitting culmination for this gospel.

The final episode stars a little-known one of the twelve named Thomas, and it plays on the theme of what faith means, what seeing is all about and how the resurrected life does not depend on physical signs.

John then concludes his gospel using the same methods he has used to build his account. We will walk through these stories carefully and embrace anew the dimensions of life that John has suggested Jesus came to convey. Resurrection is not about physical resuscitation. John will make that clear. It is about entering and participating in the "new being." It is about the transformative power that is found in Jesus, that which issues in new dimensions of what it means to be human. We turn now to these four narratives that will serve to bring our study of this gospel to its original conclusion.

CHAPTER 28

Magdalene: Do Not Cling to What Is, Journey into What Can Be

I t was a strange way to begin the story of the resurrection. Mary Magdalene had been an obscure character in John's gospel thus far, having been introduced into his text only in the previous chapter as one standing at the foot of the cross. No one reading this gospel alone had ever heard of her before. She was first mentioned in the synoptic tradition in the eighth decade of the Common Era when Mark identified her as one of those standing by looking at the cross "from afar" (Mark 15:40). Matthew, writing a decade after Mark, quotes Mark exactly, and adds nothing further to her biography. Luke, however, some ten or so years after Matthew, added a strange note, introducing her much earlier in his narrative as a woman out of whom Jesus had cast seven demons (Luke 8:2). He made no effort to explain what that reference was all about. In the first century, demons were the explanation for almost any sickness, physical or mental. This note, supported by no other biblical source, may have been the first step in the demonization of Magdalene that ultimately resulted in her designation as a prostitute.

That tradition entered Christian mythology with the support of popes like Gregory the Great, who made official the identification of Magdalene with the "woman of the street" who, in Luke alone (Luke 7:36–43), washes Jesus' feet with her tears and dries them with her hair, then kisses them before finally anointing them. It is undoubtedly a deliberately sensuous scene. There is absolutely no hint, however, in that Lucan story that this woman was identified in the author's mind with Mary Magdalene. Both Mark and Matthew related the story of Jesus' feet being anointed by a woman prior to his death (Mark 14:3–9, Matt. 26:6–13), but in both gospels she is not only unnamed, but her action is applauded and interpreted as a gesture of love. In neither source is she "a sinful woman." Indeed in both gospels it is said of her that "she has done a beautiful thing" (Mark 14:6, Matt. 26:12), and both add the note: "Wherever the gospel is preached in the entire world, what she has done will be told in memory of her" (Mark 14:9, Matt. 26:13).

It is worth noting that the Fourth Gospel gives us a quite different version of the story of the feet of Jesus being washed in a public place by a woman (John 12:1–8) and he names the woman. She is not Mary Magdalene, but Mary, the sister of Martha, and John has this event occur in their home in Bethany with Lazarus, their newly revived brother, present. Furthermore, this act is performed in the company of Jesus' disciples. Magdalene has not yet been mentioned in John's story, unless John intends for us to believe that Mary, the sister of Martha, and Mary Magdalene are one and the same, an idea that opens up some possibilities that, while interesting, are beyond the scope of this book.* The only other thing we learn from searching the earlier synoptic gospels is that when Magdalene does make her entrance into their story at the

---

* I made that suggestion and enumerated the reasons that led me to that conclusion in an earlier book entitled *Born of a Woman*. See bibliography for details.

crucifixion, she is identified first as one of the women who in Galilee provided for Jesus "out of their means" (Luke 8:3) and then as one of the women who followed Jesus all the way from Galilee to Jerusalem (Mark 15:41, Matt. 27:55). There is, however, in these meager references nothing that would lead us to believe that this woman would play a major role in the resurrection drama.

As I have sought to demonstrate in this book again and again, John has a way, and I believe it is a brilliant way, of creating and even re-creating characters to populate his story. Mary Magdalene is just one more in a long line of these literary creations. A bit player in the synoptic gospels, she is now cast by John in a major, even a starring role in his narrative. He fashions Mary Magdalene in such a way as to remind his readers of the Samaritan woman by the well. Both of them become evangelists to whom the message of Jesus is entrusted. The Samaritan woman goes and speaks to the people of her village, while Magdalene bears the message of the empty tomb to Peter and the disciples.

John opens his final chapter by portraying this woman named Magdalene at the tomb of Jesus. She is alone and she is weeping. The stone covering the opening to the tomb has been removed. This prompts an interruption in the story, which is the device that this gospel writer uses to enable Magdalene to convey the message of the tomb's emptiness to Peter and the "beloved disciple." For John to reset his story after this interruption, she is made to stare into the tomb a second time.

Before attempting to understand just what the author of this gospel is seeking to communicate with his development of this character, let me probe for a moment the meaning of the word "Magdalene." Mary is always referred to as Mary Magdalene, as if Magdalene were part of her name. Luke, however, suggests that Magdalene was not her name, but something she was called (Luke 8:2). There has been much speculation throughout history that Magdalene referred to her place of origin, a village that was presumably called Magdala. Such a village has even been located on the Sea of Galilee. There is, however, no definitive evidence from the time of Jesus that there was a village by this name then. Scholars have suggested that it might have been called by another name earlier and thus its place of existence was lost to history, but that would not explain why, if it had a different name, the title "Magdalene" was attached to this Mary as part of her identification. There is such a village of Magdala today, but it appears to have been created by the biblical story, rather than to have been reflected in the biblical story. (It certainly must help the tourist trade to be able to show off the village of Magdala from which Mary Magdalene supposedly hailed!) The place-name explanation, however, violates lots of other rules. We have noted earlier that people in the first century knew how to say "Jesus of Nazareth" and "Paul of Tarsus" or even "Peter of Bethsaida," yet nowhere in the biblical text is the phrase "Mary of Magdala" used. Magdalene appears rather to be an indelible piece of identification. Simon is nicknamed "the Rock" and is then called by this defining new nickname, Peter, but Magdalene never becomes Mary's name; it is rather an identifying appendage.

Magdalene, we also need to note, is one of the only two titles in the New Testament that appear to serve as a mark of personal identification. The other one is "Iscariot." We have already stated the consensus belief that Iscariot is derived from the word *sicarius,* which means political assassin; that is, Iscariot is attached to Judas as a description of the role he played in the story of Jesus. Could the word "Magdalene" in a similar fashion have been attached to Mary to give us an insight into the role she played in the story of Jesus? It might.

The Hebrew word *migdal* has the same consonants that are found in Magdalene (*m, g, d, l*) and in the correct order (the *n* of

Magdalene then added to create the new form of the word). Given that the Hebrew language has no vowels, only vowel points, a word having the same consonants might offer a significant clue into its meaning. The word *migdal* is used twice in the Hebrew scriptures—once in Genesis (35:21) and once in Micah (4:8)—and in both cases it is generally translated "tower." A *migdal* is a tall, recognizable structure of some significance designed to give the shepherd a better view of the flocks. It is not too large a stretch, I believe, to suggest that Mary Magdalene meant the "tall," "large" or "great" Mary, a title that revealed her significance in the life of the followers of Jesus. She is certainly portrayed this way in early Christian history, until her female presence in close association with Jesus bothered church leaders so deeply that they trashed her reputation, calling her a prostitute, while replacing her in the Christian story with a woman who was a "virgin," the pinnacle of sexual purity. If both of these women were named Mary and if the one called Magdalene was originally thought of as the "great" Mary, we can speculate—and that is all we can do—about the nature of her relationship with Jesus. Was she his wife? This kind of speculation has raged throughout Christian history, but mostly underground. Even in the rock opera *Jesus Christ Superstar,* Magdalene sings to Jesus, "I don't know how to love him."*

The Fourth Gospel has certainly fed that speculation, primarily because it is the only gospel where Magdalene's character is portrayed in any depth, and all of this development is found in this Johannine story of the resurrection. Why, we are led to wonder and to ask, is Magdalene pictured in this gospel as the chief mourner, indeed the sole mourner, at the tomb of Jesus? Why does she demand of the one she thinks is the gardener the right to claim the body of Jesus and to take it away? Such a role in

---

* The rock opera *Jesus Christ Superstar,* written by Andrew Lloyd Webber and Tim Rice in 1973, is still playing in various venues around the country.

Jewish society was reserved for the nearest of kin and was totally beyond the scope of propriety for a woman who was not the wife. Why does John have Magdalene address Jesus with the intimate term "Rabboni"? That would be the name a devoted pupil might use for a revered teacher, or the name the wife of a rabbi would use to address her deeply respected husband. I raise these issues to our consciousness, not to build a case for Jesus and Mary Magdalene to be viewed as husband and wife,* but simply, for our purposes in this book, to note that John portrays Magdalene as a very close associate, perhaps even as the primary female figure in the Jesus movement. His mother in this gospel, we noted previously, is actually never called by the name Mary, and she is, I have suggested, a symbol of Judaism, the mother of the Christian movement. So we are led to ask: Is this character, who is called Mary and who is also referred to as Magdalene, also a symbol of an insight, first into the meaning of Jesus and second into the meaning of Jesus' resurrection? In reading this gospel, which I have described as deeply Jewish and significantly mystical, can we entertain vastly new possibilities as to what John was trying to communicate through this character?

Take a close look first at the story. Jesus has been crucified. He is dead. He has been buried. Magdalene goes to his tomb to mourn her loss. That tomb symbolically holds her fragmented dreams of those of Jesus' followers. That tomb has served to place limits on Jesus' meaning. It stands as an ultimate barrier against

---

* Once again this is a subject I addressed in *Born of a Woman* (chapter 13), which is listed in the bibliography. I tackled this topic as a polemic against the way women have been historically treated in the Christian church. The primary negativity against the possibility that Jesus was married came originally from those who felt that the intimate association of Jesus with a woman as his wife might compromise his claim to be divine, since women were regarded as somehow "unclean" and as pollutants of holy men. This was part of the defense of celibacy as a mandatory requirement of priesthood. I am totally opposed to that mentality, both philosophically and experientially. The only chance I have to be whole, and thus "a holy man," is that I live inside the incredible and life-giving love of my wonderful wife.

all of the things for which he stood. It means that his love was finite, his forgiveness was finite, his life was finite. It is now over. Magdalene mulls over all of these things. When she arrives at the tomb it is "early" and "still dark" (John 20:1). She finds the tomb open. The stone has been removed from its entrance. A crack has appeared in the finality of finitude. Her mystical insight, however, has not yet developed. This empty tomb means to her only that the sanctity of the tomb has been violated, perhaps even that the grave has been robbed. That is what she was said to have reported to the disciples. Her despair heightens. Next, when she looks again into the tomb, she stares into the face of death, and this time she sees mystical figures. John describes them as two angels sitting at the head and foot of where the body of Jesus was supposed to lie. These mystical figures inquire as to the meaning of her tears. She tells them of her loss. Jesus is dead, she says; now his body is missing. He was, she still believes, bound by that body. She can thus be near to him only by being near to his physical remains.

John then says that Magdalene turns and sees Jesus standing there, but she does not recognize him. She thinks he is the gardener. He speaks, asking the same question that the angels asked: "Woman, why are you weeping?" Her previous answer to the angels is assumed, but she adds a new and revealing dimension in her relationship to this Jesus by saying: "Sir, if you have carried him away, tell me where you have laid him and I will take him away" (John 20:15). I want to be near the receptacle that contains all that remains of him, she says. The drama is then heightened as Mary hears her name being spoken. Death has not separated her from the person through whom she has been called to be. Her new identity, her new being, is still intact. Death has not broken it or torn it from her. She is known and loved; she has entered a new mystical awareness. She responds to the sound of her name by using a title of great affection: "Rabboni." She moves to be near him. No, says the risen and mystical Jesus. No, "do not cling to me. I have not yet ascended to the Father, . . . but I am ascending" (John 20:17). The present participle of the verb is used: "am ascending." It is as if the text were saying, I am in the process of being transformed; I am escaping all human limits to enter into that which is universal, unending and ultimate. Magdalene then goes to the disciples with this message: "I have seen the Lord" (John 20:18).

This is the first way that the author of the Fourth Gospel seeks to convey the meaning of resurrection. For him it has nothing to do with physicality. It has nothing to do with seeing the resuscitated body of Jesus with the sight of physical eyes. It has rather to do with recognizing that no tomb could hold the meaning present in the life of Jesus, just as no barrier could stand between him and those who had found new life in him.

The one who has stepped into this new dimension of life is now related to Jesus in the same way that a branch is related to a vine. No, I do not think that Mary saw angels at the head and foot of where the body was supposed to have been laid in the tomb. I do not believe she saw Jesus physically and mistook him for the gardener. I do not believe that she sought to cling to his actual body, only to be told that this was not possible. Finally, I do not believe that in any literal way Jesus was in the process of "ascending" to the God he had so regularly called "the Father."

John is painting an interior experience in external colors using objective words. Mary Magdalene is portrayed as the first witness of the resurrection. She is the first one to see that Jesus' glorification was revealed in his ability to give his life and his love away. She is the first to see that in his freedom to step beyond the human drive to survive, he reveals a new dimension of life and consciousness. This was his revelation. Beyond the defensive barriers of our survival-driven humanity there is a new dimension of life waiting to be entered. In this new dimension a mystical oneness with God and all that is can be experienced. The life I live, says Jesus in the portrait John has painted, is the life of God. The love I share is the love of God. The being I reveal is the being of God. I have entered a new humanity; I have discovered a doorway into a new being. I no longer have a need to cling either to the past or to the symbols of the reality that once was all I knew existed. I now know who I am. I know who God is. I step into that experience and claim it for my own.

That is what the story of Mary Magdalene reveals under the skillful pen of this gifted author and gospel writer. He told us much earlier, we recall, that this book is not intended to be read literally. It is the work of a Jewish mystic. One is to read it by listening to the experience that it is seeking to open, so that the reader can enter that experience and live into it. Mary Magdalene now understands the experience and so she asserts: "I have seen the Lord," but what she has also seen is the meaning of life. She steps into that life and claims it for her own. That is how Easter always dawns.

CHAPTER 29

Peter and the Beloved Disciple: Resurrection Dawns Without a Body

The second resurrection episode in the Fourth Gospel couples two people whom we have met before in John's drama, but he now casts them in an unusual way. He interrupts the story of Mary Magdalene, using her as his segue to these two disciples (perhaps believing that the male disciples must be given priority). Mary reports to them the emptiness of the tomb, and Peter and the "beloved disciple" immediately run to investigate, taking over the narrative. Magdalene now moves offstage, where she remains until this vignette is complete.

Recall briefly our earlier study of both of these Johannine characters. Peter is the disciple in whom an internal battle rages. He ultimately will not be like Judas and choose darkness, but choosing light will come only after an intense struggle. In the pages of this gospel, we have watched this struggle again and again. Now Peter is going to be the one who will examine the empty tomb, but who characteristically will not understand its meaning.

In this resurrection episode Peter is accompanied by one whom we have previously suggested is surely not a person of history, but a literary symbol of John's own creation. This unnamed character, identified only as "the disciple whom Jesus loved," was not introduced until the Last Supper, and there it was said of him that he was the closest disciple to Jesus and even the one through whom Peter had to go to get to Jesus. He is portrayed as the ideal disciple, one who, in contrast to Peter, always understands immediately. The author of the Fourth Gospel has placed these two in tandem before and, as he tells the story of the resurrection, does so again. When they receive Mary's message that the tomb has been opened, they run to see for themselves.

The assumption is that both know where the tomb is and that the distance is not great. The "beloved disciple" arrives first. He will always precede Peter. At the entrance to the tomb, however, he waits, stooping down only to peer in. There he sees the burial cloths on the ground, no longer wrapped around a deceased body. John's contrast is designed to be clear. This is not another "raising of Lazarus from the dead" story. Lazarus was a resuscitated body restored physically to the life of this world. He emerged from his tomb still bound in grave cloths. He had to be unbound and set free. Jesus, on the other hand, has clearly transcended life's ultimate limit. He has already been transformed, raised to a new status and a new dimension of life. There will be no body on display. This is a new reality being introduced; something very different is forcing its way into their consciousness. The "beloved disciple," who always sees beyond what Peter is able to see, does not rush into the tomb or into this mystery.

Then Peter arrives at the tomb and, following his normal behavior pattern, he barges in. There he sees exactly the same things that the "beloved disciple" has seen. The burial cloths have been laid aside and the cloth that covered Jesus' face has been neatly rolled up in a place by itself. That is all the evidence that was available to either of them, but it is said of the "beloved disciple" that "he believed" (John 20:7).

John concludes this episode, in which only one of the two witnesses is said to believe, by saying that "as yet they did not understand the scripture that he must rise from the dead" (John 20:10). The two disciples return to their homes and neither is ever referred to again in this gospel except in the later-appended epilogue.

Please note that in this Easter episode no one is said to have seen the resurrected Jesus. The only thing the witnesses saw was an empty tomb. They saw human limits that could not contain Jesus. There was no body, deceased or resurrected. There was only the impact of his life, an impact that death could not remove. That appeared to be enough for the ideal disciple, the "disciple whom Jesus loved," but it was not enough for Peter. With that detail, John's first story in which members of the twelve confront the meaning of resurrection comes to an end.

For now simply feel the contrast between Peter and the "beloved disciple." The former struggles; the latter believes. For Peter Easter dawns as an experience of a rising and unresolved tension, a conflict between a human yearning and a lived reality; it is an experience of a struggle to believe, of an attempt, usually unsuccessful, to see meaning beyond the limits inside which life seems to be bound. There are no apparitions that appear in this episode to move Peter along. There are no revelations designed to give birth to or even to confirm his struggling faith. All Peter sees is a grave that cannot hold Jesus, grave cloths that cannot bind him. That was enough for the "beloved disciple." Peter was, however, a harder case. Resurrection is not easy—not for him and not for us. Its truth dawns slowly. Death as the doorway to life does not seem apparent. Yet that is the way John suggests that the meaning of Easter broke into human awareness among those who came to be known as the twelve.

Perhaps John is trying to say to us that the resurrection we seek is not so much that of Jesus as it is of ourselves. That makes sense if we remember that this gospel is the work of a Jewish mystic, for no one should ever try to literalize the work of a mystic.

CHAPTER 30

Pentecost: The Second Coming of Jesus—It Was "A Little While"

I t is fascinating to watch the ultimate or definitive author of the Fourth Gospel, one whom I have described as a Palestinian Jew, who has been attracted to the merkabah mysticism tradition of the Jews, address the idea and substance of resurrection. Thus far he has had the risen Jesus appear to the eyes of Mary Magdalene, who at first mistakes him for another and then is told that she cannot cling to him because he is "ascending to the Father." Clearly this vision was not designed to convey a physical resuscitation.

Then, in the second episode, this author portrays two disciples, Peter and the "disciple whom Jesus loved." We note that in this episode there is still no body and no appearance of the risen Christ. In this narrative Peter continues to wrestle, but the "beloved disciple" believes, and his believing enables him to cross the boundary into new life.

Because the author of this gospel was Jewish, he knew the Jewish scriptures, which related narratives of Jewish heroes so beloved by God that they had passed from life into the oneness of God without enduring the pain and decay of death. Because he was a mystic, this idea of finding life in the oneness of God would also have had appeal to him. If the life of the vine flowed through the branches, then the oneness of life itself was held in common. As the Father loved the son, so the son loved those who had been given to him; and as they abided in that love, they passed from death to life. Our author now intends to tell the story of Jesus' triumph over death in a manner consistent with this Jewish understanding.

The first person in the Jewish scriptures to whom victory over death was attributed is Enoch, the father of Methuselah. His story is told in a brief paragraph in the book of Genesis that culminates with this summary: "Enoch walked with God and he was not, for God took him" (Genesis 5:21–24). In Jewish mythology, Enoch was said to have written a book describing the wonders of life in the presence of God, a book that bears his name.*

The second person whose death was treated with great mystery in the Jewish scriptures is Moses, the hero of the exodus event and the "giver of the law." The death of Moses is related in the last chapter of the book of Deuteronomy (34:1–8). In this narrative we are told that Moses is alone with God. God takes Moses from the plains of Moab to "the top of Mount Pisgah, which is opposite Jericho" (Deut. 34:1). There Moses is allowed to view all of the "promised land," the stretch that would someday include both the Northern Kingdom and the nation of Judah, as well as the area from the Negev Desert to the Mediterranean Sea. Moses was to be able to *see* the Jewish homeland, but not to enter it. This failure to gain entrance was his punishment for "putting

---

* The book of Enoch is an apocryphal text in the Ethiopic Bible that dates somewhere between the third century BCE and the first century CE. Enoch was not included in the official books of the Apocrypha but was quite influential in early Christian history. See bibliography for details.

God to the test" in the episode described as occurring at "the waters of Meribah" (Exod. 17:1–7). It was in this setting, we are told, that Moses died. Since God alone was present to witness this death, God alone had to be responsible for burying him. God did so, says our text, in a grave that "no man knows . . . to this day" (Deut. 34:6). Moses was described in this text as being 120 years of age when he died, and despite that number of years "his eye was not dim, nor his natural force abated" (Deut. 34:7). In other words, even at Moses' advanced age, he was so vital and so alive that he needed neither eyeglasses nor Viagra! In no time, however, this mysterious death and burial were transformed into a tradition in which God took him at his death, like Enoch, into the life of God that was eternal and timeless.

The third Jewish story in which someone is allowed to escape death is found in a cycle of stories about Elijah, who has been called the "father of the prophetic movement." The story of his victory over death is told in II Kings (2:1–12). Here Elijah with his chosen heir, Elisha, journeys out into the wilderness beyond the Jordan River. It is clear in the text that Elijah has come to the end of his days and that Elisha will be his successor. Along this journey the sons of the prophets say to Elisha, "The Lord will take your master from over you," to which Elisha responds, "Yes, I know it." Elisha again and again refuses to abandon Elijah, his master. He will go to the very end, quite reminiscent of the way John's gospel says the "beloved disciple" will do. They navigate the Jordan River by splitting its waters in Moses-like fashion so that they can walk across it on dry land. Before Elijah departs this life, Elisha makes a final request for "a double portion of your spirit." The request is to be granted, he is told, only if Elisha sees Elijah being taken from him. Then the story says a chariot of fire drawn by horses of fire separates these two figures and a whirlwind propels Elijah and his fiery chariot into the presence of God.

Elisha sees this happen and so a double portion of Elijah's spirit is bequeathed to him.

These Jewish hero stories, at least those regarding Moses and Elijah, were certainly familiar to the readers of the synoptic tradition, but they are not found in the Fourth Gospel. In the accounts found in the synoptic gospels of Jesus being transfigured on top of a mountain by the numinous light of God (Mark 9:1–9, Matt. 17:1–8, Luke 9:28–36), it is Moses and Elijah who appear out of heaven to talk with Jesus, having preceded him into the life of God. When Luke tells the story of Jesus' ascension (Acts 1:6–11), he clearly builds his narrative on the story of Elijah's ascension.* So I believe it is fair to assume that the Jewish author of the Fourth Gospel, who so clearly had a mystical bent, viewed what came to be called resurrection after the analogy of these Jewish traditions. To understand resurrection as the resuscitation of a deceased body back into the life of the world would have been quite foreign to him. Those physical concepts indeed appealed very little to John, for if he admitted the miraculous at all, it was as a sign that pointed beyond itself to that which eyes could not finally see and words could not finally express. Resurrection was for him an experience whose reality could not be questioned, and he approached it in a spirit of expectancy and wonder.

A second fallacy into which the author of this gospel believed the Christian tradition had fallen was the anticipation of what came to be called the "second coming" of Jesus. This idea grew in early Christian thought because the death and resurrection of Jesus had not ushered in the kingdom of God as his followers had anticipated it would. Indeed the credibility of the Easter claim depended on a

---

* I developed this theme of the deep dependency of the synoptic writers Mark, Matthew and Luke on the content, themes and liturgical use of the Hebrew scriptures in my book *Liberating the Gospels: Reading the Bible with Jewish Eyes*. It is my favorite of all the books I have written. See bibliography for details.

"second coming," namely the return of Jesus from heaven to inaugurate that kingdom and to bring human history to a close. Jesus'
risen life was regarded merely as the "first fruits" of the kingdom
(the down payment if you will), a phrase that Paul used with some
regularity (Rom. 8:23, 11:16; I Cor. 15:20, 23) and that also appears
in the epistle of James (1:18) and in the book of Revelation (14:4).
The early Christians developed a prayer around this theme that
was used so frequently and so regularly that it came to be known
as "the Lord's Prayer," though Jesus himself neither uttered it nor
commanded it to be recited. It is rather a prayer for the kingdom of
God to come, since it had not dawned with the death and resurrection of Jesus. The first epistle to the Thessalonians, believed by most
scholars to be Paul's earliest writing, also addresses the delay of the
coming of the kingdom. Some members of the Thessalonian community had died and the return of Jesus, which had been expected
in their lifetime, had still not happened. Disillusionment was setting
in and Paul had to respond to their concerns (I Thess. 4:13–18).

If the delay in the return of Jesus was a problem in the early
50s when Paul was alive and writing, how much more intense
would that concern have become by the turn of the first century
when John's gospel was completed. The contemporaries of Jesus
were no more, unless any had managed to live to be one hundred,
an age that was beyond longevity expectations in the first century. Was the "second coming" that had been built so deeply into
Christian expectations simply a mistake? Or had the Jesus story
been rather significantly misunderstood? That was the dilemma
for Christians at the time John was writing. If the Jesus story had
been misunderstood, how could John reinterpret resurrection so
as to correct the earlier impression?

John, I believe, lays the groundwork for this reinterpretation
in the Lazarus story (John 11). There we are told that Mary and
Martha sent for Jesus because they were facing the possibility of

the death of their brother before Jesus was expected to arrive. Jesus, however, rather than hastening to them, delayed his return. He stayed, says the text, "two days in the place where he was" (John 11:6). Only when Lazarus had died did Jesus return. John has Jesus assert that his delay was orchestrated so that "God could be glorified" (John 11:4). Jesus tells the disciples, "Lazarus has fallen asleep, but I go to awaken him" (John 11:11). The literal-minded disciples say, "If Lazarus has fallen asleep, he will recover" (John 11:12). Then Jesus says quite bluntly, "Lazarus is dead," and adds an enigmatic note: "I am glad I was not there so that you might believe" (John 11:15). Only then does the Lazarus story unfold, culminating in his return to life.

When we bring the previously mentioned background from the Jewish scriptures—the tradition of faith heroes escaping death— and add to it the insights of the Jewish mystical tradition, we have the context in which to move from Lazarus to the third resurrection narrative, where John has Jesus appear to the gathered disciples (John 20:19–25). The setting is the evening of the first day of the week, the same day that Mary Magdalene learned she could not cling to the physical presence of Jesus and the same day that Peter and the "beloved disciple" confronted the reality that the grave could not contain Jesus nor could the grave cloths bind him. Yet in this third episode with the gathered disciples, nothing from either of the two earlier resurrection episodes appears to have been communicated to the followers. John's four resurrection stories seem unrelated, as we saw earlier, with each communicating to us a distinct aspect of the resurrection. There is also no hint in this third narrative that one of the disciples, Thomas, is not present. That note is introduced only in the fourth story to serve a purpose we will come to shortly.

In this third episode, the Jesus who appears is clearly not physical. How do we know? John tells us that he entered a room to which the doors were locked "for fear of the Jews." Neither the appearance to Magdalene, however it is or was understood, nor the belief that had been born in the "beloved disciple" at the empty tomb appears to have made an impact on any member of the disciple band. In this episode, Jesus simply appears mysteriously in their midst, not bothering to open the locked doors. First he pronounces peace: "Peace be upon you" (John 20:19). It is the peace of the one who has overcome the world. John then removes all doubt that what they are seeing is the one who was crucified. Jesus shows them his hands bearing the print of the nails and his side which, as we noted earlier only John says, was pierced by a spear to fulfill the word of Zechariah. Then Jesus commissions them: "As the father has sent me, even so I send you" (John 20:21). This resurrection experience is not designed to convince the disciples that Jesus has been raised; it is intended to convince them that they have a responsibility to fulfill: They are the bearers of the resurrected life that must be shared with the world.

Having commissioned the disciples, we are told, Jesus "breathed on them" and said: "Receive the Holy Spirit." It was Pentecost, as this author had come to understand it. The community was to be the source of life. Its members had the power to bind the people or to unbind the people. They could offer life in all of its fullness, but those who were still hiding in their darkness—that is, those who still were hiding behind their defensive barriers—would never be able to receive that life. Our survival instinct must be separated from our being and then overcome before we can enter the oneness of God and give our lives away in love to others. Our survival needs represent the final boundary on our limitless humanity; escaping that boundary is what it means to be "born of the spirit."

The second coming of Jesus, as John saw it, was not something that would arrive in time, whether a short time or a long time. It would not come in space either, for that is an external place that can be measured. The second coming is the birth of all those who choose the light and enter into the mystical source of oneness with God. It is a step beyond survival into the experience of the spiritual freedom that issues in eternal life. God had, according to the ancient creation story of the Hebrew people, initiated human life by breathing into Adam the breath of life. So now Jesus, understood by John to be the human life in which the will of God was lived out and through whom the creating word of God was spoken, would breathe on the disciples to call them into the new dimension of life he came to bring. It was the new creation. To be "born of the spirit" was to be born into the meaning and oneness of God. It was an inner experience, not an outer one. It was to enter in a new way what it means to be human.

The author of the Fourth Gospel had been preparing his readers to understand this through his entire gospel. That is why in the prologue he has John the baptizer bear witness that he saw the spirit descend on Jesus and remain there. In the Hebrew scriptures the spirit had brooded over the waters of chaos to bring forth life (Gen. 1:2). The scriptures had proclaimed that God's spirit would not abide in human life forever, because we are flesh (Gen. 6:3). To demonstrate the reality of that promise, the spirit came only temporarily to a variety of individuals in the biblical story, to empower them to do a particular task. This temporary gift, according to John, became a permanent reality only in the life of Jesus. That is the witness of the baptizing one.

Then Nicodemus came along and was unable to escape his limits, his fears. You must be born of the spirit, the author of the Fourth Gospel maintains (John 3:5). In the feeding of the multitude episode, John informs his readers that it is "the spirit that gives life"; the "flesh" is of no avail. Jesus speaks the words of spirit and life (John 6:63). In the story of the Samaritan woman by the well and later in the story of Jesus going up to Jerusalem for the Feast of Sukkoth or Tabernacles, Jesus is portrayed as the source of living water, another Jewish synonym for the spirit. In the Farewell Discourses Jesus says again and again, When I depart, the Father will send the spirit to you, to call to your remembrance all that I have said. The spirit will teach you all things, John affirms; that is, the spirit will bear witness to the meaning of Jesus. The spirit will be the source of peace—not peace that is mere absence of conflict, not peace as the world gives, but peace that is beyond the world's conflict. It is the peace of being that which one most deeply *is,* the peace that enables one to bear pain, conflict and even death while knowing that nothing can finally destroy that person. Jesus, the Fourth Gospel maintains, has lifted each person to a new dimension of humanity, beyond the ability of the world to distort, to hurt or to kill, for as he has said, "I have overcome the world." The spirit will guide those in whom it resides into all truth. The spirit will take what is mine, says Jesus, and declare it to you (John 16:15).

It is in the context of the Farewell Discourses that the spirit is called the Counselor and the Paraclete (which means an advocate or helper). That is also when John has Jesus say over and over again the words "a little while." The spirit will not be long delayed, says Jesus. The disciples wonder what the words "a little while" mean. As they debate what the phrase means, Jesus says, "You will weep and lament, but the world will rejoice; you will be sorrowful, but your sorrow will be turned into joy . . . and no one will take your joy from you" (John 16:20–22). "I have said this in figures," Jesus continues, but "the hour is coming when I shall no longer speak in figures, but will tell you plainly of the Father" (John 16:25).

All these things are in the background of the story of Jesus appearing to the disciples. The resurrection is not the appearance of a physical apparition. It is the experience of the indwelling life of God in the form of the spirit. It comes as the life-giving breath of God flows to the disciples from Jesus, who has passed from death into life because he could give his life away in love for others. He could live the life of God. He could share in the oneness of God. He could open the door for us all to step into the reality of God. The glorification of Jesus was in the crucifixion; the return of Jesus was in the imparting of the spirit on Easter evening. From Friday to Sunday is in fact "a little while." There is to be no further wait for the second coming.

That is what resurrection means for John, and it is not something that occurred just in the life of Jesus; it occurs or it can occur in each of us. The Christian life is not about believing creeds and being obedient to divine rules; it is about living, loving and being. Resurrection comes when we are freed to give our lives away, freed to love beyond the boundaries of our fears, freed not only to be ourselves, but to empower all others to be themselves in the full, rich variety of our multifaceted humanity. Here prejudice dies. Here wholeness is tasted. Here resurrection becomes real.

CHAPTER 31

Thomas: The Final Witness, the Ultimate Claim

We come now to the last of the Fourth Gospel's four resurrection vignettes. Not surprisingly, John fashions this closing episode in a manner that has become almost his signature: He wraps the narrative around a character that he has created. This character's name is Thomas. Yes, he has appeared before in the tradition, but as a name with no substance. Thomas is first mentioned in Mark (3:18) as being one of the twelve chosen disciples. Matthew (10:3) and Luke (6:15) follow Mark's lead, making Thomas in the synoptic tradition nothing more than a name on a list. The synoptic gospels do not provide us with a single biographical detail about Thomas. John appears to have enjoyed his ability to draw personalities out of his imagination and to give them an indelible and recognizable identification. The phrase "doubting Thomas," which comes from John alone, has entered the vocabulary of the world and is used in common conversation, in political discourse, and in sermonic proclamations with no need to cite the source. This was a unique Johannine gift.

What role the disciple named Thomas might have assumed in the life of the early church is still subject to debate. Scholars were aware long ago that at some point in Christian history there appeared a book called the gospel of Thomas. This was known, not because the book existed to be read or quoted, but because other writers whose works have been preserved made references to that gospel. In the discovery of what came to be called the Dead Sea Scrolls, a text of the gospel of Thomas was finally discovered. It is a relatively brief 114-verse collection of sayings attributed to Jesus. Some of these sayings are quite similar to sayings of Jesus recorded in the synoptic gospels. The text of the gospel of Thomas contains no miracle stories, no narrative of Jesus' birth, no narrative of his death and no story of Easter. The book also has about it more of an Eastern mystical understanding of the nature of Jesus. It is not dogmatic or creedal and hence was not used in the theological battles that marked the first three hundred years of Christian history. Efforts to date the origin of this book have resulted in a range from as early as the 50s, which would make it prior to the writing of any of the canonical gospels, to a date well into the second century. The members of the Jesus Seminar, which is dedicated to driving the Christian story to its origins, greeted this find with particular excitement. These scholars not only sought to defend a very early date for this work, but they also incorporated it into the canon of the New Testament when they published their findings in a book entitled *The Five Gospels.*[*] Their work was quickly challenged by other scholars, notably by Professor Bart Ehrman of the department of religion at the University of North Carolina.[†] Perhaps the most impressive study

---

[*] This book was edited by Robert Funk and Roy Hoover. See bibliography for details.

[†] He argued this point in his published lectures on early Christianity, produced by the Teaching Company, later published by Oxford University Press under the title *Lost Christianities*. See bibliography for details.

of this work was done by Princeton professor and best-selling author Elaine Pagels, in a book entitled *Beyond Belief,* in which she argued that the Fourth Gospel was written to contradict the gospel of Thomas; and that is why, she argues, the author of the Fourth Gospel made Thomas into a major character, unlike his treatment in any other Christian source.[*] Another scholar wrote a massive tome seeking to demonstrate that Thomas was actually the "beloved disciple" and thus the author of the Fourth Gospel.[†] When one travels to India and visits in Christian circles, one discovers that Thomas has become the patron saint of the Indian Christian movement. He is all but universally believed to have been the primary missionary to India. Every Christian church in that land claims him as its founder. One of them calls itself the Mar Thoma Church, which means the Church of Saint Thomas.

There are, in addition to this resurrection story, other texts of the Fourth Gospel that single Thomas out from the others and begin to clothe him with a personality. In the Lazarus story, Thomas is identified with the name "the Twin," a designation that has led some to postulate that he was Jesus' twin, a speculation that is beyond the scope of this book. For our purposes, however, in this narrative, when Jesus is about to return to Judea, a place the disciples believed was hostile territory, it is Thomas who is made to state his willingness to accompany Jesus even if it results in his own death. "Let us also go that we may die with him" (John 11:16) are the words attributed to Thomas.

In the Farewell Discourses, Thomas appears once again. This time Jesus is talking about his departure. "I go to prepare a place for you," he says. "I will come again and take you to myself, that where I am you may be also" (John 14:3, 4). This is a reference

---

* See bibliography for details of Pagels' publication.

† James H. Charlesworth, writing in *The Beloved Disciple.* See bibliography for details.

to his second coming, and Thomas is portrayed as clearly not understanding it. When Jesus says, "You know the way where I am going" (John 14:4), it is too much for Thomas. He blurts out: "Lord, we do not know where you are going! How can we know the way?" (John 14:5). Jesus responds with one of the familiar "I AM" sayings of the Fourth Gospel: "I am the way and the truth and the life; no one comes to the Father, but by me. If you had known me, you would have known my Father also; henceforth you know him and have seen him" (John 14:6, 7). The words are clearly addressed to Thomas, who does not yet understand. He does not yet see the mystical oneness between the Father and the son. He does not yet understand the interpenetration of God and human life to which Jesus is constantly referring when he says such things as "the Father and I are one" or notes that the disciples are to abide in Jesus in the same way that Jesus abides in God. That is the last reference to Thomas in the text of the Fourth Gospel until the author makes him the star of the final resurrection story, the one we are now considering, at the end of this gospel (before the epilogue was added).

I believe it is fair to say that Thomas in this resurrection story is treated somewhat pejoratively, which supports Professor Pagels' thesis. He is made to stand out in his disbelief from all the other disciples. He does not accept their witness to an experience which he apparently has not had. He wants a personal experience, a physical demonstration. Resurrection cannot be hearsay for him. He will come to belief in Jesus only when he is able to see the evidence for himself. He insists on touching the wounds. In words used earlier in this gospel, Thomas is demanding a sign (John 2:18, 6:30).

In this characterization, Thomas becomes representative of another group in the audience of the Fourth Gospel. Here we again enter the tension of that gospel, blending together the Jesus story with the story of the Johannine community of followers, who were, when this gospel was written, the subjects of both controversy and persecution. If resurrection was to be understood as the physical resuscitation of a three-days-deceased body, it was as hard for people in the first century to believe as it is for people of the twenty-first century. Thomas was a "show me" kind of man. Give me the proof. Produce the evidence. You said that you have seen him alive, Thomas says: well I haven't, and until I see him with my own eyes I will not believe. Certainly the Johannine community knew people like Thomas, so John put those skeptics into his story using Thomas as a symbol.

We are now told for the first time that Thomas was not present when Jesus first appeared to the disciples. It comes as something of a shocking new detail, one that puts a new slant on the previous story. John simply rewinds the script and repeats the previous experience almost verbatim. Indeed he sets the stage quite overtly to indicate that this episode is a rerun.

The first appearance occurred, we are told, at evening on the first day of the week, the day of the resurrection. This second appearance will occur "eight days later" (John 20:26)—that is, given the way the Jews reckoned time, the first day of the second week. The scene is exactly the same. The doors are shut, which indicates that they have been secured, locked against the darkness of night and all the fears that darkness brings. The light of Jesus that will hurl back the darkness is a familiar Johannine theme. Jesus is not impeded in either episode from appearing in the disciples' midst. Shut doors are no barrier against his presence. Physicality does not appear to be an issue here. In both episodes we are told, "Jesus came and stood among them"; in both stories he says, "Peace be with you" (John 20:19, 20:26).

Only then do the stories diverge, with Thomas brought front and center in the second episode. In the first narrative Jesus showed the disciples his hands and his side (John 20:20). Now Thomas will have the same opportunity for verification. The text is clear. Jesus says: "Put your finger here and see my hands, and put out your hand and place it in my side; do not be faithless, but believing" (John 20:27). Thomas apparently does neither suggested action. Instead he utters the most overt affirmation of John's Jesus in this gospel. You are, Thomas exclaims: "my Lord and my God" (John 20:28). You are the messiah sent from God. In Johannine terms, the messenger is of the same essence as the one who did the sending. Thomas' confession is, in effect: I have seen God in the presence of Jesus; I have seen the word made flesh and dwelling among us. Thomas has come to understand that when we see Jesus, we see God. John's case is now made, as Thomas confirms the Fourth Gospel's understanding of who Jesus is.

Then John has Jesus clarify to the Thomases in the Johannine community and their descendants throughout history the correct understanding of the resurrection. First Jesus asks Thomas this question: "Have you believed because you have seen me?" Then he adds the words for which this story was created: "Blessed are those who have not seen and yet believe" (John 20:29). Blessed are those who are called into the Christ experience through the witness of others. Blessed are those who experience an expanded humanity that comes through those who were themselves examples of that new human consciousness. The disciples of Jesus will be recognized, Jesus said previously, by the love they have to give and by the freedom they achieve—freedom that will enable them to give their lives away in love to others. The life and love we encounter in one another and in the human Jesus is the life and love on display in the crucified one. His image bears the scars of the life he lived, the freedom he experienced, the fact that his glorification claim came not in his triumph, but in his death, not in resurrected power, but in his ability always to give life and love even as his own life was being ripped from him. That is John's Christ. That is what Thomas eventually sees. The cross is the final sign in this gospel that points beyond itself to its ultimate meaning. Thomas finally reads the sign properly. The crucified one is the presence of God among us. He is the God who is the source of life, and his call to us is to live fully.

John closes his gospel with words that make certain that this point is clear: "Now Jesus did many other signs in the presence of the disciples that are not in this book; but these are written that you might believe that Jesus is the Christ, the son of God, and that believing you might have life in his name" (John 20:30–31). To have life—not to become religious, not to achieve moral purity, not to win the contest to gain doctrinal orthodoxy, but to have life—*that* is the function of the Christ. It is to bring us to the experience of living in which we pass into new dimensions of life and cross the boundaries of fear that separate us from one another and from ourselves. That we "might have life and have it abundantly"—that is what Jesus is about; that is what Jesus brings. To be Christian is not to *believe* that message, but to *live* that message. On this note the Fourth Gospel comes to a conclusion, and we are left with the spirit that empowers us to be the body of Christ doing the work of Christ in every generation.

CHAPTER 32

The Epilogue: Resurrection Is Not Physical, but It Is Real

John's gospel has been brought to an appropriate ending. The summary statement contained in John 20:30–31, quoted as we wrapped up the preceding chapter, calls for nothing more. The portrait drawn by the Jewish mystic who perceived in Jesus unity with God has been painted. The glorification of Jesus has been acted out upon the cross, a human life moving beyond the biological survival drive to reveal a oneness with that which is transcendent. In four quick resurrection vignettes this author has capped his message. Resurrection frees us from the need to cling to the physical; resurrection reveals life that cannot be bound by a tomb or the grave cloths in which the body has been wrapped; resurrection is an invitation to step into the life of the transforming spirit, and the ultimate blessing of resurrection comes to those who do not see physical evidence and yet who believe. The purpose of Jesus has been fulfilled. He is the life-giver, the expander of our humanity, the revealer of dimensions of life which those who are not awakened by the spirit will never see. He came that we, by seeing and believing, might have the fullness of life in his name. There is no need for anything else to be said—but to the reader's surprise there is another chapter. It is an anti-climax!

We call that chapter the "epilogue" and most scholars believe it is the product of another hand, added after the various authors (who created the Fourth Gospel in at least three stages) had drawn this complex work to its conclusion. The epilogue does not integrate well into any of the strands that make up the finished gospel.

The reasons offered to guide us to this conclusion are many. First, chapter 21 does not comfortably follow chapter 20. The dramatic appearance of Jesus to Mary Magdalene, the visit to the tomb by Peter and the one whom Jesus loved—these scenes from chapter 20 do not cry out for another form of validation. The subsequent accounts in that chapter of the appearance of Jesus to the disciples without Thomas being present, and a second appearance to the disciples with Thomas now present, issue in the gift of the Holy Spirit, the pronouncement of peace and the ultimate affirmation that Jesus is "my Lord and my God." Yet none of these things seems to affect anyone who appears in the epilogue, which opens jarringly with the announcement by Peter: "I am going fishing."

Peter was not a sport fisherman looking for an afternoon of relaxation on a nearby lake or stream in search of a trout. Fishing was the job at which Peter earned his livelihood. He was announcing that it was time for him to pick up the pre-Jesus phase of his life and go back to his trade. The trauma and grief connected with the crucifixion had begun to fade. A return to normalcy was in order. Everyone who has ever gone through the experience of grief, no matter how wrenching, understands the transition to which Peter was referring. One has the sense from the opening words that the author of this epilogue is describing a time well after the crucifixion—certainly weeks, perhaps even months.

Another dislocating sign of the lack of continuity between chapters 20 and 21 is that "the disciples" have dropped to seven. In Paul's account they were twelve in number (I Cor. 15:5); in Matthew, having lost Judas, the total had dropped to eleven (Matt. 28:16). John has portrayed the exit of Judas into the night as having occurred at the meal described in chapter 13. The list of disciples in this epilogue is itself of interest. It includes Peter, Thomas, Nathaniel, the two sons of Zebedee and "two others" who are unnamed. As the story develops, however, one of the two unnamed ones appears to be identified as the "beloved disciple." If that is so, then two of these disciples—Nathaniel and the "beloved disciple"—are figures introduced only in the Fourth Gospel and intended to be more symbols than people of history. The epilogue seems not to understand this.

Another disconcerting sign is that the scene has shifted from Jerusalem to Galilee. It looks as if the disciples have returned to the familiar hills of their homeland, to their families and to their pre-Jesus occupation as fishermen. The earlier tradition reflected in Paul, Mark and Matthew had asserted that the resurrection experience was located in Galilee. The later tradition reflected by Luke and John 20 had centered it in Jerusalem. The epilogue in John appears to be an effort at harmonizing these differing traditions.

The next surprising note involves the first part of the epilogue, which has to do with a dramatic catch of fish that occurs after Jesus, who appeared unrecognized on the shore, gives the disciples the suggestion that they cast the nets on the other side of the boat. This same story, with many if not most of its specific details, was recorded earlier in the gospel of Luke (5:1–11), and in that source it had nothing to do with the resurrection. In both stories the disciples have "toiled all night and taken nothing," as Luke puts it (Luke 5:5, John 21:5). In both stories Jesus instructs them to let down their nets (Luke 5:4, John 21:6). In both stories they haul in a massive catch, so large that their nets begin to break (Luke 5:6, John 21:6). In both stories Peter is brought to a new understanding (Luke 5:8, John 21:15ff) and in both stories Peter is commissioned (Luke 5:10, John 21:17ff). In Luke's version Peter's commission is to fish for human beings, not for creatures from the sea. In John's story Peter is to be the one who feeds the sheep, the lambs of God. In Luke, however, this story is an event in the Galilean phase of Jesus' earthly life. In John it is a post-resurrection narrative.

A final strange note is that the epilogue in John anticipates the "second coming" of Jesus in the traditional manner and appears not to be aware that the corpus of John's gospel has already treated the gift of the Holy Spirit as the second coming of Jesus, fulfilling the promise made by Jesus in the body of this gospel that it will occur after only "a little while." To shift a major understanding and interpretation of the life of Jesus this completely argues strongly for a different author and a later time.

The tension between Peter and the "beloved disciple," noted so often in the corpus of John's gospel, is raised in the epilogue once more, but this time it is solved in Peter's favor. It is Peter who will be in charge of tending the flock of Christ's people. The one called the "beloved disciple" has been historicized in the epilogue, and the suggestion is that he has in fact died. A mythical impression was abroad in the wider Christian community that Jesus had promised that this "beloved disciple" would not die before the second coming. There is no such word in the Fourth Gospel, but that issue had to be addressed since obviously that disciple was no longer around and his existence had been literalized. So the author of the epilogue explains that Jesus did not actually say that the "beloved disciple" would not die before the second coming, but only that "if it is my will that he remain until I come, what is that to you?" (John 21:22). Next the claim is made that it is this "beloved disciple" who is writing these things and that his testimony is true. This is such an out-of-character assertion to have been made by the self-effacing "beloved disciple" as to be jolting to the literary psyche (John 21:24). Then the epilogue closes with its own summary statement, as if the one with which the regular gospel closed had been inadequate: "But there are also many other things which Jesus did; were every one of them to be written, I suppose that the world itself could not contain the books that would be written" (John 21:25). On this expansive note the epilogue comes to an end and we are left to try to understand what it means and why it was added.

There is first a harmonizing motif in the epilogue about which mention has already been made. Some of the divergent traditions are smoothed over. Among them are two locations, Galilee and Jerusalem, claimed by different writers as primary. The epilogue suggests that both are correct, with sequence being the problem. The resurrection tradition seems to have two themes: One is to awaken faith; the other is to commission leaders to carry out the purpose and to accept responsibility for the Jesus mission. This epilogue brings the two together. The tradition of "the third day" as the day of the resurrection is also an issue in conflict. Paul says the resurrection happens "on the third day" (I Cor. 15:4). Mark has Jesus predict resurrection three times, but each prediction says not "on the third day," but "after three days" (Mark 8:31, 9:31, 10:34). Matthew and Luke, in their renditions, change all of those Marcan references to read "on the third day."

Yet "on the third day" and "after three days" do not give us the same day! Mark and Matthew portray the resurrection announcement as occurring at the tomb on the day after the Sabbath, but no appearance of the risen Lord to the disciples occurs until they return to Galilee, which is a seven- to ten-day journey from Jerusalem and thus outside the three-day time frame. Luke says that the appearances of the risen Christ occurred periodically over a span of forty days, before they ceased and Jesus disappeared into the clouds (Acts 1:3). John's gospel has Jesus "appear" three times: first to Mary Magdalene at dawn on Easter day, second to the disciples without Thomas on the evening of that same day, and third to the disciples with Thomas "after eight days." The epilogue suggests that another appearance in Galilee occurred after a considerable length of time—long enough for the disciples to be back home, over their grief and ready to return to the normalcy of their workaday world. So the epilogue seeks to harmonize conflict on many levels. The fact that this epilogue to John's gospel is so reminiscent of an earlier Galilean story about Jesus recorded in the gospel of Luke suggests that the content of this narrative was early and that the epilogue writer simply turned it into a resurrection story.

Despite all of these interpretive problems, which cry out against any literal authenticity being attributed to the epilogue, I must say that I have a very deep appreciation for this epilogue, but for a very different reason. I am convinced that this chapter, though not an essential part of the Fourth Gospel, is based on a very early, primitive record that may reflect a tradition even earlier than any of the gospels' resurrection stories. If that can be demonstrated to be true, then we might discover in this chapter an authentic recollection of how the meaning of Jesus broke into the consciousness of the disciples (or, to say it inside the later-developing words of the tradition, how the resurrection actually happened).

I do not think that resurrection was ever meant to be a sign that would compel people to believe. I submit that a resuscitated body walking around with nail prints in his hands and feet would be a compelling sign indeed! It would not make much sense for Jesus to chastise Thomas by saying, "Have you believed because you have seen me? Blessed are those who have not seen and yet believe" (John 20:29), if that physical sign of a resuscitated body was intended to cause the birth of faith. So I see this chapter as an early description of how the resurrection was understood as a non-physical event—a description that a redactor thought was important enough to attach to the Fourth Gospel. Resurrection was not physical to John, as I have tried to demonstrate in this book. John portrays Mary Magdalene as seeing, but having nothing to which to cling; the disciples as seeing no body, but only an empty grave; then all of the disciples being filled by the Holy Spirit, which Jesus was believed to have breathed on them, and finally Thomas seeing after demanding to touch, but not actually touching at all. Resurrection was really the dawning of a new consciousness, the birth of a new vision of humanity, the mystical act of achieving oneness with that which is eternal.

In the course of my life and writing career, I have studied the resurrection narratives of the New Testament intensively. I have compared all the narratives, embracing the contradictions and seeking for hidden clues that might lead to new understandings. My goal has always been to separate the time-bound explanations of our faith story from the timeless experience that lies behind it, especially in regard to the moment we call Easter. The explanation and the experience are never the same. The experience, I believe, was real. It had to be. The Easter experience was so powerful that it transformed disciples, who had forsaken Jesus and had fled at the time of his arrest, into heroes who would die to bear witness to the life-changing truth that the Easter experience was for them. It was so powerful that it caused these Jewish disciples, who had been raised on the Shema prayer that proclaimed the oneness of God, to expand their understanding of God to such a degree as to allow them to see Jesus as a part of who God is and to see God as a part of who Jesus is. It was so powerful that it gave birth to a new holy day that within one generation rivaled the Sabbath in importance.

That is what the Easter *experience* did, but the Easter *explanation* was increasingly literalized and filled with contradictions. I reject these literalizations. The idea of the physical resuscitation of a three-days-dead man back into the life of this world does not enter the tradition of Christian writing until the ninth decade of the Common Era. The contrast between an experience that is both real and life-changing and an explanation that is unbelievable led me to the conclusion that while the resurrection is not physical, it is also *not nothing*. So what is it? In my study I asked four questions of the biblical texts. Where were the disciples when the experience called "resurrection" occurred? Who was it that stood in the midst of that experience as its primary interpreter? When did this life-changing reality or meaning dawn? What was the context in which it broke into the consciousness of the first believers? My answers consumed an entire book, which I entitled *Resurrection: Myth or Reality?*[*]

My answers were clear, at least to me, when my study was complete. First, the "where" question led me to see that whatever Easter was, it dawned on people in Galilee. This was attested by all the early Christian writers. The Jerusalem tradition was clearly a secondary, more magical, more supernatural and more miraculous telling of the story. Second, the "who" question led me to see that the one who stood in the center of the resurrection experience was Peter: That is why he was always listed first among the disciples, and that is why he was portrayed as the first to confess Jesus as the Christ at Caesarea Philippi (Mark 8:27–30), and that

---

[*]   See bibliography for details.

is why his struggle is portrayed in the Fourth Gospel as being so intense. Third, the "when" question led me to assert that the actual time between crucifixion and "resurrection" was not three days—that was rather a liturgical imposition to allow Easter to be observed on the first day of the week following the crucifixion on Friday and the Sabbath on Saturday. I suspect that contrary to the literalness of the three-day symbol, a minimum of three months and a maximum of a year originally separated the crucifixion from the dawning consciousness that Jesus was of God and death therefore could not contain him. Finally, it was the "how" question that forced me to wonder about the setting, the context, in which whatever resurrection was broke into the conscious awareness of Peter and the disciples. My clue for this I found in words that Luke alone records: "He was made known to them in the breaking of the bread" (Luke 24:35). Other hints of this context are found in the various stories of the feeding of the multitude that were told six times in the four gospels—twice in Mark, twice in Matthew, once in Luke and once in John. Inside almost all of those narratives are found the four eucharistic verbs: Jesus "took," he "blessed" (or gave thanks), he "broke" and he "gave." I found support for this idea particularly in John, who has Jesus assert: "I am the bread of life." So resurrection, I concluded, was an inner experience of transformation in which all limits were broken and through which union with that which we call God was achieved.

Over the years this internal experience was externalized, and that was when we got the details of tombs that were empty, grave cloths that had been abandoned, apparitions that appeared and angels who made announcements. Was there one place where the original experience was recorded in a less fantastic manner, but one which pointed to the inner reality? I found such a place, but only in the epilogue of John. Here the setting is Galilee. Peter is the one who sees and who opens the eyes of the others to see. The time is well after the crucifixion and realization dawns in them while they are eating together the early-morning eucharistic meal by the lake. That is when they see Jesus as having broken the barrier that binds us in mortality, finitude and time, and when they hear Jesus issuing the command that we must feed the sheep, the lambs of God's flock. One cannot know the fullness of life until one can give one's life away. One cannot know the essence of love until one can love another—not because another deserves love, but because another simply *is*. One cannot be all that one can be unless one frees others to be all that they can be. This is what Jesus means. This is what resurrection is. This is what the cross means. This is what life in the spirit is all about.

So the epilogue brings together the story of the resurrection for me, just as John's story of the cross makes clear the glorification of God in the life of Jesus for me. Jesus is the one who achieved the mystical oneness with the God who is the source of life, the source of love and the Ground of Being. So I finish John in an experience of wordless wonder. In this book I have encountered the God who is the great "I AM" and as a result I, too, can now say "I am." Even more, I can hear the voices of everyone else saying "I am." In this gift of being I live, I rejoice, I experience eternity. That is what I have received from the Fourth Gospel, the tales of a Jewish mystic.

This also becomes for me the basis upon which Christianity can be reformulated so that its message can be heard in the echoes of the language of the twenty-first century and upon which we can build "A New Christianity for a New World." To that task Christianity is now called.

Shalom!

Bibliography

Abbot, Ezra, Andrew Peabody and J. B. Lightfoot. *The Fourth Gospel.* London: Hodder and Stoughton, 1937.

Abelson, J. *Jewish Mysticism: An Introduction to the Kabbalah.* London: G. Bell, 1913.

Alstrup, Nils D. *The Johannine Church and History.* Oslo: University Press, 1992.

Altizer, Thomas J. J. *The Descent into Hell.* Philadelphia: Lippincott, 1970.

Anderson, Bernard W. *Understanding the Old Testament.* Englewood Cliffs, NJ: Prentice Hall, 1986.

Anderson, Paul N. *The Christology of the Fourth Gospel.* Tübingen, Germany: J. C. B. Mobed, 1996.

Ashton, John, ed. *The Interpretation of John.* Edinburgh: T. & T. Clark, 1986.

————. *Understanding the Fourth Gospel.* Oxford: University Press, 1991.

Baillie, Donald M. *God Was in Christ: An Essay on Incarnation and Atonement.* New York: Scribner, 1948.

Bakken, Norm. "The Gospel of John: A Parable in the Presence." *Impact* 48 (2002).

Barrett, C. K. *The Gospel According to St. John: An Introduction and Commentary on the Greek Text.* Philadelphia: Westminster Press, 1975.

————, ed. *The New Testament Background: Selected Documents.* San Francisco: Harper and Row, 1956.

Barth, Karl. *Church Dogmatics.* Vol. I. London: T. & T. Clark, 1936.

Bernard, Thomas Dehaney. *The Central Teaching of Jesus Christ: A Study and Exposition of Five Chapters of the Gospel According to St. John, 13–17.* London: Macmillan, 1900.

Bonhoeffer, Dietrich. *Theological Education Underground, 1937–1940.* Translated by Victoria J. Burnett. Philadelphia: Fortress Press, 2012.

Borg, Marcus. *Evolution of the Word: The New Testament in the Order the Books Were Written.* San Francisco: HarperOne, 2012.

———. *The Heart of Christianity: Rediscovering a Life of Faith.* San Francisco: HarperOne, 2004.

Brown, Raymond. *The Birth of the Messiah.* Garden City, NY: Doubleday, 1977.

———. *The Community of the Beloved Disciple.* New York: Paulist Press, 1979.

———. *The Gospel According to John.* 2 vols. Garden City, NY: Doubleday, 1966–1970.

Brownlee, W. H. *The Meaning of the Qumran Scrolls for the Bible.* Oxford: University Press, 1964.

Bruckham, Richard. *Jesus and the Eyewitnesses: The Gospels as Eyewitness Testimony.* Grand Rapids, MI: Eerdmans, 2006.

Bruner, Emil. *The Mediator.* Philadelphia: Lutterworth Press, 1934.

Bultmann, Rudolf. *The Gospel of John: A Commentary.* Translated by G. R. Beasley-Murray, general editors R. W. N. Hoare and J. K. Riches. Philadelphia: Westminster Press, 1973.

Caird, G. B. *St. Luke.* Pelican Series. Baltimore: Penguin Books, 1963.

Charlesworth, James H. *The Beloved Disciple: Whose Witness Validates the Gospel of John?* Valley Forge, PA: Trinity International, 1995.

———. *John and the Dead Sea Scrolls.* New York: Crossroads Press, 1990.

Conzelman, Hans. *The Theology of St. Luke.* London: Faber and Faber, 1960.

Countryman, L. William. *The Mystical Way in the Fourth Gospel: Crossing Over into God.* Philadelphia: Fortress Press, 1987.

Crossan, John Dominic. *Jesus: A Revolutionary Biography.* San Francisco: HarperCollins, 2001.

———. *The Power of Parable: How Fiction by Jesus Became Fiction About Jesus.* San Francisco: HarperOne, 2012.

Cullmann, Oscar. *Early Christian Worship.* Philadelphia: Westminster Press, 1953.

Davies, W. D., and D. Daube. *The Background of the New Testament and Its Eschatology: Essays in Honor of C. H. Dodd.* Cambridge: University Press, 1956.

Dodd, C. H. *The Epistle of Paul to the Romans.* London: Hodder and Stoughton, 1949.

———. *The Interpretation of the Fourth Gospel.* Cambridge: University Press, 1968.

Dods, Marcus. *The Gospel of St. John.* London: Hodder and Stoughton, 1910.

Drummond, James. *The Character and Authorship of the Fourth Gospel.* London: Williams and Norgate, 1903.

Dunderberg, Ismo. *The Beloved Disciple in Conflict? Revisiting the Gospels of John and Thomas.* Oxford: University Press, 2006.

Dunn, J. D. G. *Christianity in the Making: An Inquiry into the Origins of the Doctrine of the Incarnation.* Philadelphia: Westminster Press, 1980.

Ehrman, Bart. *Lost Christianities.* Oxford: University Press, 2005 (also produced in a DVD presentation by the Teaching Company, Chantilly, Virginia, 2001).

———. *The New Testament: A Historical Introduction to Early Christian Worship.* New York: Oxford University Press, 2012.

Enoch. *The Book of Enoch: Aramaic Fragments of Qumran Cave 4.* Edited by J. J. Malik and Matthew Black. Oxford: Clarendon Press, 1976.

Evans, Craig A. *Word and Glory: On the Exegetical and Theological Background of John's Prologue.* Sheffield, UK: Academic Press, 1993.

Filson, Floyd. *John: The Gospel of Life.* Layman's Bible Commentary. Louisville: John Knox Press, 1956.

Frete, Timothy, and Peter Gandy. *The Jesus Mysteries: Was the Original Jesus a Pagan God?* New York and London: Random House, 2001.

Fuller, Reginald. *The Formation of the Resurrection Narratives.* New York: Macmillan, 1971.

Funk, Robert. "Study Guide and Lectures on John." Unpublished manuscript made available through the courtesy of the Drew University Library, Madison, NJ, 1972.

Funk, Robert, and Roy Hoover. *The Five Gospels: What Did Jesus Really Say?* New York: Macmillan, 1993.

Goulder, Michael Donald. *Luke: A New Paradigm.* Sheffield, UK: Sheffield Academic Press, 1989.

———. "Nicodemus." *Journal of Theology* 44 (1991): 152–168.

Goulder, Michael D., and John Hick. *Why Believe in God?* London: SCM Press, 1983.

Grant, Robert M., ed. *Gnosticism: A Source Book of Heretical Writings in the Early Christian Period*. New York: Harper and Row, 1961.

Gruenwald, Ithamar. *Apocalyptic and Merkavah Mysticism*. London: E. J. Brill, 1980.

Guilding, Aileen. *The Fourth Gospel and Jewish Worship: A Study of the Relation of St. John's Gospel to the Ancient Jewish Lectionary System*. Oxford: Clarendon Press, 1960.

Haenchen, Ernst. *The Acts of the Apostles: A Commentary*. Philadelphia: Westminster Press, 1971.

————. *The Gospel of John*. Philadelphia: Westminster Press, 1984.

Harnack, Adolph. *The Mission and Expansion of Christianity in the First Three Centuries*. Translated by James Moffett. Freeport, NY: Books for Libraries Press, 1959.

Hawking, Stephen, and Leonard Mlodinow. *The Grand Design*. New York: Bantam Books, 2010.

Herrstrum, David Sten. *The Book of Unknowing: A Poet's Response to the Gospel of John*. Eugene, OR: Wipf and Stock, 2012.

Hoskyns, Sir Edwyn. *The Fourth Gospel*. London: Faber and Faber, 1947.

Howard, William F. *The Fourth Gospel in Recent Criticism and Interpretation*. London: Epworth Press, 1931.

James, Fleming. *Personalities of the Old Testament*. New York: Scribner, 1955.

Josephus. *The Complete Works*. Translated by William Whiston. Grand Rapids, MI: Kregal Press, 1999.

Jung, Carl. *The Answer to Job*. London: Routledge & Kegan Paul, 1954.

Kanagaraj, Jey J. *Mysticism in the Gospel of John*. Sheffield, UK: Sheffield Academic Press, 1998.

Käsemann, Ernst. *The Testament of Jesus: A Study of the Gospel of John in the Light of Chapter 17*. Philadelphia: Fortress Press, 1968.

Klussen, William, ed. *Issues in New Testament Interpretation: Essays in Honor of Otto A. Piper*. New York: Harper and Brothers, 1962.

Kysar, Robert. *The Fourth Evangelist and His Gospel: An Examination of Contemporary Scholarship*. Minneapolis: Augsburg Publishing House, 1975.

Lightfoot, R. H. *St. John's Gospel: A Commentary*. Edited by C. F. Evans. Oxford: Clarendon Press, 1956.

Lindars, Barnabas, ed. *The Gospel of John*. New Century Bible Commentary. Edinburgh: Oliphants, 1974.

Linforth, Katherine C. *The Beloved Disciple: Jacob the Brother of the Lord*. Melbourne, Australia: UniPrint, 2011.

Loader, W. R. G. "The Central Structure of Johannine Christology." *New Testament Studies* 22 (1984): 188–214.

Lowrie, William. *The Doctrine of St. John*. New York: Longmans, Green, 1899.

Lüdemann, Gerd. *Jesus After 2000 Years*. London: SCM Press, 2000.

MacGregor, G. H. C. *The Gospel of John*. Moffett New Testament Commentary. New York: Harper and Row, 1978.

———. *The Structure of the Fourth Gospel*. London: Morton, Oliver and Boyd, 1961.

Mack, Burton. *The Christian Myth: Origin, Logic, and Legacy*. New York and San Francisco: HarperCollins, 2000.

———. *The Lost Gospel: The Book of Q and Christian Origins*. New York and San Francisco: HarperCollins, 1993.

MacKintosh, H. R. *The Doctrine of the Person of Jesus Christ*. London: T. & T. Clark, 1913.

MacRae, Georg W. *Invitation to John*. Garden City: Doubleday, 1978.

Manson, T. W. *On Paul and John*. London: Macmillan, 1949.

Mantyn, J. Louis. *History and Theology in the Fourth Gospel*. New York: Harper and Row, 1968.

Meeks, Wayne. "Galilee and Judea in the Fourth Gospel." *Journal of Biblical Literature* 83, no. 2 (June 1966): 159–169.

———. "The Man from Heaven in Johannine Sectarianism." *Journal of Biblical Literature* 91, no. 1 (1972): 44–72.

Minear, Paul. "The Original Function of John 21." *Journal of Biblical Literature* 102 (1983): 88–98.

Moltmann, Jürgen. *Theology of Hope: On the Ground and the Implications of Christian Eschatology*. New York: Harper and Row, 1965.

Moule, Charles, ed. *The Significance of the Resurrection: The Message of the Resurrection for Faith in Jesus Christ*. London: SCM Press, 1968.

Niebuhr, Richard. *Schleiermacher on Christ and Religion: New Implications*. New York: Scribner, 1964.

Nineham, D. H. *St. Mark*. Philadelphia: Westminster Press, 1977.

Nock, Arthur Darby. *St. Paul*. New York: Harper and Brothers, 1937.

Odeberg, Hugo. *The Fourth Gospel, Interpreted in Relation to Contemporaneous Religious Currents.* Uppsala, Sweden: Almqvist and Wiksell, 1929.

Olsson, B. *Structure and Meaning in the Fourth Gospel: A Text-Linguistic Analysis of John 2:1–11 and 4:1–41.* Lund, Sweden: Gleerup, 1974.

Pagels, Elaine. *Beyond Belief.* New York: Random House, 2005.

———. *The Gnostic Gospels.* New York: Random House, 1979.

———. *Revelations: Visions, Prophecy and Politics in the Book of Revelation.* New York: Penguin Group, 2012.

Pannenberg, Wolfhart. *Jesus: God and Man.* London: SCM Press, 1968.

Pittenger, Norman. *Christ for Us Today.* London: SCM Press, 1968.

Ratzinger, Joseph Cardinal. *Jesus of Nazareth.* San Francisco: Ignatius Press, 2011.

Ravindra, Ravi. *The Gospel of John in the Light of Indian Mysticism.* Rochester, VT: Inner Traditions, 1990.

Robinson, John A. T. *Honest to God.* Philadelphia: Westminster Press, 1963.

———. *The Human Face of God.* Philadelphia: Westminster Press, 1973.

———. *In the End, God.* Eugene, OR: Cascade Press, 2011.

———. *The Priority of John.* London: SCM Press, 1986.

———. *Redating the New Testament.* Philadelphia: Westminster, John Knox Press, 1976.

———. "Resurrection in the New Testament." *Interpreter's Dictionary of the Bible,* vol. IV, pp. 43–53.

———. *Twelve New Testament Studies.* London: SCM Press, 1962.

Sanders, E. P. *Jesus and Judaism.* Philadelphia: Westminster Press, 1985.

Sandmel, Samuel. *The Genius of Paul.* New York: Farrar, Straus & Cudahy, 1958.

———. *Judaism and Christian Beginnings.* Oxford: University Press, 1979.

———. *Philo of Alexandria.* New York: Oxford University Press, 1979.

———. *We Jews and Jesus: Exploring Theological Differences for Mutual Understanding.* New York: Oxford University Press, 1965.

Sanford, John. *Mystical Christianity: A Psychological Commentary on the Gospel of John.* New York: Crossroads Press, 1995.

Schnackenburg, Rudolf. *The Gospel of St. John.* 3 vols. New York: Crossroads Press, 1980–1983.

Schneiders, Sandra M. *Written That You Might Believe: Encountering Jesus in the Fourth Gospel.* New York: Crossroads Press, 1999.

———. "A Case Study: A Feminist's Interpretation of John 4:1–42." In John Ashton, ed., *The Interpretation of John* (see above).

Scholem, Gershom G. *Major Trends in Jewish Mysticism.* New York: Schocken Books, 1941; Random House, 1965.

Scott, E. F. *The Fourth Gospel: Its Purpose and Theology.* Edinburgh: T. & T. Clark, 1908.

Spong, John Shelby. *Born of a Woman: A Bishop Rethinks the Virgin Birth and the Place of Women in a Male-Dominated Church.* San Francisco: Harper Collins, 1993.

———. *Christpower.* Haworth, NJ: St. Johan Press, 2008.

———. *Eternal Life: A New Vision—Beyond Religion, Beyond Theism, Beyond Heaven and Hell.* San Francisco: HarperOne, 2009.

———. *Here I Stand: My Struggle for a Christianity of Integrity, Love and Equality.* San Francisco: HarperCollins, 2000.

———. *Jesus for the Non-Religious.* San Francisco: HarperCollins, 2007.

———. *Liberating the Gospels: Reading the Bible with Jewish Eyes.* San Francisco: HarperCollins, 1996.

———. *A New Christianity for a New World: Why Christianity Is Dying and How a New Faith Is Being Born.* San Francisco. HarperCollins, 2001.

———. *Re-Claiming the Bible for a Non-Religious World.* San Francisco: HarperOne 2011.

———. *Rescuing the Bible from Fundamentalism: A Bishop Rethinks the Meaning of Scripture.* San Francisco: HarperCollins, 1991.

———. *Resurrection: Myth or Reality?* San Francisco: HarperCollins 1994.

———. *The Sins of Scripture: Exploring the Bible's Texts of Hate to Reveal the God of Love.* San Francisco: HarperCollins, 2005.

———. *Why Christianity Must Change or Die: A Bishop Speaks to Believers in Exile.* San Francisco: HarperCollins, 1998.

Steinbeck, John. *East of Eden.* New York: Viking Press, 1952.

Stibbe, M. "The Elusive Christ: A New Reading of the Fourth Gospel." *Journal for the Study of the New Testament* 44 (1991): 19–38.

———. *John.* Sheffield, UK: JSOT Press, 1993.

Strachen, R. H. *The Fourth Gospel: Its Significance and Environment.* London: SCM Press, 1941.

Strauss, David Friedrich. *Leben Jesu.* 1836. Translated and reprinted in London: SCM Press, 1973, under the title *The Life of Jesus Critically Examined.*

Talbert, Charles H. "The Myth of the Descending-Ascending Redeemer in Mediterranean Antiquity." *New Testament Studies* 22 (1976): 418–439.

Temple, William. *Readings in St. John's Gospel.* London: Macmillan, 1945.

Terrien, Samuel. *The Psalms and Their Meaning for Today.* Indianapolis and New York: Bobbs-Merrill, 1953.

Tillich, Paul. *The Courage to Be.* New Haven, CN: Yale University Press, 1952.

———. *The Eternal Now.* New York: Scribner, 1963.

———. *The New Being.* New York: Scribner, 1935.

———. *On the Boundary.* New York: Scribner, 1966.

———. *The Shaking of the Foundations.* New York: Scribner, 1948.

———. *Systematic Theology.* Vols. I, II, and III. Chicago: University of Chicago Press, 1951–1963.

Underhill, Evelyn. *The Mystical Way: A Psychological Study in Christian Origins.* London: J. M. Dent, 1913.

von Hügel, Friedrich. "John." *Encyclopedia Britannica.* 11th ed. London, 1911.

von Rad, Gerhard. *Genesis.* Philadelphia: Westminster Press, 1972.

———. *Old Testament Theology.* San Francisco: Harper and Row, 1965.

von Wahlde, Urban C. *The Earliest Version of John's Gospel.* Grand Rapids, MI: Eerdmans, 2008.

———. *The Gospel and Letters of John.* Vols. I, II, and III. Grand Rapids, MI: Eerdmans, 2010.

Warner, Marina. *Alone of All Her Sex: The Myth and Cult of the Virgin Mary.* New York: Macmillan, 1967.

Watkins, Henry William. *Modern Criticism and the Fourth Gospel.* London: John Murray Press, 1890.

Webb, Val. *Like Catching Water in a Net: Human Attempts to Describe the Divine.* London: Continuum, 2007.

———. *Stepping Out with the Sacred: Human Attempts to Engage the Divine.* London: Continuum, 2010.

Wendt, Hans Hinrich. *The Gospel According to St. John.* Translated by Edward Lummis. Edinburgh: T. & T. Clark, 1902.

Westcott, B. F. *The Gospel According to St. John.* London: John Murray, 1908.

Wiesel, Elie. *Night.* New York: Bantam Books, 1982.

Other resources used include:

Book of Common Prayer, According to the Use of the Episcopal Church. New York: Church Hymnal Corporation and Seabury Press, 1979.

Gospel Parallels: A Synopsis of the First Three Gospels. New York: Thomas Nelson, 1949.

The HarperCollins Study Bible (NRSV). Edited by Wayne Meeks. San Francisco: HarperCollins, 2006.

Hymnal, Protestant Episcopal Church in the United States of America. New York: Church Pension Fund, 1940 and 1982.

The Interpreter's Bible. 12 vols. Edited by Nolan B. Harmon. Nashville: Abingdon Press, 1953.

The New Oxford Annotated Bible (RSV). Edited by Herbert May and Bruce Metzger. New York: Oxford University Press, 1973.

Scripture Index

Subject Index

faith, and Gentile official's son,
107–16
Farewell Discourses, 15, 28, 70, 160,
161, 163–200, 201, 202, 229–30,
271, 297, 301; analogy of the
vine, 189–200; John clarifies Jesus'
death, 175–87; Peter and the commandment to love, 165–73
Fatima, 118
Feast of Dedication, 37 256
Feast of Tabernacles, 37, 93, 256, 297
feeding the multitude, 64, 125–33,
215, 225, 227, 228, 257, 296
fertility cults, 54
fishing, 308, 309–10
Five Gospels, The (Funk and
Hoover), 68 and n., 300 and n.
"followers of the way," 210
foot-washing, 160, 220–21, 225,
229, 276
Fourth Gospel. *See* John, Gospel of
fundamentalism, 65–66
Funk, Robert, 217n.

Gabriel, 81
Galatians, 78n., 137 and n.
Galilee, 23, 27, 35, 38, 80, 99, 140,
170, 192, 210, 234, 269, 277,
309–12, 314
Garden of Eden, 177, 178–79
Garden of Gethsemane, 28, 201–2
Genesis, 42–43, 71, 96–98, 177–79,
259, 279, 290
Gentile official's son, 107–16, 133
Gentiles, 145, 160, 190, 237,
255, 258
Gnosticism, 6, 32, 40
God, 5, 6, 7, 12, 18, 25, 44–49, 92,
105, 121–22, 142, 171–73, 175,

265, 298, 313–14; analogy of
the vine and 189–200; changing,
53–55; enthronement, 59; Gentile official's son and meaning of,
107–16; Jewish mysticism and
51–61; realm of, 87–89, 106,
111; word of, 43–47, 55–61,
160, 193, 202–6, 231–32,
240–41, 256, 257
Golgotha, 245, 261
Good Friday, 24, 136
Greek language, 33, 44, 65, 87,
127, 132, 219, 246
Gregory the Great, Pope, 276
Guilding, Aileen, *The Fourth Gospel and Jewish Worship*, 7

Hannah, 82
Hanukkah, 37, 256
Haran, 98
harvest, 36, 37, 135
healing stories, 38, 107–16, 118–24,
147–48, 154
Hebrew, 32, 33, 37, 44, 55, 85, 91,
130, 146, 182, 190, 203, 211,
220, 246, 278–79, 296
Heli, 82
Hellenism, 4, 6, 8, 19, 32, 33, 40,
57–58, 88–89, 190
heresy, 3, 89, 113–14, 191, 260n.
Herod, King, 22, 23, 80, 81, 234,
235–36
High Priestly Prayer, 15, 167n.,
201–6, 222
Holocaust, 17
"holy of holies," 46
Holy Spirit, 139, 187, 191, 259,
295, 308, 310, 313
Holy Week, 22